A TOUR IN IRELAND

TOURING IN IRELAND

towards the end of the Eighteenth Century

A TOUR IN IRELAND

WITH GENERAL OBSERVATIONS ON THE
PRESENT STATE OF THAT KINGDOM
MADE IN THE YEARS 1776, 1777 AND 1778

BY

ARTHUR YOUNG

Selected & Edited by

CONSTANTIA MAXWELL, M.A.

LECTURER IN MODERN HISTORY
TRINITY COLLEGE, DUBLIN

Author of
*A Short History of Ireland, Irish History
from Contemporary Sources,*
etc.

CAMBRIDGE
AT THE UNIVERSITY PRESS

1925

CAMBRIDGE
UNIVERSITY PRESS

University Printing House, Cambridge CB2 8BS, United Kingdom

Published in the United States of America by Cambridge University Press, New York

Cambridge University Press is part of the University of Cambridge.

It furthers the University's mission by disseminating knowledge in the pursuit of education, learning and research at the highest international levels of excellence.

www.cambridge.org
Information on this title: www.cambridge.org/9781107627352

© Cambridge University Press 1925

First published 1925
First paperback edition 2013

A catalogue record for this publication is available from the British Library

ISBN 978-1-107-62735-2 Paperback

NOTE

ARTHUR YOUNG'S *Tour in Ireland* first appeared in London in 1780. As all subsequent editions are now out of print, it is hoped that the following selection may be acceptable to the general reader, although the student of agriculture will naturally wish to consult a complete edition.

Arthur Young was not particular as to the spelling of names of persons and places, and often wrote these down as he heard them pronounced. Most of the names have therefore been corrected. In cases where the author's spelling approximates to the usual form, a change has been affected without comment, but where there is a marked difference, the correct form in square brackets has been added. In those few instances where identification has been impossible, Arthur Young's own spelling is given in inverted commas.

The frontispiece is taken from the first edition of the *Post-Chaise Companion* published in Dublin 1786. The illustration facing p. 84 is from a drawing made by Arthur Young which was included in the first edition of the *Tour*; that facing p. 204 is one of Tudor's *Six Views of Dublin* published in 1753.

For a list of books on Irish history at this time, the reader is referred to the *Cambridge Modern History* (VI, 913–24) and to the footnotes in Lecky's *History of Ireland in the Eighteenth Century* and in Dr O'Brien's *Economic History of Ireland* for the same period.

C. M.

DUBLIN,
September, 1925.

ARTHUR YOUNG

ARTHUR YOUNG, the son of a Suffolk clergyman, was born in 1741. He first applied himself to agriculture in 1763. Although an excellent theorist, he was an unsuccessful farmer, and was so often in financial straits, that he had serious thoughts at one time of emigrating to America. He made his mark through his writings. His *Farmer's Letters to the People of England* appeared in 1767, and his English *Tours* between 1768 and 1771. He published his *Political Arithmetic* in 1774 and commenced the *Annals of Agriculture* in 1784. In 1792 appeared his celebrated *Travels in France*, which was followed by *The Example of France a Warning to Britain* (1793). He was elected a Fellow of the Royal Society in 1774, and when Pitt created the Board of Agriculture in 1793, he was appointed to act as Secretary. He was elected a member of most of the noted European agricultural societies, and his works were translated into several languages. Arthur Young, who is one of the greatest of English writers on agriculture, died in London in 1820.

EDITOR'S INTRODUCTION

DURING the greater part of the eighteenth century there were four main obstacles to a healthy economic development in Ireland. The country was dominated by an alien landlord class; the Parliament was subordinate to that of England; Ireland was restricted in commercial matters, and the bulk of her population being Roman Catholic was bound down by the Penal Laws.

After the Cromwellian and the Williamite wars a large part of the soil was granted to English landlords, who had little sympathy with a tenantry differing from them in national outlook and religion. Many of them were absentees in England, spent their profits there, and managed their estates through middlemen who rack-rented the occupiers; those who remained either tended to listlessness or exploited the advantages of their position as a dominant class to the uttermost. As for the Parliament, not only was it hampered by outside control, but it was an unrepresentative and a corrupt body. Roman Catholics and Dissenters were excluded, and through wire pulling, borough influence and bribery the Government was able to direct its policy. In the seventeenth century, Ireland had a flourishing cattle and wool trade. Both of these were destroyed in the interests of English merchants. Ireland was not permitted to trade with the colonies, and many of her minor industries were suppressed. The people had few healthy outlets for their energies, and in consequence numbers emigrated or were forced to subsist in poverty upon the soil. This unsatisfactory condition was aggravated by the operation of the Penal Laws, which not only excluded Roman Catholics from all civil and military offices and from adequate educational facilities, but prevented them from holding land on the same terms as Protestants and militated against the acquisition by them of property and capital.

During the last quarter of the century, however, there was a marked improvement. Several of the landlords abolished the middleman system and resumed direct control over their estates. Many introduced new methods of agriculture and cattle breeding from England, drained bogs, planted trees, and encouraged the tenantry to take an interest in their holdings. A Patriot Party, under the leadership of Grattan, was formed in the Irish Parliament, and owing to its efforts and to the spirit of tolerance induced in England by recent happenings in America, legislative independence was conceded to Ireland in 1782. Grattan's Parliament was not an ideal body, for it was merely representative of a small minority and like former parliaments was corrupt, but it devoted its energies to the development of the country, and by an enlightened economic policy produced that marked prosperity which characterised Ireland before the Union. Owing to a change in economic opinion and to the threat conveyed to the Government by the organisation of a large body of National Volunteers, most of the trading restrictions were removed at about the same time. The growth of eighteenth century tolerance gained alleviation for the Roman Catholics, and the relaxation of the Penal Code bore fruit in an increased spirit of enterprise and industry among the people.

It has been the fashion to give all the credit to Grattan's Parliament for this improvement in Irish conditions. As a matter of fact, the turn in the tide of Irish prosperity actually dates from about the year 1750. Except for a period of depression, caused by the non-importation agreements in America, the linen trade, unrestricted by Government and fostered by the Irish Parliament, increased steadily in volume from this time, while the encouragement given by the Pre-Grattan Parliament to tillage by a policy of corn bounties led to a revival of agriculture. The Provision Trade benefited greatly from the cessation of civil war, and being one of the few industries that was free from Government control soon reached a flourishing condition. A considerable amount of wool was worked up in the country for home consumption, and large quantities of raw material were smuggled abroad. It is true that the agricultural labourer and the small tenant remained miserably poor, but the landlords were rich, to judge by the fine houses that they began to build in Dublin and the country, while in the ports a wealthy trading class was rising, and the outward aspect of Irish towns was being transformed. The end of the century was a period of high prices, rising rents, and a rapidly growing population.

Arthur Young determined to make a tour in Ireland in 1776. He seems to have heard a good deal about the country from Lord Shelburne and others, and he wished to satisfy his ever-growing curiosity in agricultural matters. He was admirably fitted to act as an observer of Irish conditions. Unlike Dr Twiss who came to Ireland in 1775 and was afraid to enter Connacht because he heard that there were neither roads nor inns there, and that it was inhabited by savages, Young showed no reluctance to penetrate into the most remote places and did not shirk the discomforts of travelling in an age and in a country where these were numerous. He was already an agriculturist of European repute and had no difficulty in securing introductions from Burke and other Irishmen resident in England, or in getting into touch with the Viceroy and the most prominent members of the Irish aristocracy and gentry. His spirit of enquiry ·was that of the scientific observer. He systematically covered a large area of country and wrote down in his note book all that he saw and heard. Not indiscriminately however, for he never made a note without first revolving the matter in his own mind; moreover, "where my intelligence was received from a company of gentlemen," he tells us, "I always waited for their settling among themselves any difference of opinion before I entered the minute, and if they did not agree took the average of the sums or quantities in question." Sometimes he asked that "small farmers" should be present to assist at these consultations held for his benefit, and he adds that he neglected no opportunities of making enquiries of the cottagers also and examining with his own eyes their situation and manner of living. Most travellers to Ireland at this time were content either to indulge in a sentimental arithmetic of their own, or to take figures and details on hearsay. Not so Arthur Young; when the tour was over he went to Dublin and stayed there for nine weeks, employing himself with great industry in examining and transcribing public records and accounts relating to trade and manufactures, being thus enabled to publish many details hitherto unknown to the public.

In spite of his general levelheadedness the reader will observe that Young was a man of views and prejudices. A sound system of agriculture in a country counted for much more in his eyes than the development of commerce or the expansion of a colonial Empire. The agricultural State was his ideal and he judged everything from that standpoint. He hated the old wasteful methods of farming, and thoroughly enjoyed the role of an apostle of the new scientific agriculture. He disliked many things from industrial villages to tea drinking, and says what he thinks of these things with emphasis. He was a typical reformer of the late eighteenth century "Why may not the time come," he asks, "when the whole world shall be in a state of knowledge, elegance and peace?" He had no mercy on the Penal Laws, he would do away with all restrictions on commerce, he would compel the absentees to stay at home, he would abolish all middlemen. With Dr Johnson he believed that "a decent provision for the poor is the true test of civilisation," and he gives a great deal of space to a consideration of the position of the cottier. He was not very much interested in history, antiquities or politics. His historical explanations are often scanty or confused, he frequently passes an old building or place of archaeological interest without due appreciation or without comment, and he tells us little or nothing of the political discussions preceding the establishment of Grattan's Parliament, which he must have heard something of in Dublin and in the various country houses in which he stayed. He tells us elsewhere that he had a constitutional horror of theorising, which doubtless explains his avoidance of politics, but in any case he belonged to that type of radical reformer who suffers a complete mental reaction in the face of revolution. In later life, it will be remembered that he regretted his championship of liberal tendencies in France, and he afterwards never referred to the Rebellion in Ireland which was so largely the fruit of French influence.

Although of course no single volume could be expected to touch upon every aspect of Irish life at this time, there are certain matters upon which we should have particularly welcomed comment by such an acute observer as Young. To what causes, for instance, would he have attributed the peculiar prosperity of Ulster, remarked upon by Wesley and other English writers of the period? Would he have attributed it to the Ulster Custom of Tenant Right; and how did this interesting Custom work out in practice? What solution would he have suggested for the problem presented by the large body of beggars that were roaming through Ireland at this time, causing considerable anxiety to the Government? What did he think of the immigration of the Irish poor into England? On these and similar matters he is silent.

The merits of the *Tour* far outweigh its demerits however, for here we have an accurate and fairly complete picture of Ireland as it was during the last quarter of the eighteenth century. All classes are reviewed in turn: the improving landlords, the middlemen, the squires or *buckeens* (familiar to every reader of Irish fiction), the rich graziers, the dairy farmers, the cottiers, and *spalpeens* or casual labourers. Each district is systematically examined: the semi-industrial North, the grazing counties of Tipperary, Limerick, Clare, Meath and Waterford; the sheep ranches of Roscommon; the dairy country of Wexford and Waterford, and the corn counties of Louth, Kildare, Carlow and Kilkenny. Arthur Young seems to have been especially interested in the linen industry and gives us full details of the processes of manufacture. He also describes the Irish fisheries and notes pretty fully the trading activities of the towns. Among other subjects touched upon are the agrarian troubles as evidenced by the Whiteboy movement, emigration from the North, afforestation, and the tithe evil. We get glimpses of the Palatines, the German colonists settled in Ireland at the beginning of the eighteenth century, and of the Quakers who are described as the wealthiest traders in the country. Agriculture however was his passion, and he gives most of his attention to that. "In the management of the arable ground," he declares, "the Irish are five centuries behind the best cultivated of the English counties." He attributes this backward condition to the miserable state of the cottier, as well as to a general lack of skill and to the want of capital. With the English reader in mind he lays a great deal of emphasis on the fact that Irish prosperity was of the greatest importance to England. Capital put into Irish manufactures and tillage farming would he thinks be well invested, for a wealthy Ireland would prove a magnificent market for English manufactures, and the development of the vast natural resources of the country by increasing food supplies would be an asset to Great Britain in time of war.

The student of the Irish *Tour* who is familiar with Young's *Travels in France* will miss here the liveliness of style which characterises that classic. The comparative lack of anecdote and humorous incident in the present work is due to an unfortunate accident which befell the author on his return journey to England. On the coaching route between Bath and London, his trunk was stolen by a new servant whom he had taken into his employment, and in that trunk was the private journal kept by him during his Irish tour, together with specimens of soils and minerals that he had collected. The trunk and the precious journal were never recovered, and Young was left with only a dry record, which he designates his *Minutes*, from which to work up his narrative.

Some lively Irish anecdotes are to be found in his *Autobiography*[1] however. From Lord Longford, for instance, he had tales of an Irish gentleman of good estate in his neighbourhood that, as he says, surpass anything to be found in Miss Edgeworth's *Castle Rackrent*. We record the entry in his own words:

His hospitality was unbounded, and it never for a moment came into his head to make any provision for feeding the people he brought into his house. While credit was to be had, his butler or housekeeper did this for him; his own attention was given solely to the cellar that wine might not be wanted. If claret was secured, with a dead ox or sheep hanging in the slaughter house ready for steaks or cutlets, he thought all was well. He was never easy without company in the house, and with a large party in it would invite another of twice the number. One day the cook came into the breakfast parlour before all the company: "Sir, there's no coals." "Then burn turf." "Sir, there's no turf." "Then, cut down a tree." This was a forlorn hope, for in all probability he must have gone three miles to find one, all

---

[1] Edited by Miss Betham-Edwards in 1898.

round the house being long ago safely swept away. They dispatched a number of cars to borrow turf. Candles were equally deficient, for unfortunately he was fond of dogs, all half-starved, so that a gentleman walking to what was called his bedchamber, after making two or three turnings met a hungry greyhound who, jumping up, took the candle out of the candlestick and devoured it in a trice, and left him in the dark. To advance or return was equally a matter of chance; therefore groping his way he soon found himself in the midst of a parcel of giggling maidservants. By what means he at last found his way to his shakedown is unknown.

The *Autobiography* records another anecdote which relates to the Right Hon. Silver Oliver, a gentleman who used to keep a splendid table and with whom Arthur Young had stayed during his tour. After Mr Oliver's death, the latter found himself in the neighbourhood of this gentleman's house where an auction was in progress, and putting his head into the kitchen was horrified to find it a regular "pigstye," very dark with "walls black as the inside of a chimney," no dressers or tables and the hearth heaped with turf. "Etna or Vesuvius might as soon have been found in England," he exclaims, "as such a kitchen." The *Tour* contains no such reminiscences, partly for the reasons given above, and partly perhaps because our author had received so much hospitality in Ireland that he felt that strict politeness was subsequently required. The reader will therefore be glad to have these samples from which he may form a notion as to the nature of other entries in the lost *Journal*. The Irish reader need take no offence from a few stories related at the expense of the Irish gentry, for the whole tone of the *Tour* is friendly to Ireland, and Young was always generously appreciative of the merits of the Irish landlord.

In the *Annals of Agriculture* will be found this passage written by Young in 1791:

My journeys to Ireland, the register of which I published, occupied the years 1776, 1777, 1778 and 1779 including a residence in the county of Cork of something more than a year employed in arranging and letting part of the estate of the Lord Viscount Kingsborough[1]. Of that work, I have no apprehension. Though the success in relation to profit was nothing, yet it will stand its ground, and I trust merit in some small degree the most flattering encomiums it has received in many parts of Europe.... I have since learned from the conversation of many most respectable gentlemen of Ireland, as well as from the conversation of others, that the book is now esteemed of some value to Ireland, and that the agriculture of the kingdom has been advanced in consequence of it.

The practical effect of Young's work on Irish economic development is too big a subject to open up here, but it may be mentioned that the valuable surveys of Irish counties issued by the Dublin Society, early in the nineteenth century, were among the first fruits of his influence. The Irish Tour has certainly 'stood its ground' in that it remains our chief authority for Irish economic conditions for the latter part of the eighteenth century.

[1] See note on Mitchelstown, pp. 232–33.

CONTENTS

PART II

GENERAL OBSERVATIONS

SOIL, FACE OF THE COUNTRY AND CLIMATE

ILLUSTRATIONS

also available for download in colour from www.cambridge.org/9781107627352

ಬಬಬಬಬಬಬಬಬಬಬಬಬ

A TOUR IN IRELAND

PART I

✩ ✩
✩

MINUTES OF THE TOUR

JUNE 19TH, 1776. Arrived at Holyhead. Found the packet, the *Claremont* (Captain Taylor), would sail very soon. After a tedious passage of twenty-two hours, landed on the 20th in the morning, at Dunleary[1], four miles from Dublin, a city which much exceeded my expectation[2]. The public buildings are magnificent, very many of the streets regularly laid out, and exceedingly well built. The front of the Parliament House is grand, though not so light as a more open finishing of the roof would have made it. The apartments are spacious, elegant, and convenient, much beyond that heap of confusion at Westminster, so inferior to the magnificence to be looked for in the seat of empire. I was so fortunate as to arrive just in time to see Lord Harcourt[3], with the usual ceremonies, prorogue the Parliament. Trinity College is a beautiful building, and a numerous society; the library is a very fine room, and well filled. The new Exchange will be another edifice to do honour to Ireland; it is elegant, cost £40,000, but deserves a better situation. From everything I saw, I was struck with those appearances of wealth which the capital of a thriving community may be supposed to exhibit. Happy if I find through the country in diffused prosperity the right source of this splendour! The common computation of inhabitants 200,000, but I should suppose exaggerated.

JUNE 21ST. Introduced by Colonel Burton[4] to the Lord Lieutenant, who was pleased to enter into conversation with me on my intended journey. Made many remarks on the agriculture of several Irish counties, and showed

himself to be an excellent farmer. Viewed the Duke of
Leinster's house, which is a very large stone edifice, the
front simple but elegant, the pediment light. There are
several good rooms, but a circumstance unrivalled is the
court, which is spacious and magnificent. The opening
behind the house is also beautiful. In the evening to the
Rotunda, a circular room, 90 feet diameter, an imitation
of Ranelagh, provided with a band of music. The barracks
are a vast building, raised in a plain style, of many divisions;
the principal front is of an immense length. They contain
every convenience for ten regiments.

JUNE 23RD. Lord Charlemont's house in Dublin, is equally
elegant and convenient, the apartments large, handsome,
and well disposed, containing some good pictures, particularly one by Rembrandt, of Judas throwing the money on
the floor, with a strong expression of guilt and remorse;
the whole group fine. In the same room is a portrait of
Caesar Borgia, by Titian. The library is a most elegant
apartment of about 40 by 30 feet, and of such a height as
to form a pleasing proportion; the light is well managed,
coming in from the cove of the ceiling, and has an exceeding
good effect; at one end is a pretty ante-room, with a fine
copy of the Venus de Medicis, and at the other two small
rooms, one a cabinet of pictures and antiquities, the other
medals. In the collection also of Robert Fitzgerald, Esq.[5],
in Merrion Square, are several pieces which very well deserve a traveller's attention; it was the best I saw in Dublin.
Before I quit that city I observe, on the houses in general,
that what they call their two-roomed ones are good and
convenient. Mr La Touche's[6], in Stephen's Green, I was
shown as a model of this sort, and I found it well contrived,
and finished elegantly.

Drove to Lord Charlemont's villa at Marino, near the
city, where his lordship has formed a pleasing lawn, mar-

gined in the higher part by a well-planted thriving shrubbery, and on a rising ground a banqueting room, which
ranks very high among the most beautiful edifices I have
anywhere seen; it has much elegance, lightness, and effect,
and commands a fine prospect. The rising ground on
which it stands slopes off to an agreeable accompaniment of
wood, beyond which on one side is Dublin harbour, which
here has the appearance of a noble river crowded with ships
moving to and from the capital. On the other side is a
shore spotted with white buildings, and beyond it the hills
of Wicklow, presenting an outline extremely various. The
other part of the view (it would be more perfect if the city
was planted out) is varied, in some places nothing but wood,
in others breaks of prospect. Returned to Dublin and
made enquiries into other points, the prices of provisions,
etc. The expenses of a family in proportion to those of
London are as five to eight.

Having the year following lived more than two months
in Dublin, I am able to speak to a few points, which as
a mere traveller I could not have done. The information
I before received of the prices of living is correct. Fish and
poultry are plentiful and very cheap. Good lodgings almost
as dear as they are in London, though we were well
accommodated (dirt excepted) for two guineas and a half
a week. All the lower ranks in this city have no idea of
English cleanliness, either in apartments, persons, or
cookery. There is a very good society in Dublin in a
parliament winter; a great round of dinners, and parties,
and balls and suppers every night in the week, some of
which are very elegant, but you almost everywhere meet
a company much too numerous for the size of the apartments. They have two assemblies on the plan of those of
London, in Fishamble Street, and at the Rotunda, and two
gentlemen's clubs, Anthry's and Daly's, very well regulated:
I heard some anecdotes of deep play at the latter, though

never to the excess common at London. An ill-judged and unsuccessful attempt was made to establish the Italian Opera, which existed but with scarcely any life for this one winter; of course they could rise no higher than a comic one. *La Buona Figliuola, La Frascatana*, and *Il Geloso in Cimento*[7], were repeatedly performed, or rather murdered, except the parts of Sestini. The house was generally empty, and miserably cold. So much knowledge of the state of a country is gained by hearing the debates of a parliament, that I often frequented the gallery of the House of Commons. Since Mr Flood[8] has been silenced with the Vice-Treasurership of Ireland, Mr Daly[9], Mr Grattan[10], Sir William Osborne[11], and the Prime Serjeant Burgh[12], are reckoned high among the Irish orators. I heard many very eloquent speeches, but I cannot say they struck me like the exertion of the abilities of Irishmen in the English House of Commons, owing perhaps to the reflection both on the speaker and auditor, that the Attorney-General of England, with a dash of his pen[13], can reverse, alter, or entirely do away the matured result of all the eloquence and all the abilities of this whole assembly. Before I conclude with Dublin I shall only remark, that walking in the streets there, from the narrowness and populousness of the principal thoroughfares, as well as from the dirt and wretchedness of the *canaille*, is a most disgusting and uneasy exercise.

JUNE 24TH. Left Dublin and passed through the Phœnix Park, a very pleasing ground, at the bottom of which to the left, the Liffey forms a variety of landscapes; this is the most beautiful environ of Dublin. Take the road to Luttrellstown through a various scenery on the banks of the river. That domain is a considerable one in extent, being above 400 acres within the wall, Irish measure; in the front of the house is a fine lawn bounded

by rich woods, through which are many ridings, four miles
in extent. From the road towards the house, they lead
through a very fine glen, by the side of a stream falling
over a rocky bed, through the dark woods, with great
variety on the sides of steep slopes, at the bottom of which
the Liffey is either heard or seen indistinctly; these woods
are of great extent, and so near the capital, form a retire-
ment exceedingly beautiful. Lord Irnham [14] and Colonel
Luttrell have brought in the assistance of agriculture to
add to the beauties of the place, they have kept a part of
the lands in cultivation in order to lay them down the
better to grass; 150 acres have been done, and above 200
acres most effectually drained in the covered manner filled
with stones. These works are well executed. In the county
of Dublin, good grass land lets at 40s. an acre. Mow most
of it for hay. Most of the people drink tea and consume
plenty of whisky and tobacco. Rent of cottages 26s. to 30s.
with a potato garden. No emigrations. The religion in
general Catholic. Labour throughout the year 10d. a day,
about Dublin 1s. Leaving Luttrellstown I went to St
Wolstan's [Co. Kildare], which Lord Harcourt had been
so obliging as to desire I would make my quarters, from
whence to view to the right or left.

JUNE 25TH. To Mr Clement's at Killadoon [Co. Kildare],
who has lately built an excellent house, and planted much
about it, with the satisfaction of finding that all his trees
thrive well. I remarked the beech and larch seemed to
get beyond the rest. He is also a good farmer.

JUNE 26TH. Breakfasted with Colonel Marlay at Celbridge. Walked through his grounds, which I found in
general very well cultivated.

Walked through Loughlinstown [Co. Kildare], the farm
of the late Mr Wynn Baker [15], to whom the Dublin

Society[16], with a liberality that does them great honour, gave for several years £300 annually in order to make experiments.

Viewed Lucan [Co. Dublin], the seat of Agmondisham Vesey, Esq. [17], on the banks of the Liffey; the house is re-building, but the wood on the river, with walks through it, is exceedingly beautiful.

Leaving Lucan the next place is Leixlip [18] [Co. Kildare], a fine one, on the river, with a fall, which in a wet season is considerable. Then St Wolstan's, belonging to the Dean of Derry[19], a beautiful villa, which is also on the river; the grounds gay and open, though not without the advantage of much wood, disposed with judgment. A winding shrubbery quits the river, and is made to lead through some dressed ground that is pretty and cheerful.

Mr Conolly's [20], at Castletown [Co. Kildare], to which all travellers resort, is the finest house in Ireland, and not exceeded by many in England. It is a large handsome edifice, situated in the middle of an extensive lawn, which is quite surrounded with fine plantations disposed to the best advantage. To the north these unite into very large woods, through which many winding walks lead, with the convenience of several ornamented seats, rooms, etc. On the other side of the house, upon the river, is a cottage, with a shrubbery, prettily laid out; the house commands an extensive view, bounded by the Wicklow mountains. It consists of several noble apartments. On the first floor is a beautiful gallery, 80 feet long, elegantly fitted up.

JUNE 27TH. Left Lord Harcourt's, and having received an invitation from the Duke of Leinster[21], passed through Mr Conolly's grounds to his Grace's seat at Carton. The park ranks among the finest in Ireland. It is a vast lawn, which waves over gentle hills, surrounded by plantations of great extent, and which break and divide in places so as to give much variety. A large but gentle vale winds through the whole, in the bottom of which a small stream has been enlarged into a fine river, which throws a cheerfulness through most of the scenes: over it a handsome stone bridge. There is a great variety on the banks of this vale; part of it consists of mild and gentle slopes, part steep banks of thick wood. On one of the most rising grounds in the park is a tower, from the top of which the whole scenery is beheld. The park spreads on every side in fine sheets of lawn, kept in the highest order by 1100 sheep, scattered over with rich plantations, and bounded by a large margin of wood, through which is a riding. At a small distance from the park is a new town, Maynooth, which the Duke has built; it is regularly laid out, and consists of good houses. His Grace gives encouragement to settling in it; consequently it increases, and he meditates several improvements.

Reached Kilcock [Co. Kildare].

JUNE 28TH. Breakfasted with Mr Jones of "Dolleston" [Dolanstown Ho., Co. Meath]. From hence took the road to Summerhill the seat of the Right Hon. H[ercules] L[angford] Rowley. The country is cheerful and rich, and if the Irish cabins continue like what I have hitherto seen, I shall not hesitate to pronounce their inhabitants as well off as most English cottagers. They are built of mud walls 18 inches or 2 feet thick, and well thatched, which are far warmer than the thin clay walls in England. Here are few cottiers without a cow, and some of them two. A bellyfull invariably of potatoes, and generally turf for fuel from a bog. It is true they have not always chimneys to their cabins, the door serving for that and window too. If their eyes are not affected with the smoke, it may be an advantage in warmth. Every cottage swarms with poultry and most of them have pigs. The plantations and

ornamented grounds at Summerhill are extensive and form
a very fine environ, spreading over the hills and having a
noble appearance. The house is large and handsome, with
an elegant hall, a cube of 30 feet and many very good and
convenient apartments.

Went in the evening to Lord Mornington's[22] at Dangan
[Co. Meath], who is making many improvements, which
he showed me. His plantations are extensive, and he has
formed a large water, having five or six islands much
varied, and promontories of high land shoot so far into it as
to form almost distinct lakes; the effect pleasing. There are
above 100 acres under water, and his Lordship has planned
a considerable addition to it. Returned to Summerhill.

JUNE 29TH. Left it, taking the road to Slane [Co.
Meath], the country very pleasant all the way; much of
it on the banks of the Boyne, variegated with some woods,
planted hedgerows, and gentle hills. The cabins continue
much the same, the same plenty of poultry, pigs and cows.
The cattle in the road have their forelegs all tied together
with straw to keep them from breaking into the fields;
even sheep, pigs and goats, are all in the same bondage.
I had the pleasure of meeting Colonel Burton at the
Castle, in whom I was so fortunate to find, on repeated
occasions, the utmost assiduity to procure me every species
of information, entering into the spirit of my design with
the most liberal ideas. His partner in Slane mills, Mr Jebb,
gave me the following particulars. Every farmer has a
little flax from a rood to an acre and all the cottages a spot.
If they have any land they go through the whole process
themselves and spin and weave it. From hence to Drogheda
there is a considerable manufacture of coarse cloth, which
is exported to Liverpool, about 1s. a yard.

Lord Conyngham's[23] seat, Slane Castle on the Boyne,
is one of the most beautiful places I have seen; the grounds

are very bold and various, rising round the Castle in noble hills or beautiful inequalities of surface, with an outline of flourishing plantations. Under the Castle flows the Boyne, in a reach broken by islands, with a very fine shore of rock on one side, and wood on the other. Lord Conyngham's keeping up Slane Castle and spending great sums, though he rarely resides there, is an instance of magnificence not often met with. While it is so common for absentees [24] to drain the kingdom of every shilling they can, so contrary a conduct ought to be held in the estimation which it justly deserves.

JUNE 30TH. Rode out to view the country and some improvements in the neighbourhood, the principal of which are those of Lord Chief Baron Foster [25], which I saw from "Glaston Hill," in the road from Slane to Dundalk. Adjoining to it is an extensive improvement of Mr Fortescue's [of Stephenstown, Co. Louth]; ten years ago the land was let at 3s. 6d., now it is a guinea; which great work was done by the tenants, and lime and fallow the means pursued. These and other improvements, with the general increase of prosperity, has had such an effect in employing the people, that Colonel Burton assured me, that twenty years ago if he gave notice at the mass houses that he wanted labourers, in two days he could have two or three hundred; now it is not so easy to get twenty, from the quantity of regular employment being so much increased. I observed weavers' looms in most of the cabins, went into one, and the man informed me that he could weave a web 65 or 66 yards long, and 26 inches wide, at 8d. a yard price in a week; 34 to 36 lb. of yarn makes it, which costs 15d. per lb.; he and his journeymen could earn 7s. or 8s. a week by it. He paid £4. 4s. for the grazing of a cow, a rood of potato garden, and the cabin. They were burning straw, which I forgot to remark, I have found very common where there is no turf: a most pernicious custom; it is in fact what I have often heard literally reported, that they burn their dunghills in Ireland.

Passed through several farms much improved, and found great attention given to fences, the ditches very large, and the banks well planted. Lord Boyne's [26] estate appears to be very rich, and the tenants beyond the common run. The country is well wooded, and has an appearance of some of the best parts of England.

Returning to Slane, dined with Mr Jebb and viewed the mill which is a very large edifice, excellently built; it was begun in 1763, and finished in 1766. The water from the Boyne is conducted to it by a weir of 650 feet long, and 8 feet high, of solid masonry; the water let into it by very complete flood gates. The canal is 800 feet long, all faced with stone, and 64 feet wide; on one side is a wharf completely formed and walled against the river, whereon are offices of several kinds, and a dry dock for building lighters. The mill is 138 feet long, the breadth 54, and the height to the cornice 42 feet, being a very large and handsome edifice, such as no mill I have seen in England can be compared with. The corn upon being unloaded, is hoisted through doors in the floors to the upper storey of the building, by a very simple contrivance, being worked by the water wheel, and discharged into spacious granaries which hold 5000 barrels. Beginning in 1763, for a few years, about 13,000 barrels per annum were ground, of late years up to 17,000 barrels. The corn is brought to the mill from all the country round to the distance of ten miles, the farmers send it in, and leave the price to be fixed. The raising the mill and offices complete cost £20,000 and has established in a fine corn country, a constant market, and has preserved the tillage of the neighbourhood. The flour is sent to Dublin, and the manufacturing country to the north about Newry, etc.

The parish of Monknewton, in the county of Meath lying between Drogheda and Slane, nearly midway, formerly belonging to the rich abbey of Mellifont[27] (whose beautiful Gothic ruins are in the neighbourhood), consists of very fine corn land, and mostly belongs to John Baker Holroyd, Esq.[28], of Sheffield Place, in the county of Sussex. The whole estate had been let out to two or three considerable people for 61 years, and they under-let in the usual style of the country. The leases expired in 1762 when Mr H. visited the estate, and found it as ill-used as it possibly could be. However great rents were offered. He declined the proposals of several considerable men to take the whole to under-let at rack rents as before, knowing that the same wretched husbandry and poverty must continue, if he did, although it would secure his rents most effectually. He was very well satisfied with the rents offered by persons who would reside on the estate (dividing with them the profits of the middleman)[29], and voluntarily engaged to pay for the masonry and principal timber of farm houses, barns, stables, etc. He made large ditches, planting them with quicks, round each farm. He allowed half the expense of inner fences. He provided an excellent limestone quarry in the neighbourhood, besides lime kilns on different farms. Mr H. is an hearty well-wisher to Ireland, and ready to embrace any scheme of improvement for its advantage. He wished to make some return to the country for spending the income of the estate out of it. He was ready to allow almost the whole of every expense that could be laid out on the lands, knowing the poverty of the common Irish residing tenantry, and their characters to be such, that they could not improve them as they should be. He is a great friend to agriculture, has considered the subject much, and was very anxious to introduce something like the best English husbandry on his Irish estate, but that is still at a great distance. He endeavoured to break through the barbarous custom of having the whole farm laid waste at the end of a lease[30], and every inch ploughed up, but could not carry his point further, than by giving great present advantages to the tenants, to induce them to agree, that the third part of the farms should not be ploughed the last four or five years of the lease. The soil is so good, that if used ever so ill in that time, it will recover, and there will be a very good sward. According to the common method of leasing lands in many parts of Ireland, the country is nearly waste and unprofitable, to the great prejudice of the public, during seven or eight years in every thirty-one years, the usual lease. For the tenant, not restrained by proper clauses, nor obliged to any particular management, or to manure, ploughs up every thing, and for some time before the expiration of his term, pursues the most ruinous system for the land, disposed even to lose some advantage himself, rather than his successor should have any benefit; consequently, the three or four last years the crops hardly pay expenses, and three or four years more are lost before it can be brought into any condition. Good and straight roads[31] are made through and across the estate, and bridges built where necessary. Such a disposition in the landlord to improve, must do much for the country. The estate is now divided into farms, from 70 to 150 acres, and let in general for thirty-one years, at 40s. and 35s. per acre. The lands are tithe free, and there are no taxes of any kind paid by the tenants, except assessments for making and repairing the roads of the barony, laid on by the Grand Jury at the assizes.

JULY 1ST. Left Slane, taking the road towards Kells [Co. Meath]. Reached Lord Bective's[32] in the evening, through a very fine country. The house and offices are entirely new built. Headfort is a large plain stone edifice; from the thickness of the walls, I suppose it is the custom

to build very substantially here. To the right, the town
of Kells is picturesquely situated, among groups of trees,
with a fine waving country and distant mountains, to the
left a rich tract of cultivation. In July, August and
September, they have great numbers of Connacht labourers
here. They are called *spalpeens*[33]. *Spal* in Irish is a scythe,
and *peen* a penny, *i.e.* a mower for a penny a day, but that
was eighty years ago. Lord Bective's father was one of
the greatest improvers I have heard of. He bought 10,000
acres of bog and rough land in the county of Cavan, much
at the rent of only 20*d*. an acre. He drained and improved
the bog, and brought it to be such good land that it is now
15*s*. an acre.

JULY 3RD. Took my leave of Lord Bective. Reached
Pakenham Hall [Co. Westmeath], where Lord Longford[34]
received me with the most friendly attention and gave me
very valuable information. Leases common are, thirty-one
years to Catholics, and three lives to Protestants. Great
part of the country let to middlemen, who re-let it to sub-
tenants, generally with a profit greater than they pay the
landlord.

In conversation with Lord Longford I made many
enquiries concerning the state of the lower classes, and
found that in some respects they were in good circumstances, in others indifferent. They have, generally
speaking, such plenty of potatoes as always to command a
bellyful; they have flax enough for all their linen, most of
them have a cow, and some two, and spin wool enough
for their clothes; all a pig, and numbers of poultry, and in
general the complete family of cows, calves, hogs, poultry,
and children, pig together in the cabin; fuel they have in
the utmost plenty. Great numbers of families are also
supported by the neighbouring lakes, which abound prodigiously with fish. A child with a packthread and a

crooked pin will catch perch enough in an hour for the family to live on the whole day, and his lordship has seen five hundred children fishing at the same time, there being no tenaciousness in the proprietors of the lands about a right to the fish. Besides perch, there is pike upwards of 5 feet long, bream, tench, trout of 10 lb. as red as a salmon, and fine eels. All these are favourable circumstances, and are very conspicuous in the numerous and healthy families among them.

Reverse the medal: they are ill clothed, and make a wretched appearance, and what is worse, are much oppressed by many who make them pay too dear for keeping a cow, horse, etc. They have a practice also of keeping accounts with the labourers, contriving by that means to let the poor wretches have very little cash for their year's work. This is a great oppression, farmers and gentlemen keeping accounts with the poor is a cruel abuse: so many days' work for a cabin; so many for a potato garden; so many for keeping a horse, and so many for a cow, are clear accounts which a poor man can understand well, but further it ought never to go; and when he has worked out what he has of this sort, the rest of his work ought punctually to be paid him every Saturday night. Another circumstance mentioned was the excessive practice they have in general of pilfering. They steal everything they can lay their hands on, and I should remark, that this is an account which has been very generally given me. All sorts of iron hinges, chains, locks, keys, etc. Gates will be cut in pieces, and conveyed away in many places as fast as built. Trees as big as a man's body, and that would require ten men to move, gone in a night. Lord Longford has had the new wheels of a car stolen as soon as made. Good stones out of a wall will be taken for a firehearth, etc., though a breach is made to get at them. In short, everything, and even such as are apparently of no use to them, nor is it easy to catch them, for they never carry their stolen goods home, but to some bog hole. Turnips are stolen by car loads, and two acres of wheat plucked off in a night. In short, their pilfering and stealing is a perfect nuisance! How far it is owing to the oppression of laws aimed solely at the religion of these people, how far to the conduct of the gentlemen and farmers, and how far to the mischievous disposition of the people themselves, it is impossible for a passing traveller to ascertain. I am apt to believe that a better system of law and management would have good effects. They are much worse treated than the poor in England, are talked to in more opprobrious terms, and otherwise very much oppressed.

Left Pakenham Hall.

Two or three miles from Lord Longford's in the way to Mullingar [Co. Westmeath] the road leads up a mountain, and commands an exceeding fine view of Lough Derravaragh, a noble water eight miles long, and from two miles to half a mile over; a vast reach of it, like a magnificent river, opens as you rise the hill. Afterwards I passed under the principal mountain, which rises abruptly from the lake into the boldest outline imaginable. The water there is very beautiful, filling up the steep vale formed by this and the opposite hills.

Reached Mullingar. It was one of the fair days. I saw many cows and beasts, and more horses, with some wool. The cattle were of the same breed that I had generally seen in coming through the country.

JULY 5TH. Left Mullingar, which is a dirty ugly town, and taking the road to Tullamore [King's Co.], stopped at Lord Belvidere's[35], with which place I was as much struck as with any I had ever seen. The house is perched on the crown of a very beautiful little hill, half surrounded with others, variegated and melting into one another. It is one of the most singular places that is anywhere to be seen, and spreading to the eye a beautiful lawn of undulating ground margined with wood. Single trees are scattered in some places and clumps in others; the general effect so pleasing that were there nothing further, the place would be beautiful, but the canvas is admirably filled. Lake Ennell, many miles in length, and two or three broad, flows beneath the windows. It is spotted with islets, a promontory of rock fringed with trees shoots into it, and the whole is bounded by distant hills. Greater and more magnificent scenes are often met with but nowhere a more beautiful or a more singular one.

From Mullingar to "Tullespace" [Tyrellspass, Co. Westmeath]. The road before it comes to Tullamore leads through a part of the Bog of Allen, which seems here extensive, and would make a noble tract of meadow. The way the road was made over it was simply to cut a drain on each side and then lay on gravel, which, as fast as it was laid and spread, bore the cars.

JULY 6TH. Went to Rahan [King's Co.], where Lord Shelburne[36] has placed a Norfolk bailiff, Mr Vancouver, for the management of a farm he took into his own hands. He has cut some very long drains into the bog, designs attacking it, and expects to make it excellent land. He has a fine field to work upon, for Lord Shelburne has 4000 acres of bog here.

Went from Rahan to the Glebe [Queen's Co.] a lodge belonging to Dean Coote[37], and from thence to Shaen Castle, near Mountmellick, his residence. Passed near large tracts of mountain, waste and bog, and not far from a great range of the Bog of Allen.

In conversation upon the subject of a union with Great Britain, I was informed that nothing was so unpopular in Ireland as such an idea; and that the great objection to it was increasing the number of absentees. When it was in agitation, twenty peers and sixty commoners were talked of to sit in the British Parliament, which would be the resident of eighty of the best estates in Ireland. Going every year to England would, by degrees, make them residents; they would educate their children there, and in time become mere absentees: becoming so they would be unpopular, others would be elected, who, treading in the same steps, would yield the place still to others; and thus by degrees, a vast portion of the kingdom now resident would be made absentees, which would, they think, be so great a drain to Ireland, that a free trade would not repay it. I think the idea is erroneous, were it only for one circumstance, the kingdom would lose, according to this reasoning, an idle race of country gentlemen, and in exchange their ports would fill with ships and commerce, and all the consequences of commerce, an exchange that never yet proved disadvantageous to any country[38].

Dean Coote has received from the Dublin Society several gold medals for the improvement of bog, culture of turnips, etc.

JULY 8TH. Left Shaen Castle, and took the road towards Athy [Co. Kildare]. Going through that town the road leads on the banks of the river Barrow, which winds through the vale to the right, the verdure beautiful and the country pleasant. Called on Mr Vicars at Ballinakill [Queen's Co.] a considerable grazier who farms near 2000 acres in different counties. Passed on to Mr Browne at Browneshill [Co. Carlow]. Tillage is very much increased here, and almost entirely owing to the inland premiums[39]; the people also increase much. Throughout the county of Carlow, the hiring tenant is in general the occupier, except in small pieces.

JULY 9TH. Left Browneshill, and taking the road to Leighlinbridge [Co. Carlow] called on Mr James Butler at Ballybar, a very active and intelligent farmer upon a considerable scale. He has generally 4 or 5 acres of cabbages, which he uses for his fat wethers; the produce of them he finds greater, and the sheep too like them better than turnips. He has sometimes 20 acres of turnips and hoes them all. This year none. It is a sign the cultivation is not well understood in a country when a man has one year 20 acres, and another none. A principal part of the advantage of the consumption is lost, if the cattle system is not regularly arranged with an eye to the turnip crop.

Having taken a short walk with Mr Butler, passed on to Captain Mercer's mill at Leighlinbridge. I had been told that this was one of the most considerable mills in Ireland. It is a very large and convenient one; grinds 15,000 barrels a year, and, if there was a brisker demand, could do yet more.

Nothing interesting from hence to Kilfane [Co. Kilkenny]. I saw some very good crops of wheat, but the country is bleak, and wants wood much. Reached Gervas Bushe's, Esq.[40], at that place in the evening, who received me with a politeness equalled only by the value of his intelligence.

JULY 10TH. Accompanied Mr Bushe in a ride through the neighbourhood to view the country, which is a great corn one.

Viewed Mount Juliet, Lord Carrick's[41] seat, which is beautifully situated on a fine declivity on the banks of the Nore. About the town of Kilkenny they have a practice which much deserves attention: three, four, five, seven, etc., little farmers, will take a large farm in partnership[42]. They must be equal in horses, cows and sheep, and tolerably so in other circumstances; they divide every field among

themselves equally, and do all the labour of it upon their
separate accounts; assisting each other mutually; they never
throw the whole into one stock and divide the profit,
from suspicions I suppose, they have of one another. The
river is a very fine one and has a good accompaniment of
well grown wood.

JULY 11TH. Left Kilfane. Mr Bushe accompanied me
to Woodstock, the seat of Sir W[illiam] Fownes. From
Thomastown hither is the finest ride I have yet had in
Ireland. The road leaving Thomastown leads on the east
side of the river through some beautiful copse woods,
which before they were cut must have had a most noble
effect with the river Nore winding at the bottom. The
country then opens somewhat, and you pass most of the
way for six or seven miles to "Inisteague" [Inistioge, Co.
Kilkenny], on a declivity shelving down to the river, which
takes a varied winding course.

Taking my leave of Mr Bushe, I followed the road to
Ross [New Ross, Co. Wexford][43]. Passed Woodstock, of
which there is a very fine view from the top of one of the
hills, the house in the centre of a sloping wood of 500
English acres and hanging in one noble shade to the river,
which flows at the bottom of a winding glen. From the
same hill in front it is seen in a winding course for many
miles through a great extent of inclosures, bounded by
mountains. As I advanced, the views of the river Nore
were very fine till I came to Ross, where from the hill
before you go down to the ferry, is a noble scene of the
Barrow, a vast river flowing through bold shores, in some
places trees on the bank half obscure it, in others it opens
in large reaches, the effect equally grand and beautiful.
Ships sailing up to the town, which is built on the side of
a hill to the water's edge, enliven the scene not a little.
The water is very deep and the navigation secure, so that

ships of 700 tons may come up to the town, but these noble harbours on the coast of Ireland are only melancholy capabilities of commerce; it is languid and trifling. There are only four or five brigs and sloops that belong to the place.

Having now passed through a considerable extent of country in which the Whiteboys[44] were very common, and committed many outrages, I shall here review the intelligence I received concerning them throughout the county of Kilkenny. I made many enquiries into the origin of those disturbances and found that no such thing as a leveller or whiteboy was heard of till 1760, which was long after the landing of Thurot[45] or the intended expedition of M. Conflans. That no foreign coin was ever seen among them, though reports to the contrary were circulated; and in all the evidence that was taken during ten or twelve years, in which time there appeared a variety of informers, none was ever taken, whose testimony could be relied on, that ever proved any foreign interposition. Those very few who attempted to favour it, were of the most infamous and perjured characters. All the rest, whose interest it was to make the discovery, if they had known it, and who concealed nothing else, pretended to no such knowledge. No foreign money appeared, no arms of foreign construction, no presumptive proof whatever of such a connection. They began in Tipperary, and were owing to some inclosures of commons, which they threw down, levelling the ditches, and were first known by the name of Levellers. After that, they began with the tithe proctors (who are men that hire tithes of the rectors), and these proctors either screwed the cottiers up to the utmost shilling, or re-let the tithes to such as did it[46]. It was a common practice with them to go in parties about the country, swearing many to be true to them, and forcing them to join by menaces, which they very often carried into execution. At last they set up to be general redressers of grievances, punished all obnoxious persons who advanced the value of lands, or hired farms over their heads; and, having taken the administration of justice into their hands, were not very exact in the distribution of it. Forced masters to release their apprentices, carried off the daughters of rich farmers, ravished them into marriages, of which four instances happened in a fortnight. They levied sums of money on the middling and lower farmers, in order to support their cause, by paying attornies, etc., in defending prosecutions against them, and many of them subsisted for some years without work, supported by these contributions. Sometimes they committed several considerable robberies, breaking into houses and taking the money, under pretence of redressing grievances. In the course of these outrages they burnt several houses and destroyed the whole substance of men obnoxious to them. The barbarities they committed were shocking. One of their usual punishments (and by no means the most severe) was taking people out of their beds, carrying them naked in winter, on horseback, for some distance, and burying them up to their chin in a hole filled with briars, not forgetting to cut off one of their ears.

In this manner the evil existed for eight or ten years, during which time the gentlemen of the country took some measures to quell them. Many of the magistrates were active in apprehending them, but the want of evidence prevented punishments, for many of those who even suffered by them, had not spirit to prosecute. The gentlemen of the country had frequent expeditions to discover them in arms, but their intelligence was so uncommonly good by their influence over the common people, that not one party that ever went out in quest of them was successful. Government offered large rewards for informations, which brought a few every year to the gallows, without any radical cure for the evil. The reason why it was not more effective was the necessity of any person that gave evidence against them quitting their houses and country, or remaining exposed to their resentment. At last their violence arose to a height which brought on their suppression. The popish inhabitants of Ballyragget, six miles from Kilkenny, were the first of the lower people who dared openly to associate against them; they threatened destruction to the town, gave notice that they would attack it, were as good as their word, came two hundred strong, drew up before a house in which were fifteen armed men, and fired in at the windows; the fifteen men handled their arms so well, that in a few rounds they killed forty or fifty. They fled immediately, and ever after left Ballyragget in peace: indeed, they have never been resisted at all without showing a great want of both spirit and discipline. It should, however, be observed, that they had but very few arms, those in bad order, and no cartridges. Soon after this they attacked the house of Mr Power in Tipperary, the history of which is well known. His murder spirited up the gentlemen to exert themselves in suppressing the evil, especially in raising subscriptions to give private rewards to whoever would give evidence or information concerning them. The private distribution had much more effect than larger sums which required a public declaration, and Government giving rewards to those who resisted them without having previously promised it, had likewise some effect. Laws were passed for punishing all who assembled and (and what may have a great effect) for recompensing at the expense of the county or barony all persons who suffered by their outrages.

In consequence of this general exertion above twenty were capitally convicted and most of them executed, and the gaols of this and the three neighbouring counties, Carlow, Tipperary and Queen's County have many in them whose trials are put off till next assizes, and against whom sufficient evidence for conviction, it is supposed, will appear. Since this all has been quiet, and no outrages have been committed, but before I quit the subject, it is proper to remark that what coincided very much to abate the evil, was the fall in the price of lands which has taken place lately. This is considerable, and has much lessened the evil of hiring farms over the heads of one another. Perhaps also the tithe proctors have not been quite so severe in their extortions, but this observation is by no means general, for in many places tithes yet continue to be levied with all those circumstances which originally raised the evil.

From Ross took the road towards Wexford. Laid at Taghmon [Co. Wexford] at as good an inn as the appearance of the place could allow of, though I was told it was very good. There was a bed on which I rested in my clothes, but the stable had neither rack nor manger. I should have gone on to Wexford, but found that Mr Neville, member for that town, to whom I had a letter of recommendation, in order to procure intelligence concerning the Baronies of Bargy and Forth [47] was in England. I therefore determined to turn off here, and make a circuit through them to get to Wexford.

JULY 12TH. Sallied from my inn which would have made a very passable castle of enchantment in the eyes of Don Quixote, in search of adventures in these noted baronies, of which I had heard so much. I had been told that they were infinitely more industrious and better farmers (there) than in any other part of Ireland, and this account was confirmed to me by several common Irish farmers I met with upon the road.

It was not long before I was in the Barony of Bargy and I was much surprised to see no great appearance of anything better than common. Potatoes not the food of the people the year through as in other parts of Ireland.

They live on them only in the winter and have oatmeal the rest of the year. Farms in Bargy generally from 40 to 100 acres. Here I understood there was a part of the barony of Shelmaliere inhabited by Quakers, rich men and good farmers. A farmer I talked to said of them, "*the Quakers*[48] *be very cunning, and the devil a bad acre of land will they hire.*" From this account I wished for a recommendation to one of these sagacious Friends. I observed all the way I went, that the cabins were generally much better than any I had seen in Ireland. Large ones, with two or three rooms, in good order and repair, all with windows and chimneys and little sties for their pigs and cattle. As well built as common in England.

Entering Forth I did not perceive any difference. I went to St Margaret's and introduced myself to Colonel Nun who gave me the following particulars with the assistance of a neighbouring farmer. Leases generally three lives or 31 years. Carry their corn to Wexford. The people increase prodigiously. Rent of a cabin and an acre £3. Generally have a cow and pigs and plenty of poultry. Religion generally Catholic. Many lads go to Newfoundland in May and come home in October, and bring from £15 to £24. Pay £3 passage out and £1. 10s. home. The people are uncommonly industrious, and a most quiet race. In fifteen or twenty years there is no such thing as a robbery. The little farmers live very comfortably and happily, and many of them are worth several hundred pounds. They all speak a broken Saxon language and not one in a hundred knows anything of Irish. They are evidently a distinct people, and I could not but remark their features and cast of countenance varied very much from the common native Irish. The girls and women are handsomer, having much better features and complexions. Indeed the women among the lower classes in general in Ireland, are as ugly as the women of fashion are handsome.

On the coast a considerable fishery of herrings. Every creek has 4 or 5 boats. None barrelled by the people, but the merchants of Wexford barrel them for the West Indies[49].

From St Margaret's I took the road to Wexford, the whole way through the barony of Forth. I saw nothing but straw hats for men as well as women, and found afterwards that they were worn through the whole county, and they give a comic appearance to every group one meets. Laid at the King's Arms at Wexford, a very clean and good inn. There are 14 or 15 small ships belonging to this port, but a bar at the mouth of the harbour prevents large ones coming in.

JULY 13TH. Got to Lord Courtown's[50], who with an attention highly flattering took every means to have me well informed. His seat at Courtown [Co. Wexford] is a very agreeable place, and in some respects a very singular one, for the house is within 600 yards of the sea, and yet it is almost buried in fine woods, which from their growth and foliage show no aversion to their neighbour, who is so often pernicious to all their brethren. Lord Courtown is a very good farmer. His sandy lands by the coast he marls richly, the finest wheat I have yet seen in Ireland was on this sand.

JULY 14TH (Sunday). To church, and was surprised to find a large congregation. This is not often the case in Ireland out of a mass house. Gallop on the strand; it is a fine firm beautiful sand for miles. The paddies were swimming their horses in the sea to cure the mange, or keep them in health. The following particulars of the husbandry of the neighbourhood his Lordship's brother gave me.

At Courtown, and around Gorey, farms in general are

small. The soil is a skirting of sand against the sea, the rest is gravel, and gravelly loam. A good deal of mountain, which in its wild state does not let for more than 3s. The little farmers improve it much by fallow and lime, which they bring from Carlow, twenty-five miles. When improved it is worth 16s. an acre, and they pay that for it at the expiration of the lease. No peas or beans sown. Not a turnip in the country among common farmers, though the finest sands and grounds imaginable for them; nor clover. A little flax is sown, generally after potatoes, and the culture of it increases gradually. It is not a sheep country, and no such thing as folding known. Lime is not used, except in the mountains from Carlow, but marl is very general, a good blue sort, which they spread amply on the sod, and plough it for wheat. They dairy much here, some having twenty cows, for butter chiefly. They all keep many pigs, and the more upon account of their dairies. Tillage is performed all with horses, four in a plough, and do half an acre a day. All their chaff is lost in winnowing their corn in the fields. In hiring and stocking farms, they will take them with scarce anything but a few cows and horses, yet they pay their rents very well and few of them fail. Tithes are valued every year, and the tenth taken as a composition, wheat at 18s. a barrel, barley, 8s., oats, 6s. The tenth lamb 2s. 6d. No tea in the labourers' cabins, but in those of little farmers they have it, and it increases much. Leases generally three lives to Protestants, and 31 years to Catholics. The system of middlemen going out—none in new let lands. Barley carried to Wexford for exportation, and wheat to Dublin by means of bounty on inland carriage. The people increase considerably. All keep cows, and generally a horse and a pig or two, with plenty of poultry reared on potatoes. They live on oat cakes when potatoes are not in season; the little farmers, that have 40 or 50 acres, eat a good deal of meat; fish is a great article with the poor, particularly herrings and cod. In general much improving, and more industrious than formerly. In about four years, forty or fifty persons emigrated to America. They are beginning to improve mountain and bog, which from being worth nothing before, now let at above 20*s.* an acre. No farms hired in partnership.

The Whiteboys were violent for about three months in 1775, chiefly from Kilkenny and Carlow, but suppressed immediately by the spirited associations of the gentlemen.

JULY 15TH. Leaving Courtown, took the Arklow road. Passed a finely wooded park of Mr Ram's and a various country with some good corn in it. Passed to Wicklow prettily situated on the sea. Reached [Newtown] Mount Kennedy [Co. Wicklow] the seat of General Cuninghame. He is in the midst of a country almost all his own, for he has 10,000 Irish acres here. His domain and the grounds about it are very beautiful. Not a level can be seen. Every spot is tossed about in a variety of hill and dale.

JULY 16TH. Rode in the morning to "Drum" [Glen of Dunran], a large extent of mountain and wood on the General's estate. It is a very noble scenery. A vast rocky glen, one side bare rocks to an immense height, hanging in a thousand whimsical yet frightful forms, with vast fragments tumbled from them, and lying in romantic confusion; the other a fine mountain side covered with shrubby wood. About Mount Kennedy the country is inclosed with various mountains and high lands. There are considerable tracts of mountain land improved. They pare and burn the mountain as the only way to improve, though contrary to an absurd Act of Parliament against it. The wool of the country is all wrought up by the inhabitants, spun, combed and wove into flannel and friezes, and to such an extent that the mountain farmers pay half their rents by this manufacture. On the mountains many goats are kept for the milk, which is drunk very much by people from Dublin, who take lodgings for drinking goats' whey. Tithes are paid by composition. The crops are viewed and they agree for one year. The people increase much. Farms much taken in the mountains by partnership. Three or four will take 100 acres and divide among themselves as in Kilkenny. They have plenty of potatoes. All keep a cow, some more. Their fuel is turf from the mountains. They are universal pilferers of everything they can lay their hands on. Great liars, but full of quickness and sagacity, and grateful to excess.

JULY 17TH. Took my leave of General Cuninghame, and went through the Glen of the Downs in my way to Powerscourt [Co. Wicklow][51]. The Glen is a pass between two vast ridges of mountains covered with wood, which have a very noble effect. The vale is no wider than to admit the road, a small gurgling river almost by its side, and narrow slips of rocky and shrubby ground which part them. In the front all escape seems denied by an immense conical mountain[52], which rises out of the Glen and seems to fill it up. The scenery is of a most magnificent character. On the top of the ridge to the right Mr La Touche has a banqueting room. Passing from this sublime scene, the road leads through cheerful grounds all under corn, rising and falling to the eye, and then to a vale of charming verdure broken into inclosures, and bounded by two rocky mountains, distant darker mountains filling up the scene in front. This whole ride is interesting, for within a mile and a half of Tinnehinch (the inn to which I was directed), you come to a delicious view on the right: a small vale opening to the sea, bounded by mountains, whose dark shade forms a perfect contrast to the extreme beauty and lively verdure of the lower scene, consisting of gently swelling lawns rising from each other, with groups of trees between, and the whole so prettily scattered with white farms, as to add every idea of cheerfulness. Kept on towards Powerscourt, which presently came in view from the edge of a declivity. You look full upon the house, which appears to be in the most beautiful situation in the world, on the side of a mountain, half-way between its bare top and an irriguous vale at its foot.

Breakfasted at the inn at Tinnehinch, and then drove to the Park to see the waterfall. Returning to Tinnehinch, I went to Enniskerry, and gained by this detour in my return to go to the Dargle, a beautiful view which I should otherwise have lost. The road runs on the edge of a declivity, from whence there is a most pleasing prospect of the river's course through the vale and the woods of Powerscourt, which here appear in large masses of dark shade, the whole bounded by mountains. Turn to the left into the private road that leads to the Dargle, and presently gives a specimen of what is to be expected by a romantic glen of wood, where the high lands almost lock into each other, and leave scarce a passage for the river at bottom, which rages, as if with difficulty forcing its way. It is topped by a high mountain, and in front you catch a beautiful plat [i.e. patch or plot] of inclosures bounded by the sea. Enter the Dargle. It is a narrow glen or vale formed by the sides of two opposite mountains; the whole thickly spread with oak wood. At the bottom (and the depth is immense) it is narrowed to the mere channel of the river, which rather tumbles from rock to rock than runs. The extent of wood that hangs to the eye in every direction is great, the depth of the precipice on which you stand immense, which with the roar of the water at bottom forms a scene truly interesting.

Return to the carriage, and quit the Dargle, which upon

the whole is a very singular place, different from all I have
seen in England, and, I think, preferable to most. Cross
a murmuring stream clear as crystal, and, rising a hill, look
back on a pleasing landscape of inclosures, which, waving
over hills, end in mountains of a very noble character.
Reach Dublin.

JULY 18TH. Once more to Lord Harcourt's at St Wol-
stan's where I was so fortunate as to meet Colonel Burton.
He gave me a fresh packet of recommendations into the
north of Ireland and taking my leave of his Excellency
passed Maynooth to "Kilrue" [Kilbrew House, Co.
Meath]. From Celbridge to Maynooth is a line of very
fine corn. Passed Dunboyne, from thence to Kilbrew.
Mr Lowther to whom I had a letter, not being at home
I was forced to take refuge in a cabin, called an inn at
Ratoath. Preserve me Fates from such another!

JULY 19TH. Left Ratoath. Got to Baron Hamilton's[53]
at Hampton [Hall] near Balbriggan [Co. Dublin], by
breakfast. His house is new built and stands agreeably by
a fine shore with a full view of the mountains of Mourne
[Co. Down] at 16 leagues distance, and the isles of Skerries
near him, much improving his view. He favoured me with
the following account.

About Hampton, farms rise from 40 acres to 100 and
150 acres. No taking in partnership. Tillage mostly with
horses. In hiring farms they will take 100 acres with £200.
Tithes are generally compounded. Many lands are hired
to be re-let. Population increases very fast, and the country
in every respect improves amazingly. A cottage and half
an acre 40s. to £3, for a cow 30s., generally have two
cows. A bellyfull of potatoes and oat meal for stir-about;
keep two or three pigs, and a great deal of poultry. They
are universally much better off than twenty years ago.

Cattle of all sorts is a very inferior object here. This place is in Fingal[54], which is a territory from near Dublin, extending along the coast, inhabited by a people they call Fingalians; an English colony planted here many years ago, speaking nearly the same language as the barony of Forth, but more intermixed with Irish in language, etc. from vicinity to the capital.

The Baron carried me to Balbriggan, a little sea port of his, which owes its being to his care and attention. It subsists by its fishing boats, which he builds; has twenty-three of them, each carrying seven men, who are paid wages, but divide the produce of their fishery. The vessel takes one share, and the hands one each, which amounts on an average to 16s. a week. The port owes its existence to a very fine pier which Baron Hamilton has built, within which ships of 200 tons can lay their broadsides, and unload on the quay. Such vessels bring coals and culm [coal dust] from Wales, etc.

Left Balbriggan, and went to Ballygarth [Co. Meath] the seat of [Thomas] Pepper, Esq. In conversation on the common people, Mr Pepper assured me he never found them more dishonest than in other countries. They would thieve slightly till they found him resolute in punishing all he discovered, even his turnips have suffered very little depredation.

JULY 20TH. To Drogheda [Co. Louth][55], a well-built town, active in trade, the Boyne bringing ships to it. It was market-day, and I found the quantity of corn, etc., and the number of people assembled, very great; few country markets in England more thronged.

To the field of battle on the Boyne[56]. The view of the scene from a rising ground which looks down upon it is exceedingly beautiful, being one of the completest landscapes I have seen. It is a vale, losing itself in front between bold declivities, above which are some thick woods and distant country. Through the vale the river winds and forms an island, the point of which is tufted with trees in the prettiest manner imaginable; on the other side a rich scenery of wood, among which is Dr Norris's house. To the right, on a rising ground on the banks of the river, is the obelisk, backed by a very bold declivity. Pursued the road till near it, quitted my chaise, and walked to the foot of it. It is founded on a rock which rises boldly from the river. It is a noble pillar, and admirably placed. I seated myself on the opposite rock, and indulged the emotions which, with a melancholy not unpleasing, filled my bosom, while I reflected on the consequences that had sprung from the victory here obtained. Liberty was then triumphant. May the virtues of our posterity secure that prize which the bravery of their ancestors won! Peace to the memory of the Prince to whom, whatever might be his failings, we owed that day memorable in the annals of Europe!

Returned part of the way, and took the road to Collon [Co. Louth], where the Lord Chief Baron Foster received me in the most obliging manner, and gave me a variety of information uncommonly valuable. He has made the greatest improvements I have anywhere met with. The whole country twenty-two years ago was a waste sheepwalk, covered chiefly with heath, with some dwarf furze and fern. The cabins and people as miserable as can be conceived; not a Protestant in the country, nor a road passable for a carriage. In a word, perfectly resembling other mountainous tracts, and the whole yielding a rent of not more than from 3s. to 4s. an acre. Mr Foster could not bear so barren a property, and determined to attempt the improvement of an estate of 5000 acres till then deemed irreclaimable. He encouraged the tenants by every species of persuasion and expense, but they had so ill an opinion

of the land that he was forced to begin with 2000 or
3000 acres in his own hands. He did not however turn
out the people, but kept them in to see the effects of his
operations. These were of a magnitude I have never
heard before. He had for several years 27 lime kilns
burning stone, which was brought four miles, with culm
from Milford Haven. The stone was quarried by from
sixty to eighty men regularly at that work. While this
vast business of liming was going forwards, roads were also
making, and the whole tract inclosed in fields. In order
to create a new race of tenants, he fixed upon the most
active and industrious labourers, bought them cows, etc.
and advanced money to begin with little farms, leaving
them to pay it as they could. These men he nursed up in
proportion to their industry, and some of them are now
good farmers with £400 or £500 each in their pockets.
He dictated to them what they should do with their lands,
promising to pay the loss, if anything should happen, while
all the advantage would be their own. They obeyed him
implicitly, and he never had a demand for a shilling loss.

He fixed a colony of French and English Protestants on
the land, which have flourished greatly. In Collon are
fifty families of tradesmen among whom sobriety and
industry are perfectly established. Many of these lands
being very wet, draining was a considerable operation.
This he did very effectually, burying in the drains several
millions of loads of stones. The mode in which the Chief
Baron carried on the improvement was by fallowing. He
stubbed the furze, etc. and ploughed it, upon which he
spread from 140 to 170 barrels of lime per acre. For
experiment he tried as far as 300 barrels, and always found
that the greater the quantity, the greater the improvement.
After the liming, fallowed the land for rye, and after the
rye took two crops of oats. His great object was to show
the tenantry as soon as he could, what these improvements

would do in corn, in order to set them to work themselves. He sold them the corn crops on the ground at 40s. an acre. The three crops paid him certainly the expense of the liming; at the same time they were profitable bargains to the tenants. With the third corn crop the land was laid down to grass. Upon this operation, after the manuring, ditching and draining, the old tenants very readily hired them. Some seeing the benefit of the works, executed them upon their own lands, but their landlord advanced all the money, and trusted to their success and honesty for the payment. This change of their sentiments induced him to build new farm houses, of which he has erected above thirty, all of lime and stone, at the expense of above £40 a house. The farms are in general about 80 acres each. He also allotted a considerable tract of many acres for plantations, which are well placed and flourishing. Mr Foster, his son, takes much pleasure in adding to them, and has introduced one thousand seven hundred sorts of European and American plants. The country is now a sheet of corn. A greater improvement I have not heard of.

This great improver, a title more deserving estimation than that of a great general or a great minister, lives now to overlook a country flourishing only from his exertions. He has made a barren wilderness smile with cultivation, planted it with people, and made these people happy. Such are the men to whom monarchs should decree their honours, and nations erect their statues.

In his Lordship's circuits through the north of Ireland, he was upon all occasions attentive to procure information relative to the linen manufacture[57]. It has been his general observation that where the linen manufacture spreads, the tillage is very bad. Thirty years ago the export of linen and yarn about £500,000 a year. Now £1,200,000 to £1,500,000. Respecting the thieving disposition of the common people, which I had heard so much of, the Chief

Baron was of an entire different opinion. From his own experience he judged them to be remarkably honest. In working his improvements he has lived in his house without shutters, bolts or bars, and with it half full of *spalpeens*, yet never lost the least trifle, nor has he met with any depredations among his fences or plantations. Raising rents he considers as one of the greatest causes of the improvement of Ireland; he has found that upon his own estates it has universally quickened their industry, set them to searching for manures, and made them in every respect better farmers. But this holds only to a certain point; if carried too far, it deadens, instead of animating industry. He has always preferred his old tenants, and never let a farm by advertisement to receive proposals. That the system of letting farms to be re-let to lower tenants was going out very much: it is principally upon the estates of absentees, whose agents think only of the most rent from the most solvent tenant.

In conversation upon the Popery Laws[58], I expressed my surprise at their severity. He said they were severe in the letter, but were never executed. It is rarely or never (he knew no instance) that a Protestant discoverer gets a lease by proving the lands let under two-thirds of their real value to a Papist. There are severe penalties on carrying arms or reading Mass, but the first is never executed for poaching (which I have heard) and as to the other, mass houses are to be seen everywhere. There is one in his own town. His Lordship did justice to the merits of the Roman Catholics by observing that they were in general a very sober, honest and industrious people. This account of the laws against them brought to my mind an admirable expression of Mr Burke's in the English House of Commons—"*Connivance is the relaxation of slavery, not the definition of liberty.*"

The kingdom more improved in the last twenty years

than in a century before. The great spirit began in 1749 and 1750. He was assured that the emigrations[59], which made so much noise in the north of Ireland, were principally [of] idle people, who, far from being missed, left the country the better for their absence. They were generally Dissenters, very few Churchmen or Catholics.

JULY 21ST. To Dundalk [Co. Louth][60]. The view down on this town very beautiful; swelling hills of a fine verdure with many rich inclosures backed by a bold outline of mountain. Laid at the Clanbrassil Arms, and found it a very good inn. The place, like most of the Irish towns I have been in, full of new buildings, with every mark of increasing wealth and prosperity. A cambric manufacture was established here by Parliament, but failed; it was, however, the origin of that more to the north.

JULY 22ND. Left Dundalk. Took the road through Ravensdale. Here I saw many good stone and slate houses, and some bleach greens, and I was much pleased to see the inclosures creeping high up the sides of the mountains, stony as they are. Rents in Ravensdale 10s., mountain land 2s. 6d. to 5s. Large tracts rented by villages, the cottiers dividing it among themselves, and making the mountain common for their cattle.

Breakfasted at Newry [Co. Down][61]—the Globe, another good inn. This town appears exceedingly flourishing, and is very well built; yet forty years ago, I was told, there were nothing but mud cabins in it. This great rise has been much owing to the canal to Lough Neagh. I crossed it twice; it is indeed a noble work. I was amazed to see ships of 150 tons and more lying in it, like barges in an English canal. Here is a considerable trade.

Take the road to Markethill [Co. Armagh]. I am now got into the linen country, and the worst husbandry I have met with. My Lord Chief Baron is right. All the farms are very small, let to weavers, etc. This road is abominably bad, continually over hills, rough, stony, and cut up. It is a turnpike, which in Ireland is a synonymous term for a vile road; which is the more extraordinary, as the bye ones are the finest in the world. It is the effect of jobs and imposition, which disgrace the kingdom; the presentment roads show what may be done, and render these villainous turnpikes the more disgusting.

Called at Lord Gosfort's[62] [at Markethill], to whom I had been introduced by Lord Harcourt; but he was not yet come from Dublin; his steward, however, gave me the few following particulars. In spinning a woman will do 5 or 6 hanks a week, and get 30s. for it by hire, as wages for half a year. A girl of twelve years old three half-pence or 2d. a day. A man will earn by weaving coarse linen 1s. 2d. and 1s. 6d. by fine linen. The manufacturers live better than the labourers. They earn 3s. 6d. a week in winter, and 4s. in summer. Cloth and yarn never so dear as at present, and people all employed—none idle. Religion mostly Roman. Manufacturers generally Protestants. The manufacturers' wives drink tea for breakfast. No cattle but for convenience among the small farmers. No farms above 100 acres, and those stock ones, for fattening cows and bullocks. Very few sheep in the country.

Reached Armagh in the evening. Waited on the Primate.

JULY 23RD. His Grace rode out with me to Armagh[63], and showed me some of the noble and spirited works by which he has perfectly changed the face of the neighbourhood. The buildings he has erected in seven years, one would suppose, without previous information, to be the work of an active life. A list of them will justify this observation. He has erected a very elegant palace, 90 by

60 feet, and 40 feet high, in which an unadorned simplicity reigns. The barracks were erected under his Grace's directions, and form a large and handsome edifice. The school is a building of considerable extent, and admirably adapted for the purpose: a more convenient or a better contrived one, is nowhere to be seen. This edifice entirely at the Primate's expense. The church is erected of white stone, and having a tall spire makes a very agreeable object in a country where churches and spires do not abound— at least such as are worth looking at. Three other churches the Primate has also built, and done considerable reparations to the cathedral. He has been the means also of erecting a public infirmary, which was built by subscription, contributing amply to it himself. A public library he has erected at his own expense, given a large collection of books and endowed it. He has further ornamented the city with a market house and shambles, and been the direct means, by giving leases upon that condition, of almost new building the whole place. He found it a nest of mud cabins, and he will leave it a well-built city of stone and slate. I heard it asserted in common conversation, that his Grace, in these noble undertakings, had not expended less than £30,000, besides what he had been the means of doing, though not directly at his own expense.

In order that I might be well informed about the linen manufacture, his Grace was so obliging as to send for one of the most considerable merchants in the city who very intelligently gave me all the particulars I wanted. About Armagh, the farms are very small; the only object the linen manufacture. This is the case all the way to Newry, also to Monaghan, but in that county the farms are somewhat larger. Towards Lurgan, Dungannon and Stewartstown [Co. Tyrone] much the same. Scarce any of them have potatoes and oats to feed their families; great importations from Louth, Meath, Monaghan, Cavan and Tyrone, besides what comes occasionally from England and Scotland.

I was informed that the produce of the flax depended on the oiliness of it, and that the goodness of the linen on not being too much bleached, which is only an exhalation of the oil. They generally pull (their flax) the latter end of July and the beginning of August, and immediately ripple it to get the seeds off, and then lay it into water from six or seven to twelve days, according to the softness of the water, trying it before they take it out; the softer the water the shorter the time, generally bogs or pools, the bog the best. They lay it so thick as to fill the pool. When they take it out, they spread it on meadow ground from ten to fifteen days, according to weather; if that is very bad, much of it is lost. Upon taking it up, they dry by laying it in heaps on a hurdle fixed upon posts, and making a fire of turf under it. As fast as it dries, they beat it on stones with a beetle, then they scutch it to separate the heart or the *shoves* from the rest. Mills are invented for this, which if they use, they pay 1s. 1d. a stone for it, which is cheaper than what their own labour amounts to. They next send it to a flax-heckler, which is a sort of combing it, and separates into two or three sorts; here generally two, tow and flax. In this state it is saleable.

We next come to the manufacture. The stone-rough after heckling will produce 8 lb. flax for coarse linen. The 8 lb. will spin into 20 dozen of yarn or 20 hanks or 5 spangles fit for a ten hundred cloth; 7½ spangles will weave into a piece of linen of 25 yards long and a yard wide. Thus 1½ stone of flax will make that piece; but the tow remains, 4¾ lb., of which they make a coarser linen. Thirty stone the produce of an acre makes therefore twenty such pieces. The price of this cloth is from 10½d. to 11½d. a yard brown, the state in which they sell it. The fixed price for weaving is 2½d. a yard, but this is when the poor are not able to raise it and work for hire for those who advance them the yarn. A great deal is done in this manner as well as by those who raise the flax and go through the whole of the operation. When the weaver has made his piece of cloth, he goes into the market of Armagh, which is every Tuesday, and sells it to the draper as he would any other commodity, always receiving the money on the spot, as there is no credit. The draper names the price, and the man takes or refuses it. There are many drapers, so that the man tries whom he pleases: there is no combination against the seller, but rather a competition. The draper generally has the bleach greens, and the expense to him of bleaching is £4. 10s. to £5 a pack of thirty pieces, or 3s. to 3s. 2d. a piece. Then he either sends it to factors in London or Dublin, or sells it at the Linen Hall in Dublin. Some go over to Chester Fair themselves, and dispose of it there.

In general the manufacture was at the height in 1770 and 1771. In 1772 and 1773 there was a great decline, both in price and quantity. In 1774 very low, till May, when a sudden rise from a speculation of sending to America, and for the demand of the Spanish flota, which was detained a year for want of coarse linens, not being able to be supplied from Germany as usual, and since May, 1774, it has continued very flourishing, but is not yet equal to what it was. The decline in 1772 and 1773, owing to the destruction of credit, and to the want of a market; but let me observe that a convulsion in credit necessarily contracts the market. Another circumstance was the price of bread in England, which they think, was so high that the English could not afford to buy much of these coarse linens, of which they are the great consumers. Germany they consider as the great rival, and not Scotland. The emigrations were chiefly in 1772 and 1773. Many weavers and spinners, with all their families, went. Some farmers, who sold their leases, went off with sums from £100 to £300 and carried many with them. They stopped going when the war broke out. In 1772 and 1773 many turned farming labourers, which is not the case when the trade is high. The religion generally Roman, some Presbyterians. Protestants emigrated most. The Oakboys and Steelboys[64] had their rise in the increase of rents and in oppressive county cesses.

JULY 24TH. Took my leave of his Grace. Took a ride to see the neighbouring country by Killylea Hill, Fellows Hall, Wood Park Lodge, Lisloony, Tynan and Glaslough. It is a cheerful beautiful country and well worth a traveller's time to take this ride in order to see it.

JULY 25TH. Returned through Armagh. Dined with Mr Workman at Maghan [Co. Armagh]. About that place they are in general very well off as to living. Their food is stir-about, potatoes, bread of maslin [*i.e.* mixed grain] or wheat, and some meat once a fortnight. They are well clothed and have plenty of fuel. The weavers universally earn much more than the few country labourers there are. The spinners earn from 3*d.* to 4*d.* a day. The weavers earn 10*d.* to 1*s.* 4*d.* Weavers very often turn labourers, which is attributed to so many being, contrary to law, bound apprentices for two years instead of five, by which means they are bad hands and can only do the very coarsest work. As to health, from the sedentary life, they rarely change their profession for that. They take exercise of a different sort, keeping packs of hounds, every man one, and joining; they hunt hares: a pack of hounds is never heard, but all the weavers leave their looms, and away they go after them by hundreds. This much amazed me, but assured it was very common. They are in general apt to be licentious and disorderly; but they are reckoned to be rather oppressed by the county cesses for roads, etc. which are not of general use.

In the evening reached Mr Brownlow's[65] at Lurgan, to whom I am indebted for some valuable information. Upon enquiring concerning the emigrations, I found that in 1772 and 1773 they were at the height, that some went from this neighbourhood with property but not many. They were in general poor and unemployed. They find here that when provisions are very cheap, the poor spend much of their time in whisky houses. The weavers earn by coarse linens 1s. a day, by fine 1s. 4d., and it is the same with the spinners, the finer the yarn the more they earn, but in common a woman earns about 3d.

This being market day at Lurgan, Mr Brownlow walked to it with me, that I might see the way in which the linens were sold. The cambrics are sold early, and through the whole morning; but when the clock strikes eleven the drapers jump upon stone standings, and the weavers instantly flock about them with their pieces. The bargains are not struck at a word, but there is a little altercation, whether the price shall be one-halfpenny or a penny a yard more or less, which appeared to me useless. The draper's clerk stands by him, and writes his master's name on the pieces he buys, with the price, and, giving it back to the seller, he goes to the draper's quarters, and waits his coming. At twelve it ends; then there is an hour for measuring the pieces, and paying the money, for nothing but ready money is taken, and this is the way the business is carried on at all the markets. Three thousand pieces a week are sold here, at 35s. each on an average, or £5250, and per annum £273,000, and this is all made in a circumference of not many miles.

The town parks about Lurgan let at 40s. an acre, but the country in general at 14s. The husbandry is exceedingly bad, the people minding nothing but flax and potatoes.

Leaving Lurgan I went to Waringstown [Co. Down], and waiting upon Mr Waring had some conversation with him upon the state of the country. He was of opinion, that the emigrations had not thinned the population, for at present they are crowded with people; but he thinks if the war ends in favour of the Americans, that they will go off in shoals. Very few Roman Catholics emigrated. The rising of the Steelboys was owing, as they said, to the increase of rents, and complaints of general oppression; but Mr Waring remarked, that the pardons which were granted to the Oakboys, a few years before, were principally the cause of those new disturbances.

Cross the road to Mr Clibborn's, who gave me much information of the greatest value concerning the linen manufacture. In bleaching (the linen) is steeped in cold river water, or sometimes not at all; then to the wash mills for washing; then boiled in barilla ashes (or America or Russia potash) imported from Alicante to Newry or Belfast. Washed thoroughly after this and spread on grass for four days; lift it and boil it again as before; then to the grass again, and repeated till nearly white for rubbing. Next put it into a scald of soap, and from thence into the rub boards, if coarse cloth one rub sufficient, but for fine three or four. After rubbing, washed, and put to sower in vitriol and water, twenty-four hours will do, but ten days no injury; fine cloth three serves, one after every rub, but for coarse one rub is sufficient. This sowering merely for cleansing and purging. After sowering it has a scald of soap, from which well washed, wrung, and made ready for starch and blue, then dried and beetled, which is done by a mill, after which done up with a screwing machine for sale. These the particulars commonly known among bleachers; there are secrets in the trade which they of course do not communicate, but not so many, I apprehend, as generally supposed, for where there are few, or even

none, but with an appearance of them, all is supposed by
the vulgar to be mystery. Upon the above account I have
only to remark, that the rubbing appears to me an operation
for giving the cloth beauty at the expense of strength. It is
a most severe operation, being drawn between boards full
of teeth, which are made for the professed purpose of adding
to the friction, and the effect is such, that large quantities
of nap are constantly taken out of the machine. This is
a very fine invention for wearing out a manufacture as soon
as made. Mr Clibborn was ready enough to confess that
this work is carried too far, but the London drapers, he
says, demand thick cloths, and this operation, contracting
the breadth of the piece, gives it a thick appearance, which
they are fond of. The beetling does not appear to me to
be near so severe an operation. It is a continued system
of perpendicular strokes upon the cloth wound round a
cylinder, for the purpose of smoothing it, and giving it a
gloss. It is sold at Dublin; half the manufacture to London
from Newry, Belfast, or Dublin. Cambric all sold in
Dublin, it increases much. England the great consumption
of Irish linens. No rivals in the Irish seven-eighths and
three-fourths yard wide, but in the dowlas and diaper the
German, and in sheeting the Russians. The dowlas and
sheeting are made in King's and Queen's County, and
Westmeath. Hands are plentiful for the demand, notwithstanding the emigrations, but the men do not work more
than half what they might do owing to the cheapness of
provisions making them idle, as they think of nothing more
than the present necessity. The present high price of linens
and yarn attributed to the increased demand at Manchester
for yarn; also to the Spanish market for linen being almost
a new trade; likewise to foreign linens coming dearer to
market than formerly.

Leaving Waringstown reached Hillsborough [Co.
Down] that night; passed through Dromore, a miserable

nest of dirty mud cabins. Lord Hillsborough [66] has marked the approach to his town by many small plantations on the tops of the hills, through which the road leads. The inn of his building is a noble one for Ireland.

JULY 27TH. Reached Lisburn [Co. Antrim] and waited on the Bishop of Down. Leaving Lisburn took the road to Belfast [67]. From Lisburn to Belfast on the river Lagan there are twelve or thirteen bleach greens. The counties of Down and Antrim are computed to make to the amount of £800,000 a year and near one-third of it in this vale.

JULY 28TH. Took the road to Portaferry [Co. Down] by "Newtown" [Newtown Ards], where I breakfasted. It is an improving place belonging to Mr Stewart who has built a very handsome market house, and laid out a square around it. Reached Portaferry, the town and seat of Patrick Savage, Esq., who took every means of procuring me information concerning that neighbourhood.

The whole barony of the Ards [68] are fishermen, sailors and farmers, by turns. This little port has a tolerable share of trade. They have twelve ships which go annually to Lough Swilly herring fishery. Coals are brought from Whitehaven, and from Gothenborg and Norway timber and iron. Trade increases, and the place is much more flourishing than it was. Cattle very trifling, only small stocks for convenience. The principal religion is Presbyterian [69]. If a weaver has, as most have, a crop of flax, the wife and daughter spin it and he weaves it; if he is not a weaver but employed by his farm, they carry the yarn to market. All along the coast of Ards and in Strangford Lough, sea wrack is collected by the country people with great diligence for burning into kelp; it yields at present from 40s. to 50s. a ton, the bleach greens have much of it and the rest of it exported to England.

The plentifulness of the country about Portaferry, Strangford, etc. is very great. This will appear from the following circumstances: pigeons 2*s*. a dozen; rabbits 4*d*. a couple; turbot 4*s*., sole 10*d*. a pair; bret and haddock 1*d*. each; lobsters 5*s*. a dozen; oysters 19*d*. a hundred; John Dory, gurnet, whiting, 4*d*. a dozen; mackerel, mullet, partridges and quails in plenty; wild ducks 10*d*. to 1*s*.; widgeon 6*d*. a couple; barnacle 10*d*. each; teal 6*d*. a couple; plover 3*d*.

This country is in general beautiful, but particularly so about the straits that lead into Strangford Lough. From Mr Savage's door the view has great variety. To the left are tracts of hilly grounds, between which the sea appears, and the vast chain of mountains in the Isle of Man distinctly seen. In front the hills rise in a beautiful outline, and a round hill projects like a promontory into the straits, and under it the town amidst groups of trees; the scene is cheerful of itself, but rendered doubly so by the ships and herring boats sailing in and out. To the right the view is crowned by the mountains of Mourne, which whenever seen, are of a character peculiarly bold, and even terrific.

JULY 30TH. Crossed the straits in Mr Savage's boat, and breakfasted with Mr Aynsworth, collector of the customs [at Strangford]. He gave me the following particulars of the barony of Lecale [Co. Down].

Great quantities of barley sown. No turnips. Their manures are marl, shells, sea wrack. Marl has been used greatly for many years, it is white marl from the bottom of bogs, and some of it immediately under the surface; they carry it on horseback in bags, which hold each 4 bushels, and they lay about 450 to 500 bags per acre. They are reckoned very much to have exhausted their land, for upon the credit of a marling they will take twenty corn crops running, and as a proof of this I was told, that the Deanery of Down, which consists of tithes in Lecale, was £2200 a year thirty-five years ago, whereas it is now no more than £1600, owing to the decline of the Lecale crops, and this from the abuse of marl. Very little grass land, and scarce any cattle, but cows to every farm for convenience. The farmers are generally, not only in Lecale, but the whole county, much better and wealthier than formerly. The linen manufacture is carried on very generally through the barony. In Downpatrick, there are 500 webs sold every week. Upon the marling coming in, there was a corn coasting trade opened from Strangford, and it flourished considerably, but fell off pretty much, as has been mentioned with respect to the Deanery of Down. The trade has, however, been upon the increase for about four years; from the 11th of September, 1775, to July the 1st, 1776, there were 100 cargoes of wheat and barley, about 50 tons each on an average, to Liverpool, White-haven, Lisbon, etc. and to Dublin. To the port of Strangford, which includes Downpatrick, Dundrum, Killyleagh, Killough, Portaferry, Comber and Newtown, there belong thirty vessels, from 35 to 150 tons burden besides fishing vessels.

I took the road to Downpatrick, through a various country; Down[patrick] Bay is on the left [*sic*], and exhibits an amazing variety of islands, creeks and bays, which appear among cultivated hills in a most picturesque manner.

JULY 31ST. Reached Belfast[70] in the forenoon, and was then fortunate enough to meet with Mr Holmes (and) several other gentlemen [to whom I had introductions]. Gained upon the whole the information I wished; it consisted of the following particulars.

The imports of Belfast consist in rum, brandy, geneva, and wines. Till within these two years much grain, since that none, but have on the contrary exported some. Coals from Britain. Iron, timber, hemp, and ashes from the Baltic. Barilla from Spain for the bleach greens. Tea, raw sugars, hops, and porter the principal articles from Great Britain. From North America, wheat, staves, flour, and flax seed; all which cut off at present. The exports are beef, butter, pork, to the West Indies and France. The great article, linen cloth to London; formerly some to America. The balance much in favour of the place. Derry, Newry, and Belfast, the linen export towns; two-thirds from Belfast, a little from Derry, the rest from Newry. There are three sugar houses here. The number of ships belonging to Belfast about fifty sail from 20 to 300 tons. A vessel of 200 tons, half-loaded, may come to the Quay, there being $9\frac{1}{2}$ to 10 feet water; larger vessels lay two miles and a half down. The trade of Belfast was at its height in 1770; 1771, 1772, and 1773, were the worst years; 1774, and 1775 it has been mending; but 1774, and 1775 not equal to 1770, and 1771, by one-third. It is curious to see from hence how the trade of this place has vibrated with the linen manufacture, that being just the account I have received of the progress of that fabric. Calculated that the trade of Belfast in general increased one-third in fifteen years, ending in 1770, or 1771.

Belfast being the place from whence the emigrations were the greatest, I made many enquiries concerning them, and found that they have for many years had a regular emigration of about 2000 annually; but in 1772 the decline of the linen manufacture increased the number; and the same cause continuing, in 1773 they were at the highest, when 4000 went. In 1774 there were but few, and in 1775 there were none, nor any since. Some that went had property, and so had some of those that always went. In general they were the most idle and worthless, and not reckoned any loss to the country.

In 1771 there were 300 looms in Belfast, but in 1774 there were only 180. There is a considerable slaughter at this place. In 1775 cured 6000 barrels of beef, at 40s. a barrel, in the town; and 5500 of pork at 50s. The principal part of the grazing land the lower part of Antrim from Ballymena towards Larne, and Ballymoney; some from Meath and even from Sligo. Six or seven years ago they exported 500 barrels of pork. In 1775, 7000 [barrels]. In 1776, it will be 10,000 [barrels]. When oatmeal above 1d. or 1¼d. a pound, the poor live entirely upon potatoes and milk; no meat; but herrings in the season. Price of provisions, etc. at Belfast are: potatoes 9d. a bushel; pigeons 6d. a couple; rabbits ditto; salmon 2d. a lb.; lobsters 6d.; plaice ¾d. per lb.; oysters 1s. to 4s. per hundred; fresh cod 1d. per lb.; barnacle 1s.; widgeon 1s. a pair; oatmeal ¾d. per lb.; lime 1s. per barrel; coals 13s. a ton. Labour the year round 1s. 1d. in the town, 8d. in the country. Seamen 30s. a month, and ship provisions. Spinners earn 3d. a day. Weavers 1s. 1d.; they never go for labourers.

Belfast is a very well built town of brick, they having no stone quarry in the neighbourhood. The streets are broad and straight, and the inhabitants, amounting to about 15,000, make it appear lively and busy. The public buildings are not numerous nor very striking, but over the exchange Lord Donegall is building an assembly room, 60 feet long by 30 broad, and 24 feet high; a very elegant room. A card room adjoining, 30 by 22 and 22 feet high; a tea room of the same size. His lordship is also building a new church, which is one of the lightest and most pleasing I have anywhere seen; it is 74 by 54 and 30 feet high to the cornice, the aisles separated by a double row of columns; nothing can be lighter or more pleasing. The town belongs entirely to his lordship. Rent of it £2000 a year. His estate extends from "Drumbridge" [Drumbeg], near Lisburn, to

Larne [Co. Antrim], twenty miles in a right line, and is ten broad. His royalties are great, containing the whole of Lough Neagh, which is, I suppose, the greatest of any subject in Europe. His eel fishery at Toome, and "Port New," on the river Bann, lets for £500 a year, and all the fisheries are his to the [salmon] leap at Coleraine. The estate is supposed to be £31,000 a year, the greatest at present in Ireland. Inishowen, in Donegal, is his, and is £11,000 of it. In Antrim, Lord Antrim's[71] is the most extensive property, being four baronies, and 173,000 acres.

AUG. IST. Crossed the mountains by the new road to Antrim. The linen manufacture spreads over the whole country; consequently the farms are very small, being nothing but patches for the convenience of weavers.

From Antrim to Shanes Castle the road runs at the end of Lough Neagh[72], commanding a noble view of it; of such an extent that the eye can see no land over it. It appears like a perfect sea, and the shore is broken sand banks, which look so much like it, that one can hardly believe the water to be fresh. Upon my arrival at the castle, I was most agreeably saluted with four men hoeing a field of turnips round it, as a preparation for grass. These were the first turnip hoers I have seen in Ireland, and I was more pleased than if I had seen four emperors. The castle is beautifully situated on the lake, the windows commanding a very noble view of it. Mr O'Neill[73] not only received me with the most flattering politeness, but was extremely assiduous for my correct information. He is a very considerable farmer. Farms as in all the linen counties are generally very small. Scarce any of them but are weavers, or the employers of weavers, but they have such a custom of splitting their farms among their children, that one of six acres will be divided. Mr O'Neill has found this to be a source of the greatest misery and inconvenience, for the portions are so small that they cannot live on them; the least accident, such as the death of a cow, etc. reduces them to want, so that neither rent nor any common demand can be paid.

There is a custom here called *rundale*[74] which is a division of their farms into spaces by balks, without fences, which they take here and there, exactly like the common fields of England. It is a most pernicious custom, which gives to all these farms the mischiefs of our open field system in England. I believe it prevails down in Wexford, etc. where I mentioned farms in partnership without sufficiently explaining this circumstance. The increase of the people is very great, extravagantly so, and is felt severely by emigration being stopped at present.

The Hearts of Steel[75] lasted three years; began in 1770 against rents and tithes, and from that went to all sorts of grievances. All was night work, with many firearms. It was in reality owing to the impudence and levelling spirit of the Dissenters. The Roman Catholics were the most quiet. Tithes, however, were a real grievance; the proctors let the first, and perhaps the second year with them run by bond, and they oppressed them by holding the bond over their heads. These tithe farmers are a bad set of people.

AUG. 3RD. Passing Randalstown [Co. Antrim] had a constant view of Slemish [1437 feet], a remarkable mountain rising from a range of other mountains. To Leslie Hill where I found Mr Leslie, a warm admirer of husbandry and practising it on a scale not often met with. He has made considerable improvements of bog; very near his house was one of 20 feet deep, which he has entirely reclaimed. Mr Leslie's crops of wheat were the finest I had seen in Ireland, nor do I remember finer in England. The common husbandry around Leslie Hill is like that of the rest of the manufacturing part of Ireland. The food of the poor people is potatoes, oatmeal and milk. They generally keep cows. Upon the whole they are in general much better off than they were twenty years ago, and dress remarkably well. The manufacture (linen) is at present very flourishing.

AUG. 4TH. Accompanied Mr Leslie to his brother's within three miles of the Giant's Causeway[76] where I had the pleasure of learning several particulars concerning the country upon the coast. Much of the country is in the *rundale* and likewise in the *changedale* system. The little farmers are all weavers, and spin great quantities of yarn for the Derry market. There is a considerable salmon fishery on the coast.

Rode from Mr Leslie's to view the Giant's Causeway. It is certainly a very great curiosity, as an object for speculation, upon the manner of its formation. Whether it owes its origin to fire, and is a species of lava, or to crystallisation, or to whatever cause, is a point that has employed the attention of men much more able to decide upon it than I am, and has been so often treated, that nothing I could say could be new.

AUG. 5TH. Departed for Coleraine [Co. Londonderry]. There the Right Hon. Mr Jackson assisted me with the greatest politeness in procuring the intelligence I wished about the salmon fishery, which is the greatest in the kingdom. Viewed both fisheries above and below the town, very pleasantly situated on the river Bann. The salmon spawn in all the rivers that run into the Bann about the beginning of August, and, as soon as they have done, swim to the sea, where they stay till January, when they begin to return to the fresh water, and continue doing it till August, in which voyage they are taken. The nets are set the middle of January, but by Act of Parliament no nets nor weirs can be kept down after the 12th of August. All the fisheries on the river Bann let at £6000 a year. From the sea to the rock above Coleraine, where the weirs are built, belongs to the London Companies[77]; the greatest part of the rest to Lord Donegall[78]. The young salmon are called *grawls*, and grow at a rate which I should suppose scarce any fish commonly known equals, for within the year some of them will come to 16 and 18 lb. but in general 10 or 12 lb. Such as escape the first year's fishery are *salmon*; and at two years old will generally weigh 20 to 25 lb. This year's fishery has proved the greatest that ever was known, and they had the largest haul, taking 1452 salmon at one drag of one net. I had the pleasure of seeing 370 drawn in at once. They have this year taken 400 ton of fish; 200 ton sold fresh at 1*d*. and 1½*d*. a lb. and 200 ton salted, at £18 and £20 per ton, which are sent to London, Spain, and Italy. The fishery employs eighty men, and the expenses in general calculated to equal the rent.

The linen manufacture is very general about Coleraine. The emigrations from this neighbourhood were in general of idle, loose, disorderly people. It is at present, I was informed, too populous, and if the emigrations are not renewed, the ill effects will be severely felt. The whole county of Derry belongs to the London Companies and the Bishop (of Derry)[79], except some trifling properties. There is a little trade at Coleraine in hides, butter and fish, and some meal is imported, which sounds strange after hearing that so many oats had been exported.

AUG. 6TH. To Newtown Limavady [Co. Londonderry]. Went by Magilligan. At Magilligan is a rabbit warren which yields on an average 3000 dozen per annum, last year 4000, and 5000 have been known. The skins are sent to Dublin, selling from £1500 to £1800 a year. The warren is a sandy tract on the shore, and belongs to the Bishop. The poor (of Newtown Limavady) live on potatoes, milk and oatmeal, with many herrings and salmon; very little flesh. In ten or fifteen years their circumstances are improved. They live and dress better and have better cabins. The emigrations were very great from hence of both idle and industrious and carried large sums with them. Not too populous at present. They have a great spirit of dividing their farms however small, from which many inconveniences arise.

From Limavady to Derry [Londonderry][80] there is very little uncultivated land. Reached Derry at night, and waited two hours in the dark before the ferry boat came over for me.

AUG. 7TH. Rowed from Fahan [Co. Donegal] to Inch Island across the Lough [Swilly]. The scenery amazingly fine, the lands everywhere high and bold, with one of the noblest outlines anywhere to be seen. Inch is a prodigiously fine extensive island, all high lands, with cultivation spreading over it; little clusters of cabins with groups of wood. The water of a great depth and a safe harbour for any number of ships. Here is the great resort of vessels for the herring fishery. It begins the middle of October, and ends about Christmas; it has been five years rising to what it is at present; last year 500 boats were employed in it. The farmers and coast inhabitants build and send them out, and either fish on their own account, or let them, but the latter most common. In a middling year each boat will take 6000 herrings a night, during the season, six times a week, the price on an average 4s. 2d. a 1000 from the water; home consumption takes the most, and the shipping, which lies here for the purpose, the rest.

Mr Alexander (one of the principal merchants of Derry)

began the fishery in 1773, when he employed two sloops only, each of 40 tons. In 1774, he employed the two sloops and a brig of 100 tons, the latter of which he sent to Antigua with 650 barrels, besides what he sold at home, and loaded the sloops in bulk for the coast trade. In 1775, he had the same brig and three sloops, and loaded all four in bulk for the coast trade, one of which on her voyage was put ashore at Blacksod [Bay], in the county of Mayo, and though the sloop was not the least injured, the country [people] came down, obliged the crew to go on shore, threatening to murder them if they did not, and then not only robbed the vessel of her cargo, but of every portable material. The cargo was 40 ton, or 160,000 herrings. Besides what was sent coastwise this year, he exported on board his ship, the *Alexander*, 340 tons, not in the herring trade, 1750 barrels to the West Indies. Here has been a vast increase of the fishery in the hands of one person, which shows clearly what might be done if larger capitals were employed.

In 1775 there were about 1800 barrels exported besides Mr Alexander's. There were that year fish enough in the Lough for all the boats of Europe. They swarmed so, that a boat which went out at seven in the evening, returned at eleven full, and went out on a second trip. The fellows said it was difficult to row through them, and every winter the plenty has been great, only the weather not equally good for taking, which cannot go on in a stormy night.

AUG. 8TH. Left Derry, and took the road by Raphoe, to the Rev. Mr Golding's, at Clonleigh [Co. Donegal]. The view of Derry, at the distance of a mile or two, is the most picturesque of any place I have seen; it seems to be built on an island of bold land rising from the river, which spreads into a fine basin at the foot of the town. The adjacent country hilly; the scene wants nothing but wood to make it a perfect landscape. Passing Raphoe, found the husbandry in the neighbourhood of Clonleigh as follows.

The soil is for the most part light loamy land, with single large stones, and very wet with springs, with considerable tracts of bog. They generally sow flax, dress and spin it in their families. When cloth sells well, they get it wove by the weavers who are also little farmers. At other times they sell the flax in yarn at market, many of them never having any woven at all. The spinners in a little farm are the daughters and a couple of maid servants, that are paid 30s. a half year, and the common bargain is, to do a hank a day of 3 or 4 hank yarn. Much more than half the flax of the country is worked into cloth; a great deal of flax is imported at Derry, this country not raising near enough for its own manufacture, their own is much the finest. Their tillage is exceeding bad, the land not half ploughed. The farmers generally re-let some of their lands to cottiers at a great increase of rent. The poor people live upon oatmeal, milk, potatoes, and herrings, but the poorest eat very little meat. A farmer of £10 a year will have a good meal of beef or bacon every Sunday; in general they all live much better than they did formerly. Very little cloth made farther than "Ballymaffey" [Ballybofey] but all over Donegal much spinning.

The county of Tyrone is various. The finest parts are about Dungannon, Stewartstown, etc. on Lough Neagh. From Strabane to Omagh much good (land); from Omagh to Armagh all cultivated. From Strabane to Dungannon almost all mountains. The Bishop of Raphoe[81] is a considerable farmer, and cultivates and hoes turnips.

AUG. 9TH. To Convoy [Co. Donegal] where I was so unfortunate as to find Mr Montgomery from home. Passing on to Ballybofey I met that gentleman's oxen, drawing sledge cars of turf[82], single with collars, and worked to the full as well as the horses. They deserved wheels however. Got to a miserable cabin on the road, the widow Barclay's, which I had been assured was an exceeding good inn, but escaped without a cold, or the itch.

AUG. 10TH. Got to Alexander Montgomery's, Esq., at Mountcharles, Lord Conyngham's agent, by breakfast; found he was so deeply engaged in the fisheries on this coast, that I could not have got into better hands; with great civility he gave me every intelligence I wished. As an introduction to it, he took me a ride to the bays on the coast, where the fisheries are most carried on, particularly Inver Bay, McSwynes Bay and Killybegs Bay. The coast is perfectly sawed by bays; the lands are high and bold, particularly about Killybegs, where the scenery is exceedingly romantic.

In Inver Bay there is a summer fishery for herrings, which begins the latter end of July, and ends the beginning of September. All the other places are winter fisheries. In the common practice, a boat is divided into seven shares, the boat one. These boats belong in general to the common inhabitants of the country, farmers, etc. The herrings are cured in bulk, that is, packed into the holds of the vessels, from 20 to 100 tons each, and are sold all over the coast of Ireland. In the sale of the herrings, the merchant suffers greatly, by the competition of the Gothenborg and Scotch fishery. At Cork, great quantities of Gothenborg herrings are imported, which though they pay a duty of 4s. a barrel, yet, as 2s. 4½d. is drawn back on the re-exportation, and with an advantage of packing the herrings, of 20 Gothenborg barrels into 25 Irish ones, and consequently having the drawback on 25, though the duty is only paid on 20, with all these circumstances, great quantities of them are sent to the West Indies, to the prejudice of the Irish fishery. Another mischief is, that though there is a bounty of 2s. 4d. a barrel exported, yet such are the fees and old duty, that the merchant receives only 11½d. and that so clogged and perplexed with forms and delays, that not many attempt to claim it. The drawback on the foreign herrings is paid immediately on the merchant's oath, but the Irish bounty not till the ship returns, with I know not how many affidavits and certificates from consuls and merchants, it may be supposed perplexing when it is not claimed. The Scotch have a bounty per barrel, on exportation, which they draw on sending them to Ireland, by which means they are enabled, with the assistance of a higher bounty on their vessels, to undersell the Irish fishery in their own markets, while the Irish merchant is precluded from exporting to either Scotland or England; this is a very hard case, and certainly may be said to be one of the oppressions on the trade of Ireland, which a legislature, acting on liberal and enlarged principles, ought to repeal. The trade of smoking herrings, which is considerable in England, might be carried on here to much greater advantage, if there was wood to do it with. In the Isle of Man they have smoke houses, supplied with wood from Wales; it is a strange neglect, that the landlords do not plant some of the monstrous wastes in this country with quick growing copse wood, which would, in five or six years, enable them to begin the trade.

In respect to the linen manufacture, it consists in all this country in spinning yarn only. Most of the yarn goes to Derry. The soil about Mountcharles is various. A great deal of stiff blue clay which is perfectly tenacious of water. Much bog and a great range of high mountains near it, which break the clouds with a westerly wind, and occasion much rain. There are very great extents of mountain all the way from Mountcharles to Ards by Lough Finn which is thirty Irish miles in a right line. It is a range of mountains, but most of the valleys are slightly cultivated, though corn does very badly in them from the wetness of the climate. Upon the dry mountains they have flocks of sheep, not large ones, but every poor man keeps some, the wool their profit, and sell them at two or three years old. Tithes are generally compounded in the gross. The middlemen were common but not now. The poor people live upon potatoes and herrings nine months in the year along the coast, and upon oat bread and milk the other three. Very little butter, and scarce any meat. They all keep cows, most of them a pig or two, and a few hens, and all a cat or a dog. They are in general circumstances not improved. In different places in Lord Conyngham's estate in [the barony of] Boylagh are many lead mines mixed with silver [83], none of them wrought. Miners who have examined say there is much silver in the ore.

AUG. 11TH. Left Mountcharles, and passing through Donegal, took the road to Ballyshannon. Came presently to several beautiful landscapes, swelling hills, cultivated, with the bay flowing up among them. Afterwards likewise to the left, they rise in various outlines, and die away insensibly into one another. Before I got to Ballyshannon, remarked a bleach green, which indicates weaving in the neighbourhood.

Viewed the salmon leap at Ballyshannon, which is let for £400 a year. The town prettily situated on the rising ground on each side the river [Erne]. Crossing the bridge, stopped for a view of the river, which is a very fine one, and was delighted to see the salmon jump, to me an unusual sight; the water was perfectly alive with them. Rising the hill, look back on the town; the situation beautiful; the river presents a noble view. Come to Belleek, a little village, with one of the finest waterfalls I remember anywhere to have seen. Reached Castle Caldwell [Co. Fermanagh] at night, where Sir James Caldwell [84] received me with a politeness and cordiality that will make me long remember it with pleasure.

AUG. 12TH. The following account of the country around Castle Caldwell, Sir James favoured me with. The county of Fermanagh may be divided into six parts, one-sixth the lake at no rent. Mountains and bogs two-sixths. Great numbers of farms are taken in partnership in *rundale*, indeed the general course is so. Upon a farm of 100 acres, there will be four, five or six families; but families will take such small spots as 5 or 6 acres. There is a great deal of letting lands in the gross to middlemen who re-let it to others. These middlemen are called *terney begs*, or *little landlords*, which prevail very much at present. These men make a great profit by this practice. The people in all the neighbourhood increase very fast. They are all in general much more industrious, and in better circumstances than they were some years ago. Their food, for three-fourths of the year, chiefly potatoes and milk, and the other quarter oatmeal; in the winter they have herrings. They have all a bellyfull of food whatever it is, as they told me themselves, and their children eat potatoes all day long, even those of a year old will be roasting them. All keep cows, and some cocks and hens, but no turkeys or geese. The common people are remarkably given to thieving, particularly grass, timber, and turf; and they bring up their children to *hoking* potatoes, that is, artfully raising them, taking out the best roots, and then replanting them, so that the owner is perfectly deceived when he takes up the crop. There is very little weaving in this country, except what is for their own use, but spinning is universal in all the cabins. In the mountain tracts, the rents are paid by yarn, young cattle and a little butter. They spin a good deal of wool, which they make into druggets, the warp of tow yarn, and the weft of wool.

Nothing can be more beautiful than the approach to Castle Caldwell; the promontories of thick wood, which shoot into Lough Erne, under the shade of a great ridge of mountains, have the finest effect imaginable. As soon as you are through the gates, turn to the left, about 200 yards to the edge of the hill, where the whole domain lies beneath the point of view. It is a promontory, three miles long, projecting into the lake, a beautiful assemblage of wood and lawn. A bay of the lake breaks into the eastern end, where it is perfectly wooded: there are six or seven islands among them (that of Boa three miles long, and one and a half broad), yet they leave a noble sweep of water, bounded by the great range of the Turaw mountains. To the right, the lake takes the appearance of a fine river, with two large islands in it, the whole unites to form one of the most glorious scenes I ever beheld. Take my leave of Castle Caldwell, and with colours flying and (Sir James') band of music playing go on board his six-oared barge for Enniskillen. That evening reached Castle Coole [Co. Fermanagh].

AUG. 15TH. Rode to the Topped Mountain [909 feet] from whence is an immense prospect of many counties, and commanding Lough Erne from one end to the other, being above forty miles long. The great sheet is towards Castle Caldwell; that to Belturbet [Co. Cavan] is so thickly strewed with islands, that the water has more the appearance of several woods. Weaving (here) is but just coming in, but increases much; the spinning is common all over the country in every cabin by the women and girls. They do not quite raise flax enough to supply their own demand. The people increase very fast in this neighbourhood, and are in better circumstances than they were some years ago.

AUG. 16TH. To Belleisle [Co. Fermanagh], the charming seat of the Earl of Ross[85]. It is an island in Lough Erne of 200 Irish acres, every part of it hill, dale and gentle declivities. It has a great deal of wood, much of which is old, and forms both deep shades and open cheerful groves.

AUG. 17TH. Rowed to Knockinny the deer park, three miles across the lake through a maze of woody islands. The fish in this part of the lake are perch, pike to 40 lb., trout, eels, bream, etc. Large flights of swans sometimes appear here in winter and are sure signs of a severe one.

Reached Florence Court [Co. Fermanagh], Lord Enniskillen's[86] seat, situated on an eminence under a great ridge of mountains. The people (here) increase considerably, notwithstanding the emigrations which were great till within these two years. Their circumstances vastly improved in twenty years. They are better fed, clothed and housed, more sober and industrious in every respect. Their food is potatoes and oaten bread and a bit of beef or bacon for winter. All keep cows, and most of them pigs, and some poultry; many turkeys and geese. No drinking tea. The religion some Catholic, but a great many Protestants. In twenty years there is a rise of 2d. a day in labour. In provisions there has been a considerable rise.

AUG. 18TH. Took the road by Swanlinbar[87] for Farnham [Co. Cavan]. That spa of the north of Ireland is a little village, which appears to be but a poor residence for the numbers that resort to it. I took the Killashandra road. Passed Mr Henry's, a house very agreeably situated amidst woods. Many lakes are in this country; I passed several large ones, which communicate with each other by a river. The road crosses a variety of bog and moory ground perfectly improvable; lime cheap, but little seems to be

done or doing. At Mr Nesbit's enter a rich woodland
country. The Bishop of Kilmore's[88] palace is on a considerable hill. The woods of Farnham appear very finely
from hence. Reached that place in the evening, time
enough for a ride with the Earl[89] on the borders of his
lakes. These are uncommonly beautiful; they are extensive, and have a shore extremely varied.

Upon the whole Farnham is one of the finest places
I have seen in Ireland. The water, wood and hill are all
in a great style and abound in a variety of capabilities.
Cabbages Lord Farnham has cultivated three years. If he
was to farm forty years, he would never be without them
for his cows, his plough bullocks, and for finishing those
fat beasts which have had the summer grass. He thinks
them far better than turnips, that an acre will go farther,
is easier cultivated, and got from the land with less damage:
nor is this opinion founded from any ignorance of turnips,
his Lordship lived several years in Norfolk and attended
to the immense advantages reaped in that county from the
cultivation of them. He introduced them at Farnham the
same time as cabbages. They are difficult to cultivate in
Ireland from the ignorance of the people in hoeing. His
Lordship has made great improvements in some of his
lands by means of hollow draining. Very wet clays over-
run with rushes and other aquatic rubbish, he has converted
into dry sound healthy pastures. The principal drains are
filled with stones, the lesser ones with sod. The breed of
strong horses he has also been very attentive to improve.

The soil about Farnham is in general a good loam.
There is a great deal of bog and mountain, which with
lakes amount to half the county. Farms are generally about
100 acres and these re-let from 2 to 10 acres, to the poor
people, who are cottiers, and pay their high rent by
labouring. They plough all with horses, three or four in
a plough, and all abreast. Here let it be remarked, that

they very commonly plough and harrow with their horses *drawing by the tail*[90]. It is done every season. Nothing can put them beside this, and they insist, that take a horse tired in traces, and put him to work by the tail, he will draw better; quite fresh again. Indignant reader! This is no jest of mine, but cruel, stubborn, barbarous truth. It is so all over Cavan.

Tithes are generally hired by proctors, who view the farmer's crops, and compound with them, making a considerable profit by it. They screw up the tenants and poor people very severely. The people are in general in much better circumstances than some years ago; more industrious, better fed, clothed and lodged. They increase very much. Potatoes and milk and butter are their food, and oaten bread when the potatoes are not in season; scarce any flesh meat among the poor. The linen manufacture consists principally in spinning, which is universal all over the country for girls and women, but weaving is by no means general, nor does it increase in this neighbourhood.

AUG. 20TH. Took my leave of Farnham and passed by Cavan to Granard [Co. Longford]. The country all the way from Cavan to near Carrickglass within two miles of Longford is exceedingly bare of trees. Reached Ballinlough, the seat of W. G. Newcomen, Esq., who has many trees and well planted hedgerows about him. He favoured me with the following particulars.

The rent of the whole county of Longford may be reckoned at 12*s.* an acre, on an average, of all that is cultivated, and one-sixth part bog and mountain, which yields no rent. In Leitrim there are many mountain improvements, by setting fire to the heath in summer, liming it the following spring, marling upon that, and then plant potatoes; get great crops, and make fine land of it. *Rundale*, or the hiring of farms in partnership, is very common, three or four families will take 100 acres. A great part of the country is let to tenants who do not occupy, but re-let at advanced rents to the poor people. The system of cattle most common is to buy yearlings at 40s. and keep them till three or four years old, and sell them lean at £5 to £5 10s. buying in some every year, and selling out the same number. Fatting cows is also very common. Ploughing all with horses, a pair abreast, but no *drawing by the tail*. This practice they utterly deny here. Tithes taken generally by the proctors, who are very civil to gentlemen, but exceedingly cruel to the poor. The country evidently increases very much in population. The people are in better circumstances than they were twenty years ago, better clothed, better fed, and more industrious, yet at present it is found, and I have had the same remark made to me at many other places, that they only work to eat, and when provisions are plenty, will totally idle away so much of their time, that there is scarce any such thing as getting work done. The religion is principally Roman. No emigrations. There is a better yeomanry than is common in Ireland. Many farmers of from 100 to 250 acres. All the cottiers have some land; all keep cows, and many pigs and geese. I remarked for some time of late that the geese are plucked, and upon enquiry, that every goose yielded three farthings or a halfpenny in feathers per annum. They make a dreadful ragged figure. The poor live upon potatoes and milk, it is their regular diet, very little oat bread being used, and no flesh meat at all, except on an Easter Sunday, or Christmas Day. Their potatoes last them through the year; all winter long only potatoes and salt. The linen manufacture spreads through Longford. There are three bleach greens in the county. The weaving increases. Spinning is universal throughout all the cabins, and likewise through all the county of Leitrim, but there is not so much weaving as in Longford.

AUG. 21ST. To Strokestown [Co. Roscommon], the seat
of Thomas Mahon, Esq. Passed through Longford, a
cheerless country, over an amazing quantity of bog, and
all improvable. Crossed the Shannon, which is here a
considerable river, and entered Connacht. The first
appearance of Strokestown woods are very noble, from a hill
which looks down on them. They are very extensive, of
a great growth, and give a richness to the view, which is
a perfect contrast to the dreary scene I had passed. A great
part of Roscommon, particularly from Athlone to Boyle,
thirty miles long and ten broad, is sheep walk, and lets on
an average 12s. an acre. It is generally walk, only patches
of potatoes and corn for the workmen. These sheep walks
I had heard so much of, that I was eager in my enquiries
concerning them. They were some years ago divided into
much larger farms than at present, for there were men
who had 20,000 sheep, whereas now 6000 or 7000 is the
greatest stock. The farms rise to 3000 acres, few under
400 or 500. They stock commonly at the rate of two
sheep an acre, and reckon the profit to be lamb and wool.
These sheep walks decrease as the people become more
numerous. Parts are ploughed up, but very few instances
of sheep gaining upon tillage. The cottiers are never
suffered to keep sheep, but have cows grazed for them, as
in other parts. The wool[91] goes mostly to Cork, where it
is spun into worsted and exported. This is the account
I had in this country. Farms about Strokestown consist
generally of *rundale* ones. Upon 200 or 300 acres,
there will be ten to fifteen families, nor is it thought
here a bad system. Much the greatest part of the land is
grass.

The linen manufacture of spinning is spread not only
through Roscommon, but all Connacht, and in Roscommon
they raise flax enough for their own use; weaving is
creeping in by degrees, about a twentieth part of their yarn

is woven in the country, into linens of 10 or 12 hundred, and sheetings half quarter wide. The yarn spun is mostly 2 hank yarn. The people are upon the increase, but not much; they are better fed than twenty years ago, and better clothed, but not more industrious, or better housed. They live on potatoes and milk, and butter. Scarce any but what keep a cow or two; they are not allowed to keep pigs in general, but many will a tolerable quantity of poultry. The men dig turf, and plant potatoes, and work for their landlord, and the women pay the rent by spinning.

Mr Mahon's woods are all of his own planting, and having besides 100 acres, a vast number of hedgerows well planted round many inclosures, which join those woods, they all take the appearance of uniting into one great range of plantations, spreading on each side the house. It is one of the strongest instances of a fine shade being speedily formed in the midst of a bleak country that I have anywhere met with, being a perfect contrast to all the neighbourhood. He began thirty-five years ago with ash, which trees are now 70 to 80 feet high, but the generality of the plantations are from seventeen to thirty years old, and are for that age, I think, the finest woods I ever saw. They consist of ash, oak, English and French elm, beech, maple, spruce, Scotch and silver fir, larch, etc.

At Clonalis, near Castlereagh, lives O'Connor, the direct descendant of Roderick O'Connor[92], who was king of Connacht six or seven hundred years ago; there is a monument of him in Roscommon church, with his sceptre, etc. I was told as a certainty, that this family were here long before the coming of the Milesians[93]. The possessions formerly so great are reduced to £300 or £400 a year. The common people pay him the greatest respect, and send him presents of cattle, etc. upon various occasions. They consider him as the prince of a people involved in one common ruin.

Another great family in Connacht is MacDermot, who calls himself Prince of Coolavin [94]. He lives at Coolavin in Sligo, and, though he has not above £100 a year, will not admit his children to sit down in his presence. Lord Kingsborough, Mr Ponsonby [95], Mr O'Hara, Mr Sandford, etc. came to see him, and his address was curious: "*O'Hara! you are welcome; Sandford, I am glad to see your mother's son* (his mother was an O'Brien): *as to the rest of ye, come in as ye can.*" Mr O'Hara, of Nymphsfield, is in possession of a considerable estate in Sligo, which is the remains of great possessions they had in that country: he is one of the few descendants of the Milesian race.

Since the bounty on the inland carriage of corn to Dublin, much is sent from the county of Roscommon, and even farther from Sligo and Mayo, and this business of carriage was mentioned to me as a proof of the great excellency of the Irish car. They carry from 9 cwt. to 12 cwt. with a single horse that is not worth above £5. The distance from hence is sixty-seven miles, and they are nine days going and returning.

AUG. 23RD. Leave Strokestown, and take the road to Elphin [Co. Roscommon], through a country principally sheep walks. The soil dry sound gravel and stony land. To Lord Kingston's [96] [at Boyle, Co. Roscommon], to whom I had a letter but unfortunately for me he was at Spa. Walked down to Longford Hill, to view [Lough Key]; it is one of the most delicious scenes I ever beheld, a lake of five miles by four, which fills the bottom of a gentle valley almost of a circular form, bounded very boldly by the mountains. Those to the left rise in a noble slope; they lower rather in front, and let in a view of Strand mountain, near Sligo, above twenty miles off. To the right, you look over a small part of a bog to a large extent of cultivated hill, with the blue mountains beyond.

Dined at Boyle, and took the road to Ballymote [Co. Sligo]. Crossed an immense mountainy bog, where I stopped and made enquiries. Found that it was ten miles long and three and a half over, containing thirty-five square miles. These hilly bogs are extremely different from any I have seen in England. In the moors in the north, the hills and mountains are all covered with heath, like the Irish bogs, but they are of various soils, gravel, shingle, moor, etc. and boggy only in spots, but the Irish bog hills are all pure bog to a great depth, without the least variation of soil, and a bog being of a hilly form is a proof that it is a growing vegetable mass and not owing merely to stagnant water.

Reached Ballymote in the evening, the residence of the Hon. Mr Fitzmaurice, where I expected great pleasure in viewing a (weaving) manufactory of which I heard much since I came to Ireland. Tired with the inactivity of a common life he (Mr Fitzmaurice) determined not only to turn manufacturer, but to carry on business in the most spirited and vigorous manner that was possible. In the first place he took every means of making himself a complete master of the business; he went through various manufactures, enquired into the minutiæ, and took every measure to know it to the bottom. This he did so repeatedly, and with such attention in the whole progress, from spinning to bleaching, and selling, that he became as thorough a master of it, as an experienced manager; he has woven linen, and done every part of the business, with his own hands. As he determined to have the works complete, he took Mr Stansfield, the engineer, so well known for his improved saw-mills, into his pay. He sent him over to Ballymote, in the winter of 1774, in order to erect the machinery of a bleach mill, upon the very best construction; he went to all the great mills in the north of Ireland to inspect them, to remark their deficiencies, that they might be improved in the mills he intended to erect. This knowledge being gained, the work was begun, and as water was necessary, a great basin was formed, by a dam across a valley, by which means 34 acres were floated, to serve as a reservoir for dry seasons, to secure plenty at all times. All the machinery of the mill is perfectly well constructed, and worthy of the artist who formed it; in general it is upon the common principle of other bleach mills, only executed in a manner much superior to any other in Ireland.

In the first year, 1774, not having a bleach green, he only kept the looms going, to sell the linen green; sixty-five in that year worked 1730 webs, each 50 yards long and seven-eighths broad, on an average 10 hundred linen. In 1775, the number of looms was eighty, and they worked 2110 pieces of the same linen. At present the number is ninety, and preparations are made for there being one hundred and twenty by this time twelve-month, and Mr Fitzmaurice has no doubt of having three hundred in two years' time. In establishing and carrying on this manu-factory, the increase has been by weavers from the north, for whom he builds houses as fast as he can, and has many more applying than he can supply by building. The full rent he fixes for a stone and slate cottage; that costs him £50 is 40s. if the weaver is idle; but in proportion to the number of webs he weaves his rent is lowered; besides which encouragement, he gives premiums for the best weaving and spinning throughout the manufactory. In order to show how far this system of employment is of importance to the neighbourhood, I may observe that the eighty looms, besides the eighty weavers, employed eighty persons more, which are usually women, quilling, warping, and winding; the quilling by children, and half as many children for quilling [*sic*]. In all eighty men, eighty women and forty children.

He has planned much greater works; has procured a
patent for a market, which he designs to establish; to build
a large handsome market house, at an expense of £1000; to
pull down all the old cabins in the town and rebuild them
in regular streets of good houses for weavers and mechanics.
To convert a large house at present used in the manufactory into a handsome inn. A large house for a master
weaver and lastly a mansion house for himself in the style
of a castle, and suitable to the ancient ruins, situation and
grounds. These are great works for the ornament and
improvement of a country, and united with the flourishing
progress of the manufactory, promise to make Ballymote
a considerable place. Too much praise cannot be given
to a man, who in the prime of life, when pleasure alone
usually takes the lead, should turn his attention and
expense to objects of such national utility and importance,
which have for their aim the well being, happiness and
support of a whole neighbourhood.

Upwards of £40,000 per annum in yarn is exported
from Sligo to Manchester and Liverpool. It is supposed
that there is as much yarn exported raw from Ireland, as
is manufactured in it. The first step taken by the manufacturer is to steep the yarn in lukewarm water for a day
or two; it is then boiled twelve hours in a strong lee of
barilla ashes, after which it is bleached for three weeks or
a month, and when dry, is dressed and softened by being
hung in a frame, and rubbed in a clipped stick, after which
it is sorted into different degrees of fineness, first by weight,
and then by the eye, when it is ready to be delivered to the
weaver, with the *reed* and *geers* adapted to manufacturing
it. The *grist* or fineness of the yarn, determines the *set*
or fineness of the *reed* through which it is to be wrought.
The *reed* is divided into *beers*, each *beer* containing 20
splits, each *split* two threads. These threads are called the
warp. The threads thrown across by the shuttle are called

the *woof*. Five *beers* are what is commonly called a *hundred*, the number of which *hundred* is regulated by the skill of the manufacturer, so as to make the cloth thick or thin in the breadth: and the number of these *hundreds* constitutes the fineness and value of the cloth. Very little weaving in Sligo, but a little scattered spinning everywhere. £80,000 of yarn last year exported from the port of Sligo. One-sixth of the county bog and mountain, the rest 15s. an acre. The farms rise to large ones, that are grazing, but all the tillage is carried on by cottiers or very inconsiderable ones.

AUG. 26TH. To the Right Hon. Joshua Cooper's at "Mercra" [Markree Castle, Co. Sligo] who not only received me with the utmost politeness but was so obliging as to send for a neighbouring gentleman, in order between them, with other assistance, to answer all my questions. Farms in culture are exceedingly small, the poor people divide and take them in partnership four or five to a ploughland of 100 acres, but they subdivide down to 5 or 6 acres, and in general all the tillage is done by these little occupiers. There are some large grazing farms up to above 1000 acres. One-seventh of the county may be reckoned bog, and unimproved mountain. Mayo one-third, perhaps half, bog and mountain. Galway more than one-third bog, mountain and lakes.

The sheep system is not of consequence, for there are scarce any flocks kept. Twenty years ago the baronies of Corran and Tireragh were continued sheep walks, but now the former is all potatoes and barley, and much of the latter is broken up, so that upon the whole tillage has gained very much on grass. Horses are used for tillage only, four in a plough abreast, and some harrowing still done *by the tail*. They will plough half an acre a day, or more commonly three days to an acre. They know nothing of cutting chaff, but let the wind blow that of their crops away. The people increase very fast most undoubtedly. Their circumstances in general are infinitely better than twenty years ago. They are clothed and fed better, and are much more industrious. *Spalpeens* going from hence decline much and will soon be entirely out. There were some emigrations to America, but not considerable, and some of them are come back again. The religion in general Catholic; but more Protestants than in any other county in Connacht. In the baronies of Leyny and Corran, there are many Milesian Irish; in Mayo more still, all of the Spanish breed. The food of the poor people is potatoes, milk and herrings, with oaten bread in summer; all keep cows, not pigs, and but a few poultry. They have an absolute bellyful of potatoes, and the children eat them as plentifully as they like. All of them have a bit of cabbages. They prefer oat bread both to potatoes and to wheat bread. All afford whisky. The common people are so amazingly addicted to thieving everything they can lay their hands on, that they will unshoe their horses in the field, in the barony of Leyny; they are also liars from their cradle, but wonderfully sagacious, cunning and artful.

Within ten miles of this, in Leitrim, is a great country of good coal near the surface; but for want of being well worked, sells at 7s. a ton; and near Ballysadare is a lead mine, but not worked with success, though very rich. As to the linen manufactory, it has made some progress; there are six bleach greens in the county, and there are many weavers. Spinning is universal in all the cabins. A woman will earn $2\frac{1}{2}d$. at it. The rents are mostly paid by yarn.

Sligo [97] is the only sea port of this country, and the state of its trade may be taken as no bad explanation of the improvement of the country around it with which it communicates.

*A view of the Duties on Imports and Exports
in the Port of Sligo.*

		£	s.	d.		£	s.	d.
1756	Imports	1208	11	4	Exports	26	11	7
1760	„	518	9	8	„	45	6	3
1765	„	1458	9	4	„	102	17	0
1770	„	1122	2	4	„	523	6	7
1775	„	2256	8	1	„	956	0	6

Mr Cooper has remarked that the great improvement of this part of Ireland commenced about the year 1748 and that rents now are, to what they were before that period, as fifteen to six.

Left Markree and went to Ballysadare [Co. Sligo], where I had great pleasure in viewing the falls. To Tanrego, the seat of Lewis Irwin, Esq., situated in the barony of Tireragh which is twenty-seven miles long, and cultivated from one and a half to three in breadth, by the sea side. They burn vast quantities of kelp in the whole barony, 300 tons, all in summer. In winter or spring they manure with it. The mountains nearest to the sea, are chiefly stocked with sheep, and farther in, with young cattle near the bog. There is a good deal of limestone, and the land is dry, and to appearance, and in fact, good; it fattens bullocks; it is attributed to the lead mines which this part is supposed to be full of. Three-fourths of Sligo, bog and uncultivated mountain.

Upon the sea shore are immense beds of oyster shells, which are burnt into lime for building and plastering, as they take much less fuel; these hills received no little increase from all the gentlemen of the interior country coming to the sea coast to eat oysters, where, having filled themselves sufficiently in the mornings, they got drunk in the evening; this was in the *un*civilized times. Most of the gentlemen of this country were Cromwell's soldiers,

and many Welsh families, Jones', Morgan's, Wynn's, etc.
In the barony of Tireragh, flax is universally cultivated;
a man with 20 acres will have a rood, which is sown with
5 gallons of seed; all the females spin, but the number of
weavers is inconsiderable. Walked down to the coast of
Tanrego, immediately opposite Knocknarea [Mountain],
which rises very boldly; the Bay of Ballysadare comes up
under it.

To Fortland [near Easky, Co. Sligo] the seat of —
Browne, Esq.; to whom I am obliged for the following
particulars. The barony of Tireragh, black mould on
limestone, lets at 18*s*. average. The farms are various,
generally taken in partnership, which is found a most
mischievous custom, and destructive to all good husbandry.
The seaweed the only manure, and they depend entirely
on it, and apt to do that too much, neglecting other parts
of management. The circumstances of the people are not
at all improved in twenty years, they are not better fed or
clothed, or in any respect better off than formerly. Nor
are they at all industrious; even of seaweed they do not
make one half the advantage they could; they might get
an hundred loads where they get one. They increase in
number very greatly, so as to be evidently crowded; this
has been the case particularly since inoculation was introduced, which was about ten years ago. They live upon
potatoes and milk and for three months in the year on
oatmeal. Mr Browne is convinced from every observation,
that the potatoes are a very wholesome and nourishing
food. The linen manufacture consists only in spinning,
which is universal in all the cabins, and it is so much, that
they are assisted by it, in paying their rents. In the barony
of Tireragh there are a few grazing farmers, but not many.
Not a third of the county is bog and mountain, but more
than half Mayo is so. The shore is a very fruitful one in
seaweed, which is burnt into kelp in summer. From the

slate quarry to Inishcrone [Co. Sligo] nine miles, they make 200 tons of kelp. It is made all the way from this country to Galway.

AUG. 27TH. To Ballina [Co. Mayo] where I experienced the most polite reception from the Right Hon. Mr King. The views of the distant mountains are very fine, the country is almost encompassed by them. Those of Donegal to the right, a great ridge, which separates Tireragh to the left, Nephin [2646 feet] noble in the front, and Knocknarea [1098 feet] behind. At Ballina is a salmon fishery, let for £520 a year, which is one of the most considerable in the kingdom. Mr Gore of Ballina has been mentioned to me as one of the most considerable in cattle of any person in Connacht; he was not at home, but his son-in-law, the Right Hon. Mr King was so kind as to procure me the particulars of his domain.

Mr Gore's breed of horned cattle is fine. Some years ago he sold heifers at £50 apiece, and now from ten to twenty guineas; the breed not declined, but purchasers not quite so mad as they were. Yearling bulls twenty guineas. This breed he got from Yorkshire thirty or forty years ago. His breed of sheep is also excellent, being much improved by rams from England. He improves much moory land and bog, generally 10 or 15 acres a year, by limestone gravel and marl. Average rent of Tireragh 12s. Walked in the evening to a most noble garden, walled and planted by Mr King; it is one of the completest I have seen in Ireland.

AUG. 28TH. Took my departure from Ballina, and waited on the Bishop of Killala[98]. I wished to have some information concerning that vast wild and impenetrable tract of mountain and bog, the barony of Erris. His Lordship and Mr Hutchinson were so kind as to give me every particular in their power. The only cultivated part is the peninsula called the Mullet, where they plant a good deal of potatoes, barley and flax, by means of seaweed, and there is a rabbit warren, the skins of the rabbits yielding £100 a year. The rest of it is without cultivation, except in small patches here and there. It is supposed, generally speaking, to be without limestone or limestone gravel, but probably no great search has been made in so dreary a region. It is no easy matter to get in or out of it in winter, and very few persons ever attempt it from November to Easter, having impassable bogs in the way. There were 896 families in the barony in 1765, 400 of which are inhabitants of the Mullet: 47 Protestant, and 849 Popish. The Bishop of Killala has built a house in the Mullet for a clergyman, who resides there; the living is between £50 and £60 a year, and 40 acres of land, which the Bishop has given from the see lands. This may truly be called a sphere for content and the philosophic virtues to exert themselves in; there is not a post-house, market town, or justice of peace, in the whole barony, which is also the case with another barony in this county, Costello. There are many herds of small cattle, and some sheep kept, which are sold from thence. There is not a tree in the whole barony of Erris; a man going out of it to pay his rent, etc., his son with him, a lad of near twenty, when he came near Killala, and saw a tree, " *Lord, Father! what is that?* " But, bare of wood as it is at present, it was, in the sylvan age of Ireland, completely covered: for in no part of the kingdom is there found more or larger in the bogs.

The barony of Tirawley is among the best parts of the county of Mayo; 800 bullocks, most of them fat, are sold from it annually at Ballinasloe fair [Co. Galway]. The quantity of tillage is very inconsiderable, but what there is, is vastly improved by the use of seaweed. The poor people in this barony are not improved in their circumstances in eighteen years past, that the Bishop has resided

at Killala. There is some weaving, so that there is scarcely
a market at Ballina, or Killala, without some linens sold.
Spinning is universal in all the cabins, but the yarn is only
four hank yarn. They spin and weave wool enough to
clothe themselves, with drugget yard-wide for the women,
at 1s. a yard, and frieze for the men. Their food is
potatoes, cockles, herrings, and a little meal, and when the
potatoes are out, on oatmeal only. Fish very plentiful.
I partook of three gurnet, two mackerel and one whiting
at the Bishop's table, which his steward bought for $6\frac{1}{2}d.$,
enough to dine six people. There are 150 fishing boats
belonging to the Bay of Killala or Moy, and to the town,
from 20 to 25. The herrings are caught near the bar,
and in the river Moy. The fishery begins in October and
lasts only two or three weeks. They judge of the shoal
being there by the gant [gannet or solan goose], a bird that
pursues the fish. The fishery was once much more considerable than at present.

AUG. 29TH. Took my leave of the good Bishop, to whom,
and his son Mr Hutchinson, I am obliged for the preceding
particulars and many civilities.

It must not be imagined that when I speak of mountains and moors in Mayo, or its wild barony Erris, that
these lands yield no rent; they are let in the lump, and
applied to feeding cattle. They put on two year-old
bullocks, and keep them till full three, when they bring
them to the good grounds, and from thence take them to
Ballinasloe. Red deer run wild in the mountains of Erris.

To Castlebar [Co. Mayo], over an indifferent country,
and a vile stony road. About that town the husbandry is
admirable. They have three customs, which I must begin
with; item, they harrow *by the tail*, the fellow who leads
the horses of a plough, walks backward before them the
whole day long, and in order to make them advance,

strikes them in the face: their heads, I trow, are not apt
to turn. Item, they burn the corn in the straw, instead
of threshing it. Among their customs it may be worth
mentioning, that at the wakes or funeral entertainments,
both men and women, particularly the latter, are hired to
cry, that is, to howl the corpse to the grave[99], which they
do in a most horrid manner; they are not so disagreeable,
however, in Munster, as I was told. The quantity of
whisky and tobacco consumed upon these occasions is pretty
considerable.

There are very large farms in this neighbourhood, even
up to £2000 a year, but all the great ones are stock farms,
and most of the tillage of the country is performed by little
fellows, cottiers, and tenants to these large farmers. Eight
or nine years ago there were no linens here, but now 300
pieces are sold in a week; 200 looms are employed in the
town and neighbourhood, yet great quantities of yarn are
sent off. The town, which belongs to Lord Lucan[100], is
greatly rising from manufactures. The houses are well
built, yet only thirty-one years or three lives granted.

In the evening reached Westport [Co. Mayo], Lord
Altamont's[101], whose house is very beautifully situated.
From the hill above the wood, on the right of the house,
is a view of the bay with Croagh Patrick [2510 ft.]
immediately rising like the superior lord of the whole
territory and looking down on a great region of other
mountains that stretch into Joyce's Country[102].

Lord Altamont is of opinion, from a variety of experience, that the best method of breaking up heathy mountain
land, is by manuring with limestone sand. If sand is not
to be had, then the white marl from under moory bottoms,
and if there is none of that, then lime. Objects to lime, as
it brings the land infallibly to moss, which is so powerful as
to choke the grasses, but marl is an excellent manure. To
leave it for three years, or till daisies and white clover

appear, then to plough it in May or June, and again in autumn, and in the spring to plant potatoes, in the common trenching way, and after the potatoes, would sow oats successively, till the chickweed appears, which is a sign that the tillage has so enriched the land, that the crops will be too great, and then leave it for grass. If seaweed is plentiful, he would manure the potatoes with it, and then would have the first crop barley instead of oats. A large portion of these mountains are wet, owing to the lack clay[103], but the potato trenches break it, and let off the water; after which the land settles by degrees, and becomes perfectly dry. There are great tracts of many miles extent of heath mountain in this neighbourhood which are capable of the above improvements. It is very remarkable, that all the wild mountains in this country have marks, and to a great height of former culture, mounds of fences, and the ridges of the plough. Lord Altamont's great-grandfather found the estate a continued forest; in 1650, those woods were of much more than a century growth, so that no cultivation could have been here probably of three hundred years. There is a tradition in the country that it was depopulated by the plague, and upon that the wood sprung up which formed those forests. At present, there is no wood on any of the hills, except immediately about Westport.

In introducing the linen manufacture, his Lordship has made great exertions. He found it to consist principally in spinning flax, which was sent out of the country, without any looms in it, except a very few, which worked only for their own use. In order to establish it, he built good houses in the town of Westport, and let them upon very reasonable terms to weavers, gave them looms, and lent them money to buy yarn, and in order to secure them from manufacturing goods, which they should not be able readily to sell, he constantly bought all they could not sell, which for some years was all they made, but by degrees, as the manufacture arose, buyers came in, so that he has for some time not bought any great quantity.

The poor in general live on potatoes and milk nine months out of the twelve, the other three months bread and milk. All of them have one or two cows; fish is exceedingly plentiful, particularly oysters for 1s. a cart load, and sand eels, yet they eat none; herrings however are an article in their food. In their domestic economy, they reckon that the men feed the family with their labour in the field, and the women pay the rent by spinning. The increase of population is very great. Lord Altamont is of opinion that the numbers have doubled on his estate in twenty years. The farms around Westport are in general large, from 400 to 4000 or 5000 acres, all of which are stock farms, and the occupiers re-let the cultivated lands, with the cabins, at a very increased rent, to the oppression of the poor, who have a strong aversion to renting of these *terney begs*. About three-fifths of the country unimproved mountains, bog and lake. On the shore towards Joyce's Country, they actually *let their dung hills accumulate, till they become such a nuisance, that they move their cabins in order to get from them.* No wheat sown but by gentlemen for their own consumption. *They burn their corn instead of threshing it.* They plough all with horses, four in a plough, directed by a man walking backwards, who to make them move forward, strikes the beasts in the face. Young colts they harrow with *by the tail*. They winnow their corn in the road and let the wind blow away the chaff. Lord Altamont mentioned descriptive of Mayo husbandry, Acts of Parliament to prevent their pulling the wool off their sheep by hand; burning their corn; and ploughing by the tail. The rents in Mayo are trebled in forty years. No emigrations. Farms are generally let in partnership, but the term *rundale* not known. Labour generally done by cottiers, who have land let to them, or grass for cows, under agreement to work for the landlord. Provisions, which the poor eat, not risen, but butcher's meat doubled. They pluck their geese alive every year. All carriage done by horses with baskets, the bottoms of which fasten with sticks, and let out the load. The industry of the people very much increased; an astonishing change in industry, sobriety, etc. and are in much better circumstances in every respect, than twenty years ago.

They have a practice common among them, which shows an increasing civility, in the change from Irish names to English ones. Even surnames, for instances *Stranaghan*, Irish for *birds*, which they call themselves. *Markahau*, Irish for a *rider*, which name they take; *Cullane*, Irish for a *whelp*, which name they assume; others call themselves *Collins*. *Conree*, Irish for a *king*, which they call themselves; *Ruddery*, a *knight*, and many others[104]. There are many Mortimers, Piercys, etc. and within a few years, a Plantagenet, in the county of Sligo.

Eagles abound very much in this country, and do great mischief, by carrying away lambs, poultry, etc.; they also watch the salmon jumping, and seize them even out of the water, by darting with that celerity, of which they are such masters; this is so common, that men with guns are set to kill and frighten them.

AUG. 30TH. Rode to Rosshill, four miles off, a headland that projects into the Bay of Newport, from which there is a most beautiful view of the bay on both sides; I counted thirty islands very distinctly, all of them cultivated under corn and potatoes, or pastured by cattle. At a distance "Clara" [Clare Island] rises in a bold and picturesque style; on the left, Croagh Patrick, and to the right other mountains. It is a view that wants nothing but wood

AN IRISH CABIN

AUG. 31ST. To Newbrook [Co. Mayo], over a various country, part waste, and much cultivated. Reached Hollymount, Mr Lindsay's, a very considerable grazier. Farms are very extensive, up to 3000 or 4000 acres, all stock ones, with portions re-let to cottiers, who are the principal arable men here. Above half the county bog, mountain and lake.

SEPT. 1ST. To Tuam [Co. Galway]. Dined with the Archbishop[105]. All this country is a good sound limestone land and famous for sheep, but upon enquiry, I found it did not materially vary from the neighbourhood of Hollymount, or Monivea [Co. Galway] whither I was going in the evening. Reached Mr French's at that place. He has improved 60 acres of bog and 290 acres of moor, which he began in the year 1744, with a great red bog from 20 to 30 feet deep, so wet and spongy that no turf fit for burning could be found to cut in it, so very wet and loose, that a man could not go on it without jumping from tuft to tuft. No heath on it, except at the verge; the only spontaneous growth red and white moss.

In the year 1744, when Mr French came to his estate, there was no other linen manufacture than a little *bandle* linen[106], merely for their own consumption. In 1746, he undertook to establish a better fabric, and with more extensive views. He first began by erecting spinning schools, and sowing flax. In 1749, he established eight weavers and their families, and the same year built a bleach mill, and formed a green, and, to carry it on to advantage, sent a lad into the north, in order to learn the whole business. Upon his return, he managed the manufactory for Mr French. The progress of this undertaking, united with the agricultural improvements, will be seen by the following returns of the Monivea estate, at different periods.

In 1744. There were 3 farmers, and 6 or 8 shepherds and cow-herds.
In 1771.   „   248 houses, 90 looms, and 268 wheels.
In 1772.   „   257 houses, 93 looms, and 288 wheels.
In 1776.   „   276 houses, 96 looms, and 370 wheels.

Here, in a few words, is the progress of a most noble
undertaking; and I should observe, that it is doubly beneficial, from one circumstance. All these weavers are mere
cottagers in a town without any land, except a cabbage-
garden, by which means they have nothing to do with farming, but become a market to the farmers that surround them,
which is what all manufacturers ought to be, instead of
spreading over the country to the destruction of agriculture.

Another circumstance in which Mr French has given
a new face to Monivea and its environs is by planting.
He found a considerable wood of birch, which being a
shabby tree, and not improving, he cut them gradually
down, and planted oak, elm, and beech, with various other
sorts. He began this thirty years ago and no year passes
without his making some new plantation. By properly
managing this wood of 111 acres he has made it pay him
£150 a year, ever since, and there is now more than thrice
the value of timber in it, to what there was when he began.
Whatever he has planted has answered well, but the growth
of the beech is the greatest. That of the oak is very great
and more flourishing than ever Mr French expected to see
them at the time of planting. The broad leaved elm
thrives very well upon the bogs, after they are cultivated.
Mr French has tried most sorts of trees in rows along the
hedges, but none of them have succeeded, the west winds
cut them in pieces; since which he makes inclosures, and
plants them thick.

I ought not to forget observing that Mr French supports
a Charter school [107] at his own expense, wherein are from
twenty to forty children, constantly supported, clothed,
and taught to read and write, and to spin and weave.

Farms around Monivea consist principally of large stock ones, from 200 to 500 acres, with very few cabins upon them; the tillage of the country is principally carried on by villagers, who take farms in partnership. Mr French's are generally from 20 to 130 acres. There will sometimes be from ten to thirty families on a farm of 200 acres; but Mr French finds they do not thrive well if there are more than six families to one farm. The whole county limestone except the mountainous tracts on the west, beyond Lough "Carril" [Carra] and the mountains to the south of Loughrea. The richest part of the county is between Loughrea and Portumna, thence to Eyrecourt, Clonfert, and Aughrim. The third of the county is bog, lake and unimproved mountain; but most of the latter yields some trifling rent; the whole third perhaps 3*d.* an acre; the other two-thirds, 12*s.* on an average. The isles of Aran contain 7000 acres, belong to John Digby, Esq.; and let at about £2000 a year. The great tract of mountain is the three baronies of Iarconnacht, Ross, Ballynahinch, and Moycullen; they are forty miles long, and fifteen broad, and are in general uncultivated. There are some good tillage farmers towards the Shannon who sow grass seed. They also sow successive crops till the land is exhausted, and leave it for some time to graze itself. No ploughing or harrowing *by the tail*, nor any burning the corn instead of threshing, but these practices were very common thirty years ago.

There are considerable improvements of mountain and some of bog, that have been carried on by the poor villagers. They dig and burn the mountain and get by that means very fine potatoes without dung, paying 20*s.* an acre for it. If they have the land to themselves, they will, after the potatoes, get good wheat, and after that several crops of oats till the land is exhausted. In one of the bogs which a village was cutting away, the men called Mr French to it, to show him the old ridge and furrow at the bottom and he found them perfect. It was 4 feet deep. That this country was once generally cultivated, there are other signs. There are vast numbers of limestone gravel pits among the mountain heathy lands, though there is not the least tradition when they were used.

The principal stock in this country is sheep for breeding, the sale being wethers, which they sell fat at Ballinasloe; and wool, of which they clip from the ewes 4 lb. and from the wethers 5 lb., sells now at above 1s. a lb. Mr French remembers the price of wool, fifty years ago, at 6s. and 7s. a stone; 1744 was reckoned a very high year, and he sold 27 bags, at 10s. 6d. a stone; but as he got out of stock, he has not since had more than two bags. In 1745, etc. it fell to 8s. a stone. The great rise of the price of wool, Mr French attributes to the low price of spinning and the increase of tillage. The stock farmers, who are good managers, all have two farms, one as a dry one, in this neighbourhood for winter, and another in the deeper richer lands in the eastern part of the county, for summer feeding and fatting.

They plough with horses, but the gentlemen mostly with oxen; they have not the Mayo custom, of walking backwards before them, nor do they harness them all abreast, but two and two. They winnow all their corn in the field to blow away the chaff. They will take a grazing farm, with three years' rent, for stock. Land sells at twenty-one years' purchase. The rents have fallen since 1772, but are now rising, from the great price of wool, black cattle, and linen. Tithes are compounded by the proctors with gentlemen, but they screw up the poor people to the utmost. There are still many men who make it their business to hire large tracts of land in order to re-let at advanced rents. Population increases greatly, yet many of them live very poorly upon potatoes and water, with some oatmeal. There are many that have no cows, only a house and a garden. There were many emigrants from Galway[108] to America, but only of the loose idle people. The general religion is Roman Catholic, but about Monivea chiefly Protestant.

Mr Andrew French of "Rathone" [Rahoon], Galway, who I met at Monivea, favoured me with the following particulars. At Galway, there is a salmon fishery which lets at £200 a year, and in the bay of Galway they have a considerable herring fishery. There are five or six men to a boat. They fish by shares, dividing into sixty. They have had this fishery time immemorial. The plenty of fish has decreased these fifteen years. All they get is sold into the country, and the demand is so far from being answered, that many cargoes are brought in from the north. The men are far from being industrious in the business, some weeks they do not go out twice. Along the whole bay there is a great quantity of kelp burnt, 3000 tons are annually exported from Galway. The shore is let with the land against it, and is what the people pay their rent by. They use a great quantity of seaweed, drove in by storms, for manuring land. In November they carry it on, the field being ready marked out in beds for potatoes, and leaving it on them; it rots against the planting season, and gives them great crops. They also do this with fern.

One circumstance, relative to the progress of the linen manufacture in this country, the town of Galway can instance. Mr Andrew French, sixteen years ago, imported the first cargo of flax seed of 300 hogsheads, and could only sell 100 of them, whereas now the annual importation rises from 1500 to 2300. Twenty years ago there were only twenty looms in Galway, now there are one hundred and eighty. They make coarse sheetings; dowlas, and Osnaburgs[109]. There are eight or nine bleach greens in the county, but they bleach, generally speaking, only for the country consumption: the great bulk of the linens are sent green to Dublin. In the town and neighbourhood of Loughrea, there are three hundred looms employed on linens that are called *Lochreas*. All the flax worked in the county is, generally speaking, raised in it. Very many weavers are in the towns, without having any land more than a cabbage garden. The linen and yarn of the whole county has been calculated at £40,000 a year.

SEPT. 3RD. Left Monivea, and took the road to Wood-lawn [Co. Galway], the seat of Frederick Trench, Esq. Woodlawn is a seat improved entirely in the modern English taste. The house stands on the brow of a rising ground, which looks over a lawn swelling into gentle in-equalities; through these a small stream is converted into a large river, in a manner that does honour to the taste of the owner; the grounds are pleasing, and are prettily scattered with clumps and single trees, and surrounded by a margin of wood. The size of farms (here) varies; there are many small ones of from 30 to 100 acres, part grazing and part tillage; also many stock ones, up to 1000 and 1500 acres; and these graziers re-let to the cabins part of it at a very high rent, by whom are carried on most of the tillage of the country. Mr Trench remarks, that if good land is let to the poor people, they are sure to destroy it; but give them heath, or what is bad, and they will make it good. Every poor man sows some flax, but still they do not raise enough for their spinning, for that is universal. Every cabin has 8 or 9 acres, and two or three cows, or two cows and one horse; and about half have horses, two or three pigs, and many poultry; half a rood of flax, one acre potatoes, or half at a medium. They live on potatoes, oats, or barley bread, or butter; like oats much better. Their circumstances are much improved in twenty years.

SEPT. 4TH. To Kiltartan [Co. Galway], the seat of Robert Gregory, Esq. He has built a large house with numerous offices, and taken 500 or 600 acres of land into his own hands, which I found him improving with great spirit. He has fixed two English bailiffs on his farm, one for accounts and overlooking his walling and other business, and another from Norfolk for introducing the turnip husbandry. He has 12 acres this year, and what particularly pleased me, I saw some Irishmen hoeing them; the Norfolk man had taught them, and I was convinced in a moment, that these people would by practice soon attain a sufficient degree of perfection in it. Mr Gregory has a very noble nursery, from which he is making plantations, which will soon be a great ornament to the country.

SEPT. 5TH. To Dromoland, the seat of Sir Lucius O'Brien[110] in the county of Clare, a gentleman who had been repeatedly assiduous to procure me every sort of information. I should remark as I have now left Galway, that that county, from entering it in the road to Tuam till leaving it to-day, has been, upon the whole, inferior to most of the parts I have travelled in Ireland in point of beauty: there are not mountains of a magnitude to make the view striking. It is perfectly free from woods, and even trees, except about gentlemen's houses, nor has it a variety in its face. Dromoland has a pleasing variety of grounds about the house; it stands on a hill gently rising from a lake, in the middle of a noble wood. Three beautiful hills rise above it, and these command very fine views of the great rivers Fergus and Shannon at their junction, being each of them a league wide. For the following particulars I am indebted to Sir Lucius O'Brien.

Average rent of the county of Clare, 5s. The bad tracts of land in the county, are the east mountains, part of the barony of Burren, and the great peninsula, which forms

the north shore of the Shannon. Great tracts are let at
nothing at all, but there are 20,000 acres from Paradise
Hill, along the Fergus and Shannon to Limerick, which
let at 20s. an acre. These lands are called the *Corcasses*[111].
The tillage of the country is carried on by little farmers,
from £20 to £100 a year, but most of it by the poor
labourers, who are generally under-tenants, not holding of
the landlords. No peas sown, but rape in considerable
quantities in mountain grounds, or boggy, both of which
are burnt for it. The crop of seed is pressed into oil at the
mills of Sixmilebridge and Scarriff near Killaloe, but the
greatest part is bought up by the merchants of Limerick
for exportation to Holland. The rape cakes are all exported to England for manure. Flax is sown in small
quantities by the poor people for their own consumption,
and some yarn sold, but not much from the whole county.
Spinning is by no means general; not half the women spin.
Some linens, *bandle* cloths, and Clare dowlas, for exportation in small quantities, and other sorts, enough for home
consumption. Wool is spun for clothing for the people,
into worsted yarn for serges, and into yarn for stockings.
Great quantities of friezes are sold out of the county.

The principal grazing system consists in a union of both
rearing and fattening; the rearing farms generally at a
considerable distance from the rich lands on the Fergus
and Shannon. There are 4000 bullocks fattened annually
in the county of Clare, bought in at £6 and sold out at £10,
and 3000 cows, bought in at £3 and sold fat at £5; also
6000 fat wethers, sold out of the county annually at 20s.
each.

This country is famous for cider orchards. An acre of
trees yields from 4 to 10 hogsheads per annum, and what
is very uncommon in the cider counties of England, yields
a crop every year. I never beheld trees so laden with apples
as in Sir Lucius O'Brien's orchard, it amazed me that they

did not break under the immense load which bowed down the branches.

Middlemen, not common, but much land re-let, arising from the long tenures which are given. The poor live upon potatoes ten months of the year; but, if a mild winter, and a good crop, all the year on them. They keep cows very generally. Labour is usually paid for with land. Working days of Roman Catholics may be reckoned 250 in a year, which are paid for with as much land as amounts to about £6, and the good and bad master is distinguished by this land being reckoned at an high or a low rent. The state of the poor, on comparison with what they were twenty years ago, is that they are much increased in numbers, and better clad than they were, and more regularly fed, in being freed from those scarcities which were felt before the laws for the increase of tillage [112].

Relative to smuggling wool from Clare, Sir Lucius gave me several strong reasons for believing that there had not been any for some years. He was executor to a man who made a fortune by it twenty-five years ago, but he would never smuggle when above 10s. a stone. The cause of the high price of wool is the admission of woollen yarn in all the ports of England, and the increased demand in the Manchester fabric for that yarn, which demand would have operated in England as in Ireland, had the cheapness of spinning been equal. Another cause, the increase of population, and the people being better clad. Sending a pound of wool to France, smugglers compute to be 6d., which is fifty per cent. on the present prime cost. Thus the French could get wool much cheaper from England, where the prime cost is lower. There is none from Cork, for being a manufacturing town, the people would not allow it. A duty of 4d. per stone of 18 lb. on woollen and worsted yarn exported, marks the quantity which Ireland grows beyond its own consumption. Raw wool, 2000 to 10,000 stone, the rest yarn, which is nearly doubled in value by the manufacture. The quantity of broad cloth and serges, that is, old and new drapery, imported from England, equals the export of woollen yarn.

SEPT. 8TH. Left Dromoland. Sir Lucius rode with me through "Clonmelly" [townland of Clonmoney] to the hill above Bunratty Castle for a view of the Shannon from Limerick to Foynes Island, which is thirty miles, with all its bays, bends, islands, and fertile shores. It is from one to three miles broad, a most noble river, deserving regal navies for its ornament, or what are better, fleets of merchantmen, the cheerful signs of far extended commerce, instead of a few miserable fishing boats, the only canvas that swelled upon the scene; but the want of commerce in her ports is the misfortune, not the fault of Ireland [113]. Thanks for the deficiency to that illiberal spirit of trading jealousy, which has at times actuated and disgraced so many nations. The prospect has a noble outline in the bold mountains of Tipperary, Cork, Limerick, and Kerry. The whole view magnificent.

At the foot of this hill is the Castle of Bunratty, a very large edifice, the seat of the O'Briens, princes of Thomond; it stands on the bank of a river, which falls into the Shannon near it. About this castle, and that of Rosmanagher [114], the land is the best in the county of Clare; it is worth £1. 13s. an acre, and fats a bullock per acre in summer, besides winter feed.

To Limerick [115], through a cheerful country, on the banks of the river, in a vale surrounded by distant mountains. That city is very finely situated, partly on an island formed by the Shannon. The new part, called Newtown-Pery, from Mr Pery, the Speaker [116], who owns a considerable part of the city, and represents it in Parliament, is well built. There is a communication with the rest of the town by a handsome bridge of three large arches, erected at Mr Pery's expense. Here are docks, quays, and a Custom House, which is a good building, faces the river, and on the opposite banks is a large quadrangular one, the House of Industry. This part of Limerick is very cheerful and agreeable, and carries all the marks of a flourishing place.

The exports of this port are beef, pork, butter, hides, and rape seed. The imports are rum, sugar, timber, tobacco, wines, coals, bark, salt, etc. The customs and excise, about sixteen years ago, amounted to £16,000, at present £32,000, and rather more four or five years ago.

Much flour goes to Dublin from this county and Tipperary on the land carriage bounty. There is a great increase of tillage; thrice the corn grown that there was formerly. There has been much pasturage broken up on this account; some bullock land, and some sheep land. Great quantities of butter made within a few miles of Limerick. Scarce any spinning here, or in the neighbourhood, either of wool or flax. The poor live upon potatoes and milk, generally speaking, with some oatmeal. They do not all keep cows. They are in a better situation in most respects than twenty years ago. Population has much increased within twenty years. Emigrations were known from hence; two ships went commonly till the war. Between 1740 and 1750, there were only four carriages in and about Limerick, the Bishop's, the Dean's, and one other clergyman's, and one neighbouring gentleman's. Four years ago there were about 70 coaches and postchaises in Limerick, and one mile round it. In Limerick district, now 183 four-wheeled carriages; 115 two-wheeled ditto.

Land sells at twenty years' purchase. Rents were at the highest in 1765, fell since, but in four years have fallen 8s. to 10s. an acre about Limerick. They are at a stand at present, owing to the high price of provisions from pasture.

The number of people in Limerick are computed at 32,000, it is exceeding populous for the size; the chief street quite crowded; many sedan chairs in town, and some hackney chaises. Assemblies the year round, in a new Assembly House, built for the purpose, and plays and concerts common. Upon the whole, Limerick must be a very gay place, but when the usual number of troops are in town, much more so. To show the general expenses of living, I was told of a person's keeping a carriage, four horses, three men, three maids, a good table, a wife, three children, and a nurse, and all for £500 a year.

SEPT. 9TH. To Castle Oliver [Co. Limerick]. Various country, not so rich to appearances as the *corcasses*, being fed bare. Much hilly sheep walk, and for a considerable way, a full third of it potatoes and corn. No sign of de-population. Having engaged myself to Mr Oliver, to return from Killarney by his house, as he was confined to Limerick by the assizes, I shall omit saying anything of it at present.

SEPT. 10TH. Reached Anne's Grove [Co. Cork], the seat of Richard Aldworth, Esq. to whom I am obliged for the following particulars. (The country) abounds exceedingly with land-jobbers, who have hired large tracts, and re-let them to tenants, and those to under ones, but gentlemen are getting out of this system now. No graziers here. The rents are made by tillage and sheep and a few dairies. The barony of Orrery in this county (Cork) is as rich as Limerick. Duhallow has much mountains and unim-proved, vast tracts of it heath, but rears at present great numbers of young cattle and many dairies. In Carbery, there are great quantities of wild country, and much un-cultivated; provisions are extravagantly cheap from want of communications. Neither peas, beans, nor rape in the

country, but turnips and clover are creeping in among
gentlemen. Flax is sown by everybody for their own use,
which they spin, and get woven into linen for themselves,
and what they have to spare, sell in yarn. There are very
few of these weavers. The cottiers have all sheep, which
they milk for their families. The poor people reckon
their cattle by *collops* [117], that is, proportions. The heaviest
collop is six sheep, the next is a horse, the next two heifers,
and lastly the cow. Flocks rise to 500 sheep; no folding.
Dairies are considerable. They rise from 20 to 50 cows,
are employed in making butter only; in some parts of the
county they make very good cheese. The tillage of the
farmers is all done by horses; that of the gentlemen by
oxen. To 100 acres of tillage they keep about six horses;
they make up their teams, borrowing of one another. The
chaff is thrown away, as everywhere else. The poor people
in general occupy from 10 to 15 acres; but the most
common way is hiring in partnership in *rundale*, and they
have *changedale* also. Most of them have only a cabin and
a cabbage garden, and the size is usually enough for 100
plants, and their rent for it 20s.; in this case they pay their
neighbour for the grass of their cow; but I was sorry to
find that some of them have no cows. They live the year
through upon potatoes, and for half the year have nothing
but water with them. They have all a pig, and some of
them several, but kill one for themselves at Christmas.
Their circumstances are very generally better than twenty
years ago, especially in clothing, but in food no great
difference. Spinning is the general business of the women;
they spin infinitely more wool than flax.

In the little towns of Doneraile, Mitchelstown, Mallow,
Kilworth, Kanturk, and Newmarket, are clothiers, who
buy up the wool, employ combers in their houses, who
make considerable wages, and when combed, they have a
day fixed for the poor to come and take it, in order to

spin it into worsted, and pay them by the ball, by which they earn $1\frac{3}{4}d$. to $2d$. a day. The clothier exports this worsted from Cork to Bristol and Norwich. Of late they have worked a good deal of it into serges, which are sent to Dublin by land carriage, and from thence to the north, from whence it is smuggled into England by way of Scotland. The poor people's wool is worked into friezes for the use of the men. The weavers who work these friezes and serges live about the country in the cabins. Immense quantities of raw wool are sent to Cork from all parts; 500 cars have been seen in a line, and it is supposed to be sent in large quantities to France. No emigrations. All the poor people are Roman Catholics, and among them are the descendants of the old families who once possessed the country, of which they still preserve the full memory, insomuch, that a gentleman's labourer will regularly leave to his son, by will, his master's estate.

Mr Aldworth has erected a bolting mill which will grind 5000 barrels of wheat. He has also taken pains to improve the breed of sheep, by buying English ewes. The same attention he has given to swine. He began to plant hops in 1772 upon half an acre of land, a fine rich red loam a yard deep; they succeeded perfectly well. In 1773 he added two acres; in 1775 he planted another acre. This year he has a very good appearance. Has not found the climate at all against them, and is clear that it may be a very advantageous branch of culture.

SEPT. 11TH. It was with regret I left so agreeable and liberal a family as that of Anne's Grove[118]; everything about the place had a much nearer resemblance to an English than an Irish residence, where so many *fine* places want *neatness*, and where, after great expense, so little is found *complete*.

SEPT. 12TH. To Lord Doneraile's[119], to whom I am indebted for a variety of useful intelligence. The situation of his house is on a beautiful rising ground which slopes down to a winding vale. Respecting his Lordship's husbandry the following particulars deserve the attention of the reader. Three years ago he procured ewes from Leicestershire, in order to improve the breed. The sheep which were here before took three to a stone of wool, but now only two, and the wool is to the full as good as ever, and he finds that they are much more thriving and advantageous to keep, and easier fed than the sheep of the country. Sheep, his Lordship finds the most advantageous stock of all others, he keeps six to the acre winter and summer. Has tried many breeds of cattle, and finds that the long horned English cow is the best for fattening. The Kerry cow is much the best for milking in quantity of good milk. For working, he finds the small mongrel Kerry beast works the best, and moves the fastest. He works them all by the horns, in the manner practised in the south of France, four in a plough at the first ploughing. English waggons Lord Doneraile has tried and laid aside, from finding, on experience, that they are very much inferior to the common Irish car in hay harvest, dung, lime, etc. but he uses one-horse carts for many sorts of work. Turnips he has cultivated for some years, hoes them, and gets good crops; he uses them in feeding sheep, and also fattening beasts. He makes his tillage exceedingly profitable by the use of lime.

Lord Doneraile has erected a granary upon a new construction, that of a flue in the walls for a fire to air the whole building, and dry any damp corn that may happen to be in it. He dried the walls after building with it perfectly in a short time. This granary is so completely built, that not a mouse can possibly get in it; it has a thorough air, with lattice windows of wire. By the way, these flues are a proof, if one was wanting, how much moister the climate of Ireland is than that of England.

SEPT. 13TH. Left Doneraile, and went to Colonel Jephson's at Mallow [Co. Cork]. About that place they live upon potatoes generally the year through. All of them keep cows and pigs, which latter they feed on small potatoes. Their circumstances are not better than twenty years ago, for though they have now 6*d.* and then had but 5*d.* yet the rise is not proportioned to that of rents. Villages of cottiers will take farms in partnership in the manner I have often described. Leases are thirty-one years, or three lives, and many farms let to middlemen, who occupy no part of the land themselves, but re-let it. Above one-third of the county is waste land.

There are collieries about ten miles off, near Kanturk, from which coal is sold at 3*s.* a barrel; it is large and hard. Upon the river Blackwater, there are tracts of flat land in some places one quarter of a mile broad; the grass everywhere remarkably fine, and lets at 30*s.* It is the finest sandy land I have anywhere seen, of a reddish brown colour; would yield the greatest arable crops in the world, if in tillage.

There is but little manufacturing in Mallow; even spinning is not general. I walked to the spring in the town to drink the water, to which so many people have long resorted; it resembles that of Bristol, prescribed for the same cases, and with great success. In the season there are two assemblies a week. Lodgings are 5*s.* a week each room, and those seemed to be miserably bad. Board 13*s.* a week. These prices, in so cheap a country, amazed me, and would, I should fear, prevent Mallow from being so considerable, as more reasonable rates might make it, unless accommodations proportionable were provided. There is a small canal, with walks on each side, leading to the spring, under cover of some very noble poplars. If a double row of good lodgings were erected here, with public rooms, in an elegant style, Mallow would probably become a place for amusement, as well as health[120].

SEPT. 14TH. To "New Grove," the seat of Robert Gordon, Esq.[121]. New Grove is an entire new improvement of Mr Gordon's, the whole place some years ago being a waste moor, or "mountain," as it is called in Ireland. He imported a man from Norfolk, whom he gave forty guineas a year with board, who brought ploughs, hoes, etc. with him; gave him a guinea for every boy he taught to plough, and every boy who could fairly plough, had a shilling a day wages. By this means he has collected a set of excellent ploughmen, who have been of infinite use.

Six years ago, Mr Gordon established a linen manufactory, and bleach mill, upon the completest scale; a factory of 11 looms for damask, bleacher's house and other buildings, with a reservoir of water for turning the wheel; the whole well built, well contrived, and at the expense of £1200. Trusted to a manager for the conduct of the works, who broke, which put a stop to them; otherwise there would have been a flourishing manufactory established. Spinning flax coming in, but the woollen through the country; and from hence to the north-west Duhallow Barony is the great country for spinning cotton.

SEPT. 15TH. To Blarney Castle[122], S[t] J[ohn] Jefferys, Esq.; of whose great works in building a town at Blarney [Co. Cork], I cannot give so particular an account as I wish to do; for I got there just as he and his family were on the point of setting out for France. I did not however let slip the time I had for making some enquiries, and found that in 1765, when Mr Jefferys began to build this town, it consisted only of two or three mud cabins; there are now ninety houses. He first established the linen manufactory, building a bleach mill, and houses for weavers, etc. and letting them to manufacturers from Cork, who have been so successful in their works, as to find it necessary to have larger and more numerous edifices, such as a large stamping mill for printing linens and cottons, to which is annexed another bleach mill, and since there has been a third erected. The work carried on is that of buying yarn, and weaving it into linens, 10*d*. to 30*d*. white. Also diapers, sheeting, ticking, and linens and cottons of all sorts printed here, for common use and furniture. These several branches of the linen, employ 130 looms, and above 300 hands.

Another of Mr Jefferys's objects has been the stocking manufacture, which employs 20 frames, and 30 hands, in buildings erected by him; the manager employing, by covenant, a certain number of apprentices, in order by their being instructed, to diffuse the manufactory. Likewise a woollen manufactory, a mill for milling, tucking, etc. broad cloths; a gig mill for glossing, smoothing, and laying the grain; and a mill for napping, which will dress above 500 pieces a year, but will be more, when some alterations now making are finished. A leather mill for dressing shamoy, buck, or skins, fully employed. A large bolting mill, just finished, and let for £132 a year. A mill, annexed to the same, just finishing, for plating; and a blade mill for grinding edged tools. A large paper mill, which will be finished this year. He has been able to erect this multiplicity of mills, thirteen in all, by an uncommon command of water.

The town is built in a square, composed of a large handsome inn, and manufacturers' houses, all built of excellent stone, lime, and slate. A church, by the first fruits, and liberal addition of above £300 from Mr

Jefferys. A market house, in which are sold £100 worth of knit stockings per week. Four bridges, which he obtained from the county, and another (the flat arch) to which he contributed a considerable sum. In all these establishments, he has avoided undertaking or carrying on any of the manufactures upon his own account, from a conviction that a gentleman can never do it without suffering very considerably. His object was to form a town, to give employment to the people, and to improve the value of his estate by so doing; in all which views it must be admitted, that the near neighbourhood of so considerable a place as Cork very much contributed; the same means which he has pursued would, in all situations, be probably the most advisable, though the returns made might be less advantageous. Too much can scarcely be said in praise of the spirit with which a private gentleman has executed these works, which would undoubtedly do honour to the greatest fortune.

Mr Jefferys, besides the above establishments, has very much improved Blarney Castle and its environs. He has formed an extensive ornamented ground, which is laid out with considerable taste.

Accompanied Mr Jefferys, etc. to Dunkettle [Co. Cork], the seat of Dominick Trant, Esq.[123]. For the following particulars concerning the neighbourhood, I am indebted to Mr Trant.

The diet of the poor is potatoes and milk, with some fish in the herring and sprat season. Labourers' houses from 25s. to 40s. a year. Fuel, a very little coal, the rest supplied by bushes, stolen faggots, etc. as there is no turf in this part of the country. Price of labour 6d. per day through the year, on a pinch in harvest 8d. sometimes more, but within the liberties of the city generally 8d. Women 3d. and 4d. a day in reeking [i.e. heaping up] corn. Children from 1d. to 3d. in picking stones, etc.

Most employed in country business; a few at some bolting
iron and paper mills in the neighbourhood. From 14 acres
of orchard Mr Trant makes 60 hogsheads a year of cider.

SEPT. 16TH. To Cove[124] by water from Mr Trant's
quay. The first view of Haulbowline Island and Spike
Island, high rocky lands, with the channel opening to
Cove, where are a fleet of ships at anchor, and Rostellan,
Lord Inchiquin's[125] house, backed with hills, a scenery that
wants nothing but the accompaniment of wood. Arrived
at the ship at Cove. In the evening returned.

Dunkettle is one of the most beautiful places I have seen
in Ireland. It is a hill of some hundred acres broken into
a great variety of ground, by gentle declivities, with everywhere an undulating outline, and the whole varied by a
considerable quantity of wood, which in some places is
thick enough to take the appearance of close groves, in
others spreads into scattered thickets and a variety of single
groups. This hill, or rather cluster of hills, is surrounded
on one side by a reach of Cork harbour, over which it
looks in the most advantageous manner; and on the other
by an irriguous vale, through which flows the river
Glanmire. The scene is not only beautiful in those
common circumstances which form a landscape, but is alive
with the cheerfulness of ships and boats perpetually
moving.

SEPT. 17TH. To Castlemartyr [Co. Cork] the seat of the
Earl of Shannon[126]. It is an old house, but much added
to by the present earl; he has built, besides other rooms, a
dining one 32 feet long by 22 broad, and a drawing one,
the best rooms I have seen in Ireland, a double cube of
25 feet, being 50 long, 25 broad, and 25 feet high. The
grounds about the house are very well laid out; much wood
well grown, considerable lawns, a river made to wind

through them in a beautiful manner, an old castle so perfectly covered with ivy as to be a picturesque object.

Lord Shannon established a factory at "Cloghnickelty" [Clonakilty], in the year 1769, a bleach yard of 17 acres of land, with mills, etc. for bleaching the pieces that are wove in the neighbourhood. There are 94 looms at work in the town, £100 a week laid out in yarn, and at three fairs, £1800, the amount of which is £7000 a year. The cloth chiefly coarse. This establishment has had great effect in increasing the manufactures in the neighbourhood.

His Lordship has reclaimed 109 acres of furze land, which he has eradicated, and brought to a very profitable soil. Upon going into tillage, he found that the expense of horses was so great that it eat up all the profit of the farm, which made him determine to use bullocks. He did it in the common method of yokes and bows, but they performed so indifferently, and with such manifest uneasiness, that he imported the French method of drawing by the horns, and in order to do this effectually, he wrote to a person at Bordeaux to hire him a man who was practised in that method. Upon first introducing it, there was a combination among all his men against the practice, but he was determined to carry his point in this matter. He followed a course that had all imaginable success. One lively, sensible boy took to the oxen, and worked them readily. His Lordship at once advanced this boy to 8d. a day; this did the business at once; others followed the example, and since that he has had numbers who could manage them, and plough as well as the Frenchman. They plough an acre a day with ease, and carry very great loads of corn and hay, coals, etc.

Farms (about Castlemartyr) not taken in partnership so much as in other parts. Two or three will take a farm of 30 or 40 acres, but it is not general. A third part of the county is waste land. Flax is sown by few of the common people in patches. Very few flocks in this country. The poor people all keep a *collop* or two of sheep, with which they clothe themselves. They plough generally with four horses, sow with two and use ploughs of so bad a construction, that a man attends them with a strong stick leaning on the beam to keep it in the ground. Tithes are everywhere valued by the proctor by the acre. No emigrations from the county of Cork. The religion is almost universally Catholic.

There is a woollen trade at Castlemartyr. Mr James Pratt in particular buys wool in Tipperary and at Ballinasloe. The best is the Connacht. It is the finest and is short. The longest is in the county of Carlow and Tipperary. The trade has been a rising one for two years.

SEPT. 20TH. From Castlemartyr to Castle Mary [Co. Cork], the seat of Robert Longfield, Esq. who keeps a great quantity of land in his hands. Has cultivated the potatoes, called here *Bulls*, that is, the English *Cluster*, very much for cattle, but nobody will eat them; gives them to his horses and bullocks, and when he gives his horses potatoes, they have no oats. It is surprising to see how fond horses are of them; they do very well on them raw, but the best way is to boil them, as they will then fatten the horses. The bullocks are equally fond of them, and will follow him to eat them out of his hand. Sheep are the same, and will get into the fields to scrape them up. Upon the whole, Mr Longfield is persuaded that no root or crop in the world is more beneficial to a farmer than this potato.

He established the linen manufacture here three years ago, by building a bleach mill and bleach green; he has 14 looms constantly at work upon his own account, who are paid for what they manufacture by the yard. The factory employs 50 hands. A great many weavers are scattered about the country, who bring their webs, etc., to be bleached here. The flax is raised, and the yarn spun

at Clonakilty and Ross [Ross Carbery], etc. in the west
of the county. No woollen manufacture is carried on in
this country. The county of Cork two-thirds waste, at a
very low or no rent.

SEPT. 21ST. To Rostellan, the seat of Lord Inchiquin,
commanding a beautiful view of Cork Harbour, the ships
at Cove, the Great Island and the two others [*i.e.* Haulbowline and Spike Island] which guard the opening of the
harbour. Got to Cork[127] in the evening, and waited on the
Dean[128], who received me with the most flattering
attention. Cork is one of the most populous places I have
ever been in. It was market day, and I could scarce drive
through the streets, they were so amazingly thronged; on
the other days, the number is very great. I should suppose
it must resemble a Dutch town, for there are many canals
in the streets, with quays before the houses. The best-
built part is Morrison's Island, which promises well; the
old part of the town is very close and dirty. As to its
commerce, the following particulars I owe to Robert
Gordon, Esq., the Surveyor General.

Average of nineteen years' export, ending March 24th, 1773.

					£
Hides, at £1 each ...	...	...	...	...	64,000
Bay and woollen yarn	...	...	...	...	294,000
Butter, at 30s. per cwt. from 56s. to 72s.	...	...	180,000
Beef, at 20s. a barrel	...	...	...	...	291,970
Camblets, serges, etc.	...	...	...	...	40,000
Candles ...	...	...	...	...	34,220
Soap	...	...	...	...	20,000
Tallow	...	...	...	20,000
Herrings, £18 to £35,000 all their own	...	...	21,000
Glue, £20 to £25,000	...	...	...	...	22,000
Pork	...	...	...	...	64,000
Wool to England ...	...	...	...	...	14,000

Small exports, Gothenborg herrings, horns, hoofs, etc.

feather beds, palliasses, feathers, etc.   35,000

£1,100,190

Seventy to eighty sail of ships belong to Cork. The number of people mustered by the clergy, by hearth-money, and by the number of houses, payments to minister, average of the three, 67,000 souls, if taken before the 1st of September, after that 20,000 increased. There are 700 coopers in the town. Barrels, all of oak or beech, all from America; the latter for herrings, now from Gothenborg and Norway.

Cork duties, in 1751, produced	...	£62,000
„ „ 1776 „	...	£140,000

Export of woollen yarn from Cork, £300,000 a year in the Irish market. No wool smuggled, or at least very little. The wool comes to Cork, etc. and is delivered out to combers, who make it into balls. These balls are bought up by the French agents at a vast price, and exported; but even this does not amount to £40,000 a year.

Particulars of the woollen fabrics of the county of Cork received from a manufacturer. The woollen trade, serges and camblets, ratteens, friezes, druggets, and narrow cloths, the last they make to 10s. and 12s. a yard; if they might export to 8s. they are very clear that they could get a great trade for the woollen manufacturers of Cork. The wool comes from Galway and Roscommon, combed here by combers, who earn 8s. to 10s. a week, into balls of 24 ounces, which is spun into worsteds, of twelve skeins to the ball, and exported to Yarmouth for Norwich. The export price, £30 a pack, to £33, never before so high; average of them £26 to £30. Some they work up at home into serges, stuffs, and camblets; the serges at 12d. a yard, 34 inches wide; the stuffs 16 inches, at 18d. the camblets at 9½d. to 13d.; the spinners at 9d. a ball, one in a week; or a ball and half 12d. a week, and attend the family besides. This is done most in Waterford and Kerry, particularly near Killarney. The weavers earn 1s. a day

on an average. Full three-fourths of the wool is exported
in yarn, and only one-fourth worth worked up. Half the
wool of Ireland is combed in the county of Cork.

A very great manufacture of ratteens at Carrick-on-Suir,
the bay worsted is for serges, shalloons[129], etc. Woollen
yarn for coarse cloths, which latter have been lost for
some years, owing to the high price of wool. The bay
export has declined since 1770, which declension is owing
to the high price of wool. No wool smuggled[130], not even
from Kerry, not a sloop's cargo in twenty years, the price
too high; the declension has been considerable. For every
86 packs that are exported, a licence from the Lord
Lieutenant, for which £20 is paid. Upon the whole, there
has been no increase of woollen manufacture within
twenty years. Is clearly of opinion that many fabrics
might be worked up here much cheaper than in France,
of cloths that the French have beat the English out of;
these are, particularly, broad-cloths for the Levant trade,
frieze which is now supplied from Carcassone in
Languedoc, flannels, serges; these would work up the
coarse wool. At Ballinasloe Fair, in July, £200,000
a year bought in wool. There is a manufactory of knit-
stocking by the common women about Cork, for eight or
ten miles around. Besides their own consumption, great
quantities are sent to the north of Ireland.

All the weavers in the country are confined to towns,
have no land, but small gardens. *Bandle* or narrow linen,
for home consumption, is made in the western part of the
county. Generally speaking, the circumstances of all the
manufacturing poor are better than they were twenty
years ago. The manufactures have not declined, though
the exportation has, owing to the increased home con-
sumptions. Bandon was once the seat of the stuff,
camblet, and shag[131] manufacture, but has in seven years
declined above three-fourths. Have changed it for the

manufacture of coarse green linens, for the London market, but the number of manufacturers in general much lessened.

SEPT. 22ND. Left Cork and proceeded to Coolmore [Co. Cork], the seat of the Rev. Archdeacon Oliver [132], who is the capital farmer of all this neighbourhood. Mr Oliver began the culture of turnips four years ago, and found them so profitable (for feeding cattle) that he has every year had a field of them in the broad-cast method, and well hoed. This year they are exceedingly fine, clean, and well hoed, so that they would be no disgrace to a Norfolk farmer. This is the great object wanting in Irish tillage; a gentleman, therefore, who makes so considerable a progress in it, acts in a manner the most deserving praise that the whole circle of his husbandry will admit. In bringing in furzy waste land he has improved very extensively. Land about Coolmore lets from 8s. to 20s. The poor people have most of them land with their cabins, from 4 to 6 acres, which they sow with potatoes and wheat. Not many of them keep cows, but a few sorry sheep for milk; they generally have milk, either of their own, or bought, in summer, and in winter they have herrings; but live, upon the whole, worse than in many other parts of the kingdom. Farms rise to 200 or 300 acres, but are hired in partnership.

Before I quit the environs of Cork, I must remark that the country on the harbour I think preferable, in many respects, for a residence to anything I have seen in Ireland. *First*, it is the most southerly part of the kingdom. *Second*, there are very great beauties of prospect. *Third*, [here is] by much the most animated, busy scene of shipping in all Ireland. *Fourth*, a ready price (consequently) for every product. *Fifth*, great plenty of excellent fish and wild fowl. *Sixth*, the neighbourhood of a great city for objects of convenience.

SEPT. 24TH. Took my leave of Mr Oliver. I purposed going from hence to Bandon, in the way to Carbery, and so to Killarney, by Bantry and Nedeen, but, hearing that the Priest's Leap between Bantry and Nedeen was utterly impassable, the road not being finished, which is making by subscription, I changed my route, and took the Macroom road. Dined with Colonel Ayres, who informed me that the agriculture of that neighbourhood was very indifferent, and little worth noting, except the use of lime as a manure, which is practised with great success. From hence I reached Sir John Colthurst's[138] at Knightsbridge, who has a very extensive estate here.

SEPT. 25TH. Took the road to Nedeen, through the wildest region of mountains that I remember to have seen. Sir John was so obliging as to send half a dozen labourers with me, to help my chaise up a mountain side, of which he gave a formidable account; in truth it deserved it. The road leads directly against a mountain ridge, and those who made it were so incredibly stupid, that they kept the straight line up the hill, instead of turning aside to the right, to wind around a projection of it. The path of the road is worn by torrents into a channel, which is blocked up in places by huge fragments, so that it would be a horrid road on a level; but on a hill so steep that the best path would be difficult to ascend, it may be supposed terrible. The labourers, two passing strangers, and my servant, could with difficulty get the chaise up. It is much to be regretted that the direction of the road is not changed, as all the rest from Cork to Nedeen is good enough. For a few miles towards the latter place the country is flat on the river Kenmare; much of it good, and under grass or corn.

Nedeen is a little town, very well situated, on the noble river Kenmare, where ships of 150 tons may come up.

There are but three or four good houses. Lord Shelburne[134], to whom the place belongs, has built one for his agent. There is a vale of good land, which is here from a mile and a half to a mile broad; and to the north and south, great ridges of mountains said to be full of mines.

At Nedeen, Lord Shelburne had taken care to have me well informed by his people in that country, which belongs for the greatest part to himself. He has above 150,000 Irish acres in Kerry; the greatest part of the barony of Glanarought belongs to him, most of Dunkerron and Iveragh. The size of farms is various, from 40 acres to 1000; less quantities go with cabins, and some farms are taken by labourers in partnership. Some wheat is sown, but not generally by the poor people. Oats are the common crop. There are some dairies. The butter is all carried to Cork on horses' backs. The common stock of the mountains are young cattle, bred by the poor people; but the large farmers go generally to Limerick for yearlings, turn them on the mountains, where they are kept till three years old, when they sell them at Nedeen or Killarney. The poor people's heifers sell at three years old, at 30s. Their breed is the little mountain, or Kerry cow, which upon good land gives a great deal of milk. There are few sheep kept, not sufficient to clothe the poor people, who however, work up what there is into frieze. Many goats are kept on the mountains, especially by the poor people, to whom they are a very great support, for upon the mountains the milk of a goat is equal to that of a cow, and some of the kids are killed for meat.

Upon asking whether they ploughed with horses and oxen, I was told there was not a plough in the whole parish of "Tooavista" [Tuosist] which is twelve miles long by seven broad. All the tillage is by the Irish *loy*[135]; ten men dig an acre a day that has been stirred before. It will take forty men to put in an acre of potatoes in a day. The labour of the farms is generally carried on by cottiers, to whom the farmer assigns a cabin, and a garden, and the running of two *collops* on the mountain, for which he pays a rent; he is bound to work with his master for 3*d*. a day and two meals. Their food in summer, potatoes and milk; but in spring they have only potatoes and water. Sometimes they have herrings and sprats. They never eat salmon. The religion is in general Roman Catholic.

There has been a considerable fishery upon the coast of Kerry. Last year, that in the Kenmare river was the most considerable; it employed twelve boats. This year none at all; the chief in Ballinskelligs [Bay] and river Valentia. None in Kenmare for several years before: but great abundance of sprats for three years. Salmon is constant; they export about 5 tons salted. The herrings chiefly for home consumption, salted and fresh. Killarney is the principal market for wheat, which is twelve miles distant.

Lord Shelburne has a plan for improving Nedeen, to which he has given the name of Kenmare, from his friend the nobleman, with that title[136], which, when executed, must be of considerable importance. It is to build ten cabins, and annex 10 acres to each cabin, rent free for twenty-one years; also to form twenty-acred allotments for the parks to the town of Nedeen, with design to encourage settlements in it, for which 330 acres are kept in hand. The situation is advantageous, and ships of 100 tons can come up to it, with a very good landing-place. He has also fixed some English farmers.

The climate in these parts of Kerry is so mild, that potatoes are left by the poor people in the ground the whole winter through; but last winter almost ruined them, their crop being destroyed.

SEPT. 26TH. Left Nedeen, and rising the mountainous region, towards Killarney, came to a tract of mountain bog, one of the most improvable I have anywhere seen. Soon entered the wildest and most romantic country, a region of steep rocks and mountains, which continued for nine or ten miles.

From one of these heights, I looked forward to the lake of Killarney at a considerable distance, and backward to the river Kenmare. Came in view of a small part of the Upper Lake, spotted with several islands, and surrounded by the most tremendous mountains that can be imagined, of an aspect savage and dreadful. From this scene of wild magnificence, I broke at once upon all the glories of Killarney; from an elevated point of view I looked down on a considerable part of the lake, which gave me a specimen of what I might expect. The water you command (which, however, is only a part of the lake) appears a basin of two or three miles round; to the left it is enclosed by the mountains you have passed, particularly by the Torc [1764 ft.], whose outline is uncommonly noble, and joins a range of others, that form the most magnificent shore in the world; on the other side is a rising scenery of cultivated hills, and Lord Kenmare's park and woods; the end of the lake at your feet is formed by the root of Mangerton [2756 ft.], on whose side the road leads. From hence I looked down on a pretty range of inclosures on the lake, and the woods and lawns of Muckross, forming a large promontory of thick wood, shooting far into the lake. The most active fancy can sketch nothing in addition. Islands of wood beyond seem to join it, and reaches of the lake, breaking partly between, give the most lively intermixture of water: six or seven isles and islets form an accompaniment, some are rocky, but with a slight vegetation, others contain groups of trees, and the whole thrown into forms, which would furnish new ideas to a painter. Farther is a chain of wooded islands, which also appear to join the main land, with an offspring of lesser ones

scattered around. Arrived at Mr Herbert's at Muckross, to whose friendly attention I owed my succeeding
pleasure.

SEPT. 27TH. Walked into Mr Herbert's beautiful grounds.
Entered the garden, and viewed Muckross Abbey[137], one
of the most interesting scenes I ever saw. It is the ruin
of a considerable abbey, built in Henry the VIth's time,
and so entire, that if it were more so, though the building
would be more perfect, the ruin would be less pleasing.
It is half obscured in the shade of some venerable ash
trees; ivy has given the picturesque circumstance, which
that plant alone can confer, while the broken walls and
ruined turrets throw over it "*The last mournful graces of
decay.*" Heaps of skulls and bones scattered about, with
nettles, briars and weeds sprouting in tufts from the loose
stones, all unite to raise those melancholy impressions,
which are the merit of such scenes, and which can scarcely
anywhere be felt more completely. The cloisters form a
dismal area, in the centre of which grows the most prodigious yew tree I ever beheld, in one great stem, 2 feet
diameter, and 14 feet high, from whence a vast head of
branches spreads on every side, so as to form a perfect
canopy to the whole space.

From the abbey we passed to the terrace, a natural one
of grass on the very shore of the lake. Returned to breakfast and pursued Mr Herbert's new road, which he has
traced through the peninsula to Dinish Island, three miles
in length. It is carried in so judicious a manner through
a great variety of ground, rocky woods, lawns, etc., that
nothing can be more pleasing; it passes through a remarkable scene of rocks, which are covered with woods; from
thence to the marble quarry, which Mr Herbert is working;
and where he gains variety of marbles, green, red, white,
and brown, prettily veined. The road leads by a place

where copper mines were worked; many shafts appear; as much ore was raised as sold for £25,000, but the works were laid aside, more from ignorance in the workmen, than any defects in the mine. Came to an opening on the Great Lake, which appears to advantage here, the town of Killarney on the north-east shore. Look full on the mountain Glena [138], which rises in a very bold manner, the hanging woods spread half way, and are of great extent, and uncommonly beautiful.

SEPT. 28TH. Took boat on the lake, from the promontory of Dundag. I had been under a million of apprehensions that I should see no more of Killarney, for it blew a furious storm all night, and in the morning the bosom of the lake heaved with agitation, exhibiting few marks but those of anger. After breakfast, it cleared up, the clouds dispersed by degrees, the waves subsided, the sun shone out in all its splendour; every scene was gay, and no idea but pleasure possessed the breast. With these emotions sallied forth, nor did they disappoint us. Rowed under the rocky shore of Dundag. Cross to Dinish [Island]. Passing the Bridge, by a rapid stream [The Meeting of the Waters], came presently to the Eagle's Nest [1100 ft.]; it is nearly perpendicular, and rises in such full majesty, with so bold an outline, that the magnificence of the object is complete. The immense height of the mountains of Killarney may be estimated by this rock; from any distant place that commands it, it appears the lowest crag of a vast chain, and of no account, but on a close approach it is found to command a very different respect. Pass between the mountains called the Great Range, towards the Upper Lake. Row to the cluster of the Seven Islands, a little archipelago. They rise very boldly from the water upon rocky bases, and are crowned in the most beautiful manner with wood; the channels among them opening to new scenes, and the great amphitheatre of rock and mountain that surround them unite to form a noble view.

Returned by a course somewhat different, through the Seven Islands, and back to the Eagle's Nest. At that noble rock fired three cannon for the echo, which indeed is prodigious; the report does not consist of direct reverberations from one rock to another with a pause between, but has an exact resemblance to a peal of thunder rattling behind the rock, as if travelling the whole scenery we had viewed and lost in the immensity of Macgillicuddy's Reeks.

SEPT. 29TH. Rode after breakfast to Mangerton Cascade and "Drumarourk" Hill[139], from which the view of Muckross is uncommonly pleasing. Returning took boat again towards Ross Isle [Lough Leane]. Of the Isle of Innisfallen, it is paying no great compliment to say, it is the most beautiful in the King's dominions, and perhaps in Europe. It contains 20 acres of land. The general feature is that of wood; the surface undulates into swelling hills, and sinks into little vales that let in views of the surrounding lake between the hills, while the swells break the regular outline of the water, and give to the whole an agreeable confusion.

Row to Ross Castle[140], in order to coast that island. There is nothing particularly striking in it. The near approach to Tomies exhibits a sweep of wood, so great in extent, and so rich in foliage, that no person can see without admiring it. The mountainous part above is soon excluded by the approach; wood alone is seen, and that in such a noble range, as to be greatly striking; it just hollows into a bay, and in the centre of it is a chasm in the wood; this is the bed of a considerable stream, which forms O'Sullivan's Cascade, to which all strangers are conducted, as one of the principal beauties of Killarney. Returned to Muckross.

SEPT. 30TH. This morning I had dedicated to the ascent of Mangerton, but his head was so enshrouded in clouds, and the weather so bad, that I was forced to give up the scheme. Mr Herbert has measured him with very accurate instruments, of which he has a great collection, and found his height 835 yards above the level of the sea. The Devil's Punch Bowl [2206 ft.], from the description I had of it, must be the crater of an exhausted volcano. There are many signs of them about Killarney, particularly vast rocks on the sides of mountains, in streams, as if they had rolled from the top in one direction. Brown stone rocks are also sometimes found on lime quarries, tossed thither, perhaps in some vast eruption.

In my way from Killarney to Castleisland, rode into Lord Kenmare's park, from whence there is another beautiful view of the lake, different from many of the preceding; there is a broad margin of cultivated country at your feet, to lead the eye gradually in the lake, which exhibits her islands to this point more distinctly than to any other, and the backgrounds of the mountains of Glena and Tomies give a bold relief.

Upon the whole, Killarney, among the lakes that I have seen, can scarcely be said to have a rival. The extent of water in Lough Erne is much greater; the islands more numerous, and some scenes near Castle Caldwell, of perhaps as great magnificence. The rocks at Keswick are more sublime, and other lakes may have circumstances in which they are superior; but when we consider the prodigious woods of Killarney; the immensity of the mountains; the uncommon beauty of the promontory of Muckross, and the isle of Innisfallen; the character of the islands, and the uncommon echoes, it will appear, upon the whole, to be in reality superior to all comparison.

Before I quit it, I have one other observation to make, which is relative to the want of accommodations and extravagant expense of strangers residing at Killarney. I speak it not at all feelingly, thanks to Mr Herbert's hospitality, but from the accounts given me: the inns are miserable, and the lodgings little better. I am surprised somebody with a good capital does not procure a large well-built inn, to be erected on the immediate shore of the lake, in an agreeable situation, at a distance from the town; there are very few places where such an one would answer better. There ought to be numerous and good apartments; a large rendezvous-room for billiards, cards, dancing, music, etc. to which the company might resort when they chose it; an ordinary for those that liked dining in public; boats of all sorts, nets for fishing, and as great a variety of amusements as could be collected, especially within doors, for the climate being very rainy, travellers wait with great impatience in a dirty common inn, which they would not do if they were in the midst of such accommodations as they meet with at an English spa. But above all, the prices of everything, from a room and a dinner, to a barge and a band of music, to be reasonable, and hung up in every part of the house. The resort of strangers to Killarney would then be much increased, and their stay would be greatly prolonged; they would not view it post haste, and fly away the first moment to avoid dirt and imposition. A man, with a good capital and some ingenuity, would, I think, make a fortune by fixing here upon such principles.

Rents here are about 8s. an acre on an average, including much indifferent land, but not the mountains. About three-fifths of the county of Kerry is waste land. Farms are from £20 a year to £130, the large ones include considerable mountain tracts. The tillage of the country is trifling. Pasturage is applied chiefly to dairies; the common ones about 40 or 50 cows. They are all set at 40s. to 50s. a cow. Three acres allowed to a cow; some paid in butter. The dairyman has his privilege, which is a cabin, potato garden, liberty to cut turf, and a quantity of land proportioned to the number of cows. The butter is all sent to Cork on horses' backs, in truckles, and in that way the poor horses of the country will carry 8 cwt. the distance thirty-seven miles. They go in two days, and generally home in a week. Very few sheep kept; no flocks, except Mr Herbert's. It is remarkable, that no sheep in the country are better fattened than many upon Macgillicuddy's Reeks, which are the wildest and most desolate region of all Kerry. Great herds of goats are kept on all the mountains of this country, and prove of infinite use to the poor people. The inhabitants are not in general well off; some of them have neither cows nor goats, living entirely upon potatoes, yet are they better than twenty years ago, particularly in clothing. Price of provisions the same as at Nedeen, but pork not common. Turkeys, at 9*d*. Salmon, at 1*d*. Trout and perch plentiful. No pike in Kerry. Lampreys and eels, but nobody eats the former.

All the poor people, both men and women, learn to dance, and are exceedingly fond of the amusement. A ragged lad, without shoes or stockings, has been seen in a mud barn, leading up a girl in the same trim for a minuet: the love of dancing and music are almost universal amongst them.

Took my leave of Muckross, and passing through Killarney, went to Castleisland. In my way to Arabela [Co. Kerry], crossed a hilly bog of vast extent, from 1 to 6 or 7 feet deep, as improvable as ever I saw, covered with bog myrtle and coarse grass; it might be drained at very little expense, being almost dry at present. It amazed me to see such vast tracts in a state of nature, with a fine road passing through them.

To Mr Blennerhasset, member for the county, I am indebted for every attention towards my information.

About Castleisland the land is very good, ranking among the best in Kerry. From that place to Arabela, the land is as good as the management bad, every field overrun with all kinds of rubbish, the fences in ruins, and no appearance but of desolation. The state of the poor in the whole county of Kerry represented as exceedingly miserable, and, owing to the conduct of men of property, who are apt to lay the blame on what they call land pirates, or men who offer the highest rent, and who, in order to pay this rent, must, and do re-let all the cabin lands at an extravagant rise, which is assigning over all the cabins to be devoured by one farmer. The cottiers on a farm cannot go from one to another, in order to find a good master, as in England, for all the country is in the same system, and no redress to be found. Such being the case, the farmers are enabled to charge the price of labour as *low* as they please, and rate the land as *high* as they like. This is an evil which oppresses them cruelly, and certainly has its origin in its landlords, when they set their farms, setting all the cabins with them instead of keeping them tenants to themselves. The oppression is, the farmer valuing the labour of the poor at 4*d.* or 5*d.* a day, and paying that in land rated much above its value. Owing to this, the poor are depressed; they live upon potatoes and sour milk, and the poorest of them only salt and water to them, with now and then a herring. Their milk is bought, for very few keep cows, scarce any pigs, but a few poultry. Their circumstances are incomparably worse than they were twenty years ago; for they had all cows, but then they wore no linen; all now have a little flax. To these evils have been owing emigrations, which have been considerable.

OCT. IST. Rode over the mountain improvements which William Blennerhasset, Esq. of Elm Grove has made.

OCT. 2ND. To Ardfert [Co. Kerry] by Tralee, through a continuation of excellent land, and execrable management. To the west of Tralee are the "Mahagree" [Magharee] islands, famous for their corn products; they are rock and sand, stocked with rabbits; near them a sandy tract, twelve miles long, and one mile broad, to the north, with the mountains to the south, famous for the best wheat in Kerry. All under the plough. Farms are large, 100, 200, or 300 acres, but some are taken in partnership.

Arriving at Ardfert, Lord Crosbie[141], whose politeness I have every reason to remember, was so obliging as to carry me by one of the finest strands I ever rode upon, to view the mouth of the Shannon at Ballingary, the site of an old fort. It is a vast rock separated from the country by a chasm of a prodigious depth, through which the waves drive. The rocks of the coast here are in the boldest style, and hollowed by the furious Atlantic waves into caverns in which they roar. It was a dead calm, yet the swell was so heavy, that the great waves rolled in and broke upon the rocks with such violence as to raise an immense foam, and give one an idea of what a storm would be; but fancy rarely falls short in her pictures. The view of the Shannon is exceedingly noble; it is eight miles over, the mouth formed by two headlands of very high and bold cliffs, and the reach of the river in view very extensive. It is an immense scenery. Perhaps the noblest mouth of a river in Europe.

Ardfert is very near the sea, so near it, that single trees or rows are cut in pieces with the wind, yet about Lord Glandore's house there are extensive plantations exceedingly flourishing. Many fine ash and beech, about a beautiful Cistercian abbey[142], and a silver fir of forty-eight years' growth, of an immense height and size.

OCT. 3RD. Left Ardfert, accompanying Lord Crosbie to Listowel [Co. Kerry]. Called in the way to view Lixnaw, the ancient seat of the Earls of Kerry, but deserted for ten years past, and now presents so melancholy a scene of desolation, that it shocked me to see it. Everything around lies in ruin and the house itself is going fast off by thieving depredations of the neighbourhood.

Proceeded to Woodford[143], Robert Fitzgerald's, Esq. Close to the house is a fine winding river under a bank of thick wood, with the view of an old castle hanging over it. Mr Fitzgerald is making a considerable progress in rural improvements; he is taking in mountain ground, fencing and draining very completely, and introducing a new husbandry. Farms are very much in partnership, and improvements exceedingly backward on that account. The poor live on potatoes and milk all the year round, but are rather better off than they were twenty years ago.

OCT. 4TH. From Woodford to Tarbert [Co. Kerry], the seat of Edward Leslie, Esq., through a country rather dreary, till it came upon Tarbert, which is so much the contrary, that it appeared to the highest advantage. The house is on the edge of a beautiful lawn, with a thick margin of full grown wood, hanging on a steep bank to the Shannon, so that the river is seen from the house over the tops of this wood, which being of a broken irregular outline, has an effect very striking and uncommon. The river is two or three miles broad here, and the opposite coast forms a promontory, which has from Tarbert exactly the appearance of a large island. To the east, the river swells into a triangular lake with a reach opening at the distant corner of it to Limerick. The union of wood, water, and lawn forms upon the whole a very fine scene. I am indebted to Mr Leslie's good offices for the following particulars.

Farms are from 50 to 300 or 400 acres; it is common to have the poor people hire them in partnership, but only the small ones; the large are all stock farms. Every cabin has a bit of flax, which they spin and manufacture for their own use, there being some weavers dispersed about the country. A little pound yarn is sold besides to Limerick, but not much. A little wool is spun for their own use, and wove into frieze. The state of the poor is something better than it was twenty years ago, particularly their clothing, cattle, and cabins. They live upon potatoes and milk; all have cows; and when they dry them, buy others. They also have butter, and most of them keep pigs, killing them for their own use. They have also herrings. They are in general in the cottier system, of paying for labour by assigning some land to each cabin. The country is greatly more populous than twenty years ago, and is now increasing, and if ever so many cabins were built by a gradual increase, tenants would be found for them. Tithes are all annually valued by the proctors, and charged very high. There are on the Shannon about 100 boats employed in bringing turf to Limerick from the coast of Kerry and Clare, and in fishing, the former carry from 20 to 25 tons, the latter from 5 to 10, and are navigated each by two men and a boy.

OCT. 5TH. Kept the road to Adare [Co. Limerick], where Mrs Quin[144], with a politeness equalled only by her understanding, procured me every intelligence I wished for. The poor people do not all keep cows, but all have milk. All have pigs and poultry. [They] are not better off than twenty years ago. Have a potato garden, of which one-half to three-fourths of an acre carries a family through the year; they live entirely upon them, selling their pigs.

Palatines[145] were settled here by the late Lord Southwell, about seventy years ago. They have in general leases for three lives, or thirty-one years, and are not cottiers to any farmer, but if they work for them, are paid in money. The quantities of land are small, and some of them have their feeding land in common by agreement. They are different from the Irish in several particulars; they put their potatoes in with the plough, in drills, horse-hoe them while growing, and plough them out. They plough without a driver; a boy of twelve has been known to plough and drive four horses, and some of them have a hopper in the body of their ploughs, which sows the land at the same time it is ploughed. They preserve some of their German customs: they appoint a burgomaster [for instance], to whom they appeal in case of all disputes; and they yet preserve their language, but that is declining. They are very industrious, and in consequence are much happier and better fed, clothed, and lodged, than the Irish peasants. We must not, however, conclude from hence that all is owing to this; their being independent of farmers, and having leases, are circumstances which will create industry. Their crops are much better than those of their neighbours. There are three villages of them, about seventy families in all. For some time after they settled, they fed upon sour crout, but by degrees left it off, and took to potatoes, but now subsist upon them and butter and milk, but with a great deal of oat bread, and some of wheat, some meat and fowls, of which they raise many. They have all offices to their houses, that is, stables and cow-houses, and a lodge for their ploughs, etc. They keep their cows in the house in winter, feeding them upon hay and oat straw. They are remarkable for the goodness and cleanliness of their houses. The women are very industrious, reap the corn, plough the ground sometimes, and do whatever work may be going on; they also spin, and make their children do the same. Their wheat is much better than any in the country, insomuch that they get a better price than anybody else. Their industry goes so far, that jocular reports of its excess are spread. In a very pinching season, one of them yoked his wife against a horse, and went in that manner to work, and finished a journey at plough. The industry of the women is a perfect contrast to the Irish ladies in the cabins, who cannot be persuaded, on any consideration, even to make hay; it not being the custom of the country; yet they bind corn, and do other works more laborious. Mrs Quin, who is ever attentive to introduce whatever can contribute to their welfare and happiness, offered many premiums to induce them to make hay, of hats, cloaks, stockings, etc., etc. but all would not do.

Few places have so much wood about them as Adare. Mr Quin has above 1000 acres in his hands, in which a large proportion is under wood. There is a fine river runs under the house, and within view are no less than three ruins of Franciscan friaries[146], two of them remarkably beautiful, and one has most of the parts perfect, except the roof.

OCT. 7TH. To Castle Oliver [Co. Limerick] by Bruff, passing through a very fine tract of rich reddish loam. The Right Hon. Mr Oliver was assiduous to the last degree to have me completely informed. Very little land under tillage, and the grass applied chiefly to dairies. In one particular they are very attentive; they conduct the mountain streams into their grass lands, cutting little channels, to introduce the water as much as possible over the whole, and though it comes from a poor mountain of brown stone, or turf, yet the benefit they find to be very great. This is a general custom among all the little occupiers, and they are frequently coming to Mr Oliver, with complaints of each other for diverting or stealing one another's streams. The state of the poor people better in these mountainous tracts than upon the rich flats of Limerick, both from there being more employment and greater plenty of land for them. Some few farms taken in partnership. The rich land reaches from Charleville at the foot of the mountains to Tipperary, by Kilfinnane, a line of twenty-five miles, and across from Ardpatrick to within four miles of Limerick, sixteen miles. Bruff, Kilmallock and Hospital have very good land about them, the quantity in the whole conjectured to be 100,000 acres. It is in general under bullocks, but there is some tillage scattered about. The graziers are many of them rich, but generally speaking, not so much from the immediate profit as from advantageous leases. Great quantities of flax sown by all the poor and little farmers, which is spun in the country, and a good deal of *bandle* cloth made of it. This and pigs are two great articles of profit here; they keep great numbers, yet the poor in this rich tract of country are very badly off. Land is so valuable, that all along as I came from Bruff, their cabins are generally in the road ditch, and numbers of them without the least garden; the potato land being assigned them upon the farm where it suits the master best. The price they pay is very great, from £4 to £5 an acre, with a cabin; and for the grass of a cow, 40s. to 45s. They are, if anything, worse off than they were twenty years ago. A cabin, an acre of land, at 40s. and the grass of two cows, the recompense of the year's labour; but are paid in different places by an acre of grass for potatoes at £5. Those who do not get milk to their potatoes, eat mustard with them, raising the seed for the purpose. The population of the country increases exceedingly, but most in the higher lands. New cabins are building everywhere.

Mr Oliver has practised husbandry on a pretty extensive scale. A considerable part of his land is improved mountain, which he grubbed and cleared of spontaneous rubbish, and manured with limestone sand, and then cultivated some for corn, and some for turnips. Where the land is boggy, he burns, in order to get rid of that soil, which he considers as worth but little. In the breed of cattle he has been very attentive[147], purchasing bulls and cows, at the expense of twenty guineas each, of the long-horned Lancashire breed, and from them has bred others. I saw two exceeding well made bulls of a year old of his breeding, which would have made a considerable figure in Leicestershire. Turnips he has cultivated for many years, applying them chiefly to feeding deer; but he has fattened some sheep on them with good success. Hollow draining he has practised upon an extensive scale, and laid a large tract of wet land dry by it. Castle Oliver is a place almost entirely of Mr Oliver's creation, from a house surrounded with cabins and rubbish he has fixed it in a fine lawn, surrounded by good wood.

OCT. 9TH. Left Castle Oliver. Passed through Kilfinnane and Duntryleague, in my way to Tipperary. Towards Tipperary I saw vast numbers of sheep and many bullocks. All this line of country is part of the famous Golden Vale[148]. To Thomastown [Co. Tipperary], where I was so unfortunate as not to find Mr Mathews at home; the domain is 1500 English acres, so well planted, that I could hardly believe myself in Ireland. There is a hill in the park, from which the view of it, the country and the Galtees, are striking.

To the Earl of Clanwilliam's[149]. The country is all under sheep, and the soil dry sandy loam. Farms are generally large, commonly 3000 or 4000 acres, and rise up to 10,000, of which quantity there is one farm, this is Mr Macarthy's, of Spring House, near Tipperary, and is I suppose the most considerable one in the world. Here are some of the particulars of it: 9000 acres in all; £10,000 rent; 8000 sheep; 2000 lambs; 550 bullocks; 80 fat cows; £20,000 value of stock; 200 yearlings; 200 two-year olds; 200 three-year olds; 80 plough bullocks; 180 horses, mares and foals; 150 to 200 labourers; 200 acres tillage.

The quantity of tillage in this country, trifling, but the crops are large. Much bog; that of Allen comes in a line through the Queen's County to within three miles of Cashel. One fifth of Tipperary mountain, the rest 20s. an acre. Rents have fallen since 1771.

Respecting the state of the poor in this country they are paid by a cabin, and one acre and a half of land, for which they are reckoned £4, and for grass of a cow £2. 2s. They live upon potatoes and milk; generally have cows, but not all, and those who have not, buy, but very many of them have for the half year, only potatoes and salt. They all keep pigs. They are just as they were twenty years ago.

OCT. 12TH. To Lord de Montalt's[150], at Dundrum [Co. Tipperary], a place which his Lordship has ornamented in the modern style of improvement. The house was situated in the midst of all the regular exertions of the last age; parterres, parapets of earth, straight walks, knots and clipped hedges, all which he has thrown down, with an infinite number of hedges and ditches, filled up ponds, and opened one very noble lawn around him, scattered negligently over with trees, and cleared the course of a choked up river, so that it flows at present in a winding course through the grounds.

His Lordship's system of husbandry is an admirable one; it is to take farms into his own hands, as the leases expire, to keep them for improvement, and when done to re-let them. This is the true agriculture for profit for a landlord; he has upon this system improved near 2000 acres. Throwing down the old miserable fences which split the farms into little scraps of fields, and made new ditches for drains and water-courses, disposed the new fields to the best advantage, drained them with stone drains where wet, broke up such of the grass as was bad, cultivated it enough to bring it into proper order, and laid it down again to

meadow; there cannot be a better system, or more calculated at the same time to ornament a country, and
improve his own estate.

The mountain lands of Tipperary, one-seventh of the
county, the rest lets at 20s. an acre on an average. There
is some woollen manufacture scattered through it, especially
at Thurles, Tipperary, Clonmel, etc.

OCT. 13TH. Leaving Dundrum, passed through Cashel,
where is a rock and ruin on it, called the rock of Cashel [151],
supposed to be of the remotest antiquity. Towards
Clonmel [Co. Tipperary] [152], there is a great deal of
tillage. The first view of that town, backed by a high ridge
of mountains, was very pleasing. It is the best situated
place in the county of Tipperary, on the Suir, which
brings up boats of 10 tons burden. It appears to be a busy
populous place, yet I was told that the manufacture of
woollens is not considerable. It is noted for being the
birthplace of the inimitable Sterne. Within two miles of
it is Marlfield, the seat of Stephen Moore, Esq. celebrated
in Ireland for his uncommon exertions in every branch of
agriculture. His mill was built seven years ago, and cost
£15,000. It began to be worked with only 3000 barrels
of wheat in a year, which has risen gradually to 20,000
barrels in 1776, a very strong proof of the great increase of
tillage in the neighbourhood. He sends his flour to Dublin,
on the bounty, which rather more than pays the expense
of carriage, 6d. per cwt. Never exports on his own
account, but sends a little to Waterford. It goes to Dublin
in cars, which take each 8 to 10 cwt., that is from four to
five bags. Mr Moore tried English broad-wheeled waggons, with high-priced strong horses, but they did not
answer at all; he has found the cars to carry much greater
loads.

Mr Moore contracts for biscuit, which he bakes in large

quantities, and bread for the whole town of Clonmel. He has eight ovens going for biscuit. Starch he also makes large quantities of. Adjoining his flour mill, he has erected a rape mill, for making oil; the seed is all raised in the neighbourhood. The cake sells at 48s. a ton, and is exported, some to Holland, but most to England, for manure. Mr Moore's husbandry is also worthy of considerable notice. His principal attention has been given to cattle; seventeen years ago he imported Leicestershire rams, Northampton stallions, and a Craven bull from England. I examined his bulls, cows, and oxen with attention; he has a bull which deserves every commendation for shape; and three or four out of six or seven prime cows I saw, were very beautiful ones.

To Sir William Osborne's[153] [at Newtownanner Ho.], three miles the other side Clonmel. This gentleman has made a mountain improvement which demands particular attention, being upon a principle very different from common ones. Twelve years ago he met with a hearty looking fellow of forty, followed by a wife and six children in rags, who begged. Sir William questioned him upon the scandal of a man in full health and vigour, supporting himself in such a manner. The man said he could get no work. "*Come along with me, I will shew you a spot of land upon which I will build a cabin for you, and if you like it you shall fix there.*" The fellow followed Sir William, who was as good as his word. He built him a cabin, gave him 5 acres of a heathy mountain, lent him £4 to stock with, and gave him, when he had prepared his ground, as much lime as he would come for. The fellow flourished; he went on gradually; repaid the £4, and presently became a happy little cottier. He has at present 12 acres under cultivation, and a stock in trade worth at least £80. His name is John Conory. The success which attended this man in two or three years brought others, who applied for land, and Sir William gave them as they applied. The mountain was under lease to a tenant, who valued it so little, that upon being reproached with not cultivating, or doing something with it, he assured Sir William, that it was utterly impracticable to do anything with it, and offered it to him without any deduction of rent. Upon this mountain he fixed them; gave them terms as they came determinable with the lease of the farm, so that every one that came in succession had shorter and shorter tenures, yet are they so desirous of settling, that they come at present, though only two years remain for a term. In this manner Sir William has fixed twenty-two families, who are all upon the improving land, the meanest growing richer, and find themselves so well off, that no consideration will induce them to work for others, not even in harvest. Their industry has no bounds; nor is the day long enough for the revolution of their incessant labour. Some of them bring turf to Clonmel, and Sir William has seen Conory returning loaded with soap ashes.

He found it difficult to persuade them to make a road to their village, but when they had once done it, he found none in getting cross roads to it, they found such benefit in the first. Sir William has continued to give them whatever lime they come for, and they have desired 1000 barrels among them for the year 1776. Their houses have all been built at his expense, they raise what little offices they want for themselves. He has informed them, that upon the expiration of the lease, they will be charged something for the land, and has desired that they will mark out each man what he wishes to have; some of them have taken pieces of 30 or 40 acres; a strong proof that they find their husbandry beneficial and profitable. He has great reason to believe that nine-tenths of them were Whiteboys, but are now of principles exceedingly different from the miscreants that bear that name. Their cattle are feeding on the mountain in the day, but of nights they house them in little miserable stables. All their children are employed regularly in their husbandry, picking stones, weeding, etc. which shows their industry strongly; for in general they are idle about all the country. The women spin.

Too much cannot be said in praise of this undertaking. It shows that a reflecting penetrating landlord can scarcely move without the power of creating opportunities to do himself and his country service. It shows that the villainy of the greatest miscreants is all situation and circumstance. *Employ*, don't *hang* them. Let it not be in the slavery of the cottier system, in which industry never meets its reward, but by giving property, teach the value of it. By giving them the fruit of their labour, teach them to be laborious. All this Sir William Osborne has done, and done it with effect, and there probably is not an honester set of families in the county than those which he has formed from the refuse of the Whiteboys.

Suppose he builds a house to every 20 acres, and limes that quantity of land, the expense would be a few shillings over £40, or 40s. an acre. If they pay him 2s. 4d. an acre for the land, he will make just £6 per cent. for his money; a most striking proof of the immense profit which attends mountain improvements of every kind, because instead of 2s. 4d. they would consider 6s. or 7s. as a rent of favour. Four shillings and eight pence is 12 per cent. for his money; 7s. is 18 per cent. Yet in spite of such facts do the lazy, trifling, inattentive, negligent, *slobbering*, profligate owners of Irish mountains leave them, as they received them, from the hands of their ancestors, in the possession of grouse and foxes. Shame to such a spiritless conduct!

OCT. 15TH. Left Newtown[anner], and keeping on the banks of the Suir, passed through Carrick [Carrick-on-Suir, Co. Tipperary] to Curraghmore [Co. Waterford], the seat of the Earl of Tyrone[154]. This line of country, in point of soil, inferior to what I have of late gone through; so that I consider the rich country to end at Clonmel. For the following account of the husbandry of the county of Waterford I am obliged to the attention of Lord Tyrone.

That county is divided into very large farms, and the renters of them keep cows generally, which they let to dairymen. One farmer, Mr Peor, has two thousand cows, and pays £2000 a year, but they rarely let more to one man than fifty cows, usually about twenty. The dairyman's privilege is a house and 2 or 3 acres of land, or a horse and two cows in twenty. They make nothing but butter, and all keep hogs, but do not feed them with milk, selling it all. 1300 to 1500 churns full of milk, each 8 gallons, goes into Waterford every day in the year, and a prodigious quantity to Carrick. The county is by far the greatest dairying one in Ireland. The breed is the common mountain cow, poor to look at, but great milkers. Average rent of all the land under cows, 10s. One-third of the county mountain. Not a thirtieth part of the county under the plough. The tillage consists only of little patches broken up by the cabins; it has been increasing these fifteen years. About Dungarvan [Co. Waterford], there are many potatoes planted, which are sent to Dublin in boats, with loads of birch brooms, and they are said to be loaded with "*fruit*" and "*timber*," but in no part of the county do they plant grass potatoes; they plant many of the Bull or Turk sort for their pigs, but they are reckoned an unwholesome sort for the people to feed on. Upon the coast there is a great deal of seaweed and sea sand, especially beyond Dungarvan and Waterford. Flax is scarcely anywhere sown.

The poor people feed on potatoes and milk. Most of them have cows. Many of them for a part of the year only salt; but they have oat bread when potatoes are not in season. They all keep pigs, but never eat them. Their circumstances are in general greatly better than they were twenty years ago, both in food and clothing; they have now all shoes and stockings, and are decently dressed every Sunday. No hats among the women, and it is the same in other parts. Their labour is valued, and they are paid the amount in land. The religion of the lower classes is the Roman Catholic.

Emigrations from this part of Ireland principally to Newfoundland, for a season; they have £18 or £20 for their pay, and are maintained, but they do not bring home more than £7 to £11. Some of them stay and settle. Three years ago there was an emigration of indented servants to North Carolina, of 300, but they were stopped by contrary winds, etc. There had been something of this constantly, but not to that amount. The oppression which the poor people have most to complain of is the not having any tenures in their lands, by which means they are entirely subject to their employers.

Manufactures here are only woollens. Carrick[155] is one of the greatest manufacturing towns in Ireland. Principally for ratteens, but of late they have got into broadcloths, all for home consumption. The manufacture increases, and is very flourishing. There are between three and four hundred people employed by it, in Carrick and its neighbourhood.

Lord Tyrone is clear that if his estate in Londonderry was in Waterford, or that all the inhabitants of it were to emigrate from it, so as to leave him to new model it, he would be able to get full one-third more for it than he can do at present; rents in the north depending not on quality, but on price of linen. The rise in the prosperity of Ireland, about the year 1749, owing to the higher price of provisions, which raised rents and enforced industry. Butter now 9*d*. a lb., thirty years ago 2½*d*.

Lord Tyrone has improved 127 acres of hill, the soil reddish dry loam, on a slaty bottom, over-run with furze, briars and bushes. He first grubbed them up, then he levelled an infinite number of old ditches and mounds, ploughed in winter, and second ploughed in May; and 200 barrels of roach lime per acre. Upon this ploughed twice more, and sowed, part with wheat at Michaelmas, and part with barley in spring. The crops exceedingly good; 8 barrels an acre of wheat, and 18 of barley. After the wheat, barley and grass seeds were sown; the barley as good as the other, and upon the barley, part oats were sown, the crop 15 barrels, and white clover and hay seeds. Before the improvement, it let at 10*s*. an acre; after the improvement, it would let readily at 25*s*.

Curraghmore is one of the finest places in Ireland, or indeed that I have anywhere seen. The house, which is large, is situated upon a rising ground, in a vale surrounded by very bold hills, which rise in a variety of forms, and offer to the eye, in riding through the grounds, very noble and striking scenes.

OCT. 17TH. Accompanied Lord Tyrone to Waterford[156]. Made some enquiries into the state of their trade, but found it difficult, from the method in which the Custom House books are kept, to get the details I wished; but in the year following, having the pleasure of a long visit at Ballycanvan, the seat of Cornelius Bolton, Esq., his son, the member for the city, procured me every information I could wish. I was informed that the trade of the place had increased considerably in ten years, both the exports and imports. The exports of the products of pasturage, full one-third in twelve years. That the staple trade of the place is the

Newfoundland trade; this is very much increased, there is more of it here than anywhere. The number of people who go passengers in the Newfoundland ships is amazing; from 60 to 80 ships, and from 3000 to 5000 annually. They come from most parts of Ireland, from Cork, Kerry, etc. Experienced men will get £18 to £25 for the season, from March to November; a man who never went will have £5 to £7, and his passage, and others rise to £20, the passage out they get, but pay home £2. An industrious man in a year will bring home £12 to £16 with him, and some more. A great point for them is to be able to carry out all their slops, for everything there is exceedingly dear, 100 or 200 per cent. dearer than they can get them at home. They are not allowed to take out any woollen goods but for their own use. The ships go loaded with pork, beef, butter, and some salt, and bring home passengers, or get freights where they can; sometimes rum. The Waterford pork comes principally from the barony of Iverk in Kilkenny, where they fatten great numbers of large hogs; for many weeks together they kill here 3000 to 4000 a week, the price 50s. to £4 each; goes chiefly to Newfoundland.

There is a foundry at Waterford for pots, kettles, weights, and all common utensils; and a manufactory of anvils to anchors, etc., which employs 40 hands. There are two sugar-houses, and many salt-houses.

There is a fishery upon the coast for a great variety of fish, herrings particularly in the mouth of Waterford Harbour, and two years ago in such quantities there, that the tides left the ditches full of them. There are some premium boats both here and at Dungarvan, but the quantity of herrings barrelled is not considerable.

The butter trade of Waterford has increased greatly for seven years past; it comes from Waterford principally, but much from Carlow. From the 1st of January, 1774, to the 1st of January, 1775, there were exported 59,856 casks of butter. The slaughter trade has increased, but not so much as the butter. Eighty sail of ships now belonging to the port, twenty years ago not thirty.

Revenue of Waterford

1751	...	...	£17,000
1776	...	...	£52,000

The finest object in this city is the quay, which is unrivalled by any I have seen; it is an English mile long; the buildings on it are only common houses, but the river is near a mile over, flows up to the town in one noble reach, and the opposite shore a bold hill, which rises immediately from the water to a height that renders the whole magnificent. This is scattered with some wood, and divided into pastures of a beautiful verdure by hedges. I crossed the water, in order to walk up the rocks on the top of this hill; in one place, over against Bilberry Quarry, you look immediately down on the river, which flows in noble reaches from Granny Castle on the right past Cromwell's Rock, the shores on both sides quite steep, especially the rock of Bilberry. You look over the whole town, which here appears in a triangular form; besides the city, the Comeragh Mountains, "Slein-a-man" [Slievenaman, 2364 ft.], etc. come in view. Kilmacow River falls into the Suir, after flowing through a large extent of well planted country; this is the finest view about the city.

From Waterford to Passage, and got my chaise and horses on board the *Countess of Tyrone*, in full expectation of sailing immediately, as the wind was fair, but I soon found the difference of these private vessels and the post-office packets at Holyhead and Dublin. When the wind was fair the tide was foul; and when the tide was with them, the wind would not do; in English there was not a complement of passengers, and so I had the agreeableness of waiting with my horses in the hold, by way of rest, after a journey of above 1500 miles.

OCT. 18TH. After a beastly night passed on shipboard, and finding no signs of departure, walked to Ballycanvan the seat of Cornelius Bolton, Esq. Rode with Mr Bolton, jun. to Faithlegg Hill [157], which commands one of the finest views I have seen in Ireland. This hill is the centre of a circle of about ten miles diameter, beyond which higher lands rise, which, after spreading to a great extent, have on every side a background of mountain. In a northerly direction, Mount Leinster [2610 ft.], between Wexford and Wicklow, twenty-six miles off, rises in several heads, far above the clouds. A little to the right of this, "Sliakeiltha" [Slieve-coiltia, 888 ft.] (*i.e.* the woody mountain), at a less distance, is a fine object. To the left, Tory Hill, only five miles, in a regular form varies the outline. To the east, there is the long mountain, eighteen miles distant, and several lesser Wexford hills. To the south-east, the Saltees. To the south, the ocean, and the *collines* about the Bay of Tramore. To the west, Monavullagh [158] rises 2160 feet above the level of the sea, eighteen miles off, being part of the great range of the Comeragh mountains; and to the north-west Slievenaman, at the distance of twenty-four miles; so that the outline is everywhere bold and distinct, though distant. These circumstances would alone form a great view, but the water part of it, which fills up the canvas, is in a much superior style. The great river Suir takes a winding course from the city of Waterford, through a rich country, hanging on the sides of hills to its banks, and, dividing into a double channel, forms the lesser island, both of which courses you command distinctly; united, it makes a bold reach under the hill on which you stand, and there

receives the noble tribute of the united waters of the Barrow
and the Nore, in two great channels, which form the larger
island; enlarged by such an accession of water, it winds
round the hill in a bending course, of the freest and most
graceful outline, everywhere from one to three miles across,
with bold shores, that give a sharp outline to its course to
the ocean. Twenty sail of ships at Passage gave animation
to the scene. Upon the whole, the boldness of the mountain
outline; the variety of the grounds; the vast extent of
river, with the declivity to it from the point of view,
altogether form so unrivalled a scenery—every object so
commanding—that the general want of wood is almost
forgotten.

Farms about Ballycanvan, Waterford, etc., are generally
small, from 20 and 30 to 500 acres, generally about 250;
all above 200 acres are in general dairies; some of the dairy
ones rise very high. Every house has a little patch of flax
for making a little *bandle* cloth, but the quantity is not
considerable. The dairies are generally set at £2. 5s. The
dairyman's privilege to forty cows is a cow and horse, and
2 acres and a cabin, and he is allowed to rear one calf in
ten; 100 acres to forty cows; they do not keep any hogs
on account of cows. There are few sheep kept, no great
flocks. The poor people spin their own flax, but not more,
and a few of them wool for themselves. Their food is
potatoes and milk; but they have a considerable assistance
from fish, particularly herrings. Part of the year they have
also barley, oaten, and rye bread. They are incomparably
better off in every respect than twenty years ago. Their
increase about Ballycanvan is very great, and tillage all
over this neighbourhood is increased.

Among the poor people, the fishermen are in much the
best circumstances. The fishery is considerable; Waterford
and its harbour have 50 boats each, from 8 to 12 tons, six

men on an average to each. Their only net fishery is that of herrings, which is commonly carried on by shares. The division of the fish is; first, one-fourth for the boat, and then the men and nets divide the rest, the latter reckoned as three men. They reckon 10 maze of herrings an indifferent night's work; when there is a good take 40 maze have been taken, 20 a good night; the price per maze, from 1*s*. to 7*s*., average 5*s*. Their take, in 1775, the greatest they have known, when they had more than they could dispose of, and the whole town and country stunk of them, they retailed them 32 for 1*d*. 1773 and 1774 good years. They barrelled many; but in general there is an import of Swedish.

Mr Bolton cannot be too much commended for the humane attention with which he encourages his poor cottier tenantry; he gives them all leases, whatever their religion, of twenty-one or thirty-one years, or lives; even the occupier of 2 acres has a lease. It is inconceivable what an effect this has had; this is the way to give the Catholics right ideas. I was for three weeks a witness of a most spirited industry among them[159]; every scrap of rough rocky land, not before improved, they were at work upon, and overcoming such difficulties as are rarely to be found on common wastes. Many spots, not worth 5*s*. an acre, they were reclaiming to be well worth 25*s*. and 30*s*. The improvement of this part of Mr Bolton's estate may be guessed at when I mention, that on only 500 acres of it, there have been built, in six years, forty new houses, many of them handsome ones of stone and slate. For cabins, barns, etc. he gives timber for the roofs.

OCT. 19TH. The wind being fair, took my leave of Mr Bolton, and went back to the ship. Met with a fresh scene of provoking delays, so that it was the next morning, at

eight o'clock, before we sailed; and then it was not wind,
but a cargo of passengers that spread our sails. Twelve or
fourteen hours are not an uncommon passage, but such
was our luck, that after being in sight of the lights on the
Smalls, we were by contrary winds blown opposite to
Arklow sands; a violent gale arose which presently blew
a storm, that lasted 36 hours, in which, under a reefed
mainsail, the ship drifted up and down wearing [*i.e.* tacking],
in order to keep clear of the coasts. No wonder this
appeared to me, a freshwater sailor, as a storm, when the
oldest men on board reckoned it a violent one. The wind
blew in furious gusts; the waves ran very high; the cabin
windows burst open, and the sea pouring in set everything
afloat, and among the rest a poor lady, who had spread her
bed on the floor. We had however the satisfaction to find,
by trying the pumps every watch, that the ship made little
water. I had more time to attend these circumstances than
the rest of the passengers, being the only one in seven who
escaped without being sick. It pleased God to preserve us;
but we did not cast anchor in Milford Haven till Tuesday
morning the 22nd, at one o'clock.

It is much to be wished that there were some means of
being secure of packets sailing regularly, instead of waiting
till there is such a number of passengers as satisfies the
owner, and captain. With the post-office packets there is
this satisfaction, and a great one it is; the contrary conduct
is so perfectly detestable, that I should suppose the scheme
of the Waterford ones can never succeed [160]. Two years
after, having been assured this conveyance was put on a
new footing, I ventured to try it again; but was mortified
to find that the *Tyrone*, the only one that could take a
chaise or horses, was repairing, but would sail in five days;
I waited, and received assurance after assurance that she
would be ready on such a day, and then on another; in a

word, I waited twenty-four days before I sailed. Moderately speaking, I could, by Dublin, have reached Turin or Milan as soon as I did Milford in this conveyance. All this time the papers had constant advertisements of the *Tyrone* sailing regularly, instead of letting the public know that she was under a repair. Her owner seems to be a fair and worthy man, he will therefore probably give up the scheme entirely, unless assisted by the corporation, with at least four ships more, to sail regularly *with* or *without* passengers; at present it is a general disappointment. I was fortunate in Mr Bolton's acquaintance, passing my time very agreeably at his hospitable mansion; but those who, in such a case, should find a Waterford inn their resource, would curse the *Tyrone*, and set off for Dublin.

* * * * * * *

1777

Upon a second journey to Ireland this year, I took the opportunity of going from Dublin to Mitchelstown [Co. Cork][161], by a route through the central part of the kingdom which I had not before sufficiently viewed.

Left Dublin the 24th of September, and taking the road to Naas [Co. Kildare], I was again struck with the great population of the country, the cabins being so much poorer in the vicinity of the capital than in the more distant parts of the kingdom.

Mr Nevill, at Furness [Co. Kildare], had, in a very obliging manner, given directions for my being well informed of the state of that neighbourhood. He is a landlord remarkably attentive to the encouragement of his tenantry. He allows half the expense of building houses on his estate, which has raised seven of stone and slate, and nine good cabins, at £27 each. He gives annually three premiums of £7, £5, and £3 for the greatest number of trees, planted in proportion to the number of their acres, and pays the hearth money [162] of all who plant trees. He also allows his tenants 40s. an acre for all the parts of their farm that want gravelling, and does the boundary fence for them, but he is paid in his rent very well for this. The following particulars I owe to him.

Tillage is done with both horses and oxen, and, which is extraordinary, the latter are used by common farmers as well as gentlemen. Six oxen, or six horses in summer to a plough, or four in winter, do about half an acre a day. It is generally a corn country, yet are there some graziers that buy in bullocks, but more cows. Also some dairies that fatten veal for Dublin, by which they make £3 or £4 a cow; feeding them in winter when dry on straw, some on hay. They are let out to dairymen at £4 a cow. The sheep kept are generally ewe flocks for fattening, for Dublin market. Buy in at Ballinasloe, at 10s. to 15s. Sell the lamb in June or July, at 8s. to 14s., and the ewe in November, at the same price they gave; keep them chiefly on clover. No folding. Medium price of wool, for ten years past, 16s. clip, three to a stone. A great many hogs bred; keep them for fattening on potatoes; some are finished with offal corn and peas; in summer they feed them on clover. Mark this! one would think, from more than one circumstance, that a good farmer in England was speaking.

In respect of labour, every farmer has as many cottiers as ploughs, whom they pay with a cabin, and one acre of potatoes, reckoned at 30s., and a cow kept through the year, 30s. more. Every cabin has one or more cows, a pig, and some poultry. Their circumstances just the same as twenty years ago. Their food, potatoes and milk for nine months of the year; the other three wheaten bread, and as much butter as the cow gives. They like the potato fare best. Some have herrings; and others 6s. to 10s. worth of beef at Christmas. Sell their poultry; but many of them eat their pig. The sale of the fowls buys a few pounds of flax for spinning, most of them having some of that employment. They are not much given to thieving except bushes and furze, which is all they have for fuel, there being no bog nearer than that of Allen. They bring turf eight and ten miles. Women are paid 5d. a day, earn by spinning, 3d. A farming-man, £5. 10s. a year. A lad, £1. 10s. A maid, £2 to £2. 10s. Reaping, 6s. 6d. Mowing grass, 2s. 6d. to 3s.

To Kildare, crossing the Curragh[163], so famous for its turf. It is a sheep walk of above 4000 English acres, forming a more beautiful lawn than the hand of art ever made. The soil is a fine dry loam on a stony bottom; it is fed by many large flocks, turned on it by the occupiers of the adjacent farms, who alone have the right, and pay very great rents on that account. It is the only considerable common in the kingdom. The sheep yield very little wool, not more than 3 lb. per fleece, but of a very fine quality.

From Furness to Shaen Castle, in the Queen's County, Dean Coote's; but as the husbandry, etc., of this neighbourhood is already registered, I have only to observe, that Mr Coote was so kind as to shew me the improved grounds of Dawson's Court, the seat of Lord Carlow[164], which I had not seen before. The principal beauties of the place are the well grown and extensive plantations, which form a shade not often met with in Ireland.

From Shaen Castle to Gloster, in the King's County, the seat of John Lloyd, Esq., member for that county, to whose attention I owe the following particulars. But first let me observe, that I was much pleased to remark, all the way from Naas quite to Roscrea [Co. Tipperary], that the country was amongst the finest I had seen in Ireland, and consequently that I was fortunate in having an opportunity of seeing it after the involuntary omission of last year. The cabins, though many of them are very bad, yet are better than in some other counties, and chimneys generally a part of them. The people too have no very miserable appearance; the breed of cattle and sheep good, and the hogs much the best I have anywhere seen in Ireland. Turf is everywhere at hand, and in plenty; yet are the bogs not so general as to affect the beauty of the country, which is very great in many tracts, with a scattering of wood, which makes it pleasing. Shaen Castle stands in the midst of a very fine tract. From Mountrath [Queen's Co.] to Gloster, Mr Lloyd's, I could have imagined myself in a very pleasing part of England; the country breaks into a variety of inequalities of hill and dale; it is all well inclosed, with fine hedges; there is a plenty of wood, not so monopolized as in many parts of the kingdom by here and there a solitary seat, but spread over the whole face of the prospect; look which way you will, it is cultivated and cheerful.

There are great tracts of bog in the county. Estates are remarkably divided, and are in general small. The size of farms varies much, 600 acres are a very large one; usually not less than 100; very few in partnership. Very little flax. There are a few bleach yards about Clara, etc., but the business is not much upon the increase. Tillage is performed more with horses than with horned cattle; the latter only by considerable graziers. Very few hogs kept, not more than for mere convenience. The tillage of the whole country is very inconsiderable; it is chiefly pasturage, not one acre in fifteen is tilled; one reason of there not being more, is the number of farms, from 150 to 400 acres, under leases for ever, which are so highly improved by the tenants that they abstain from tillage, under the idea of its being prejudicial. Respecting the labour of a farm, the standing business is done by cottiers. A cottier is one who has a cabin, and an acre and a half of garden, charged at 30s., and the grass of one or two cows, at 25s. each, and the daily pay 6d. the year through, the account being kept by tallies, and those charges deducted. The year's labour amounts to about £6 after the cottier's time for his potatoes and turf is deducted; the remaining 40s. is paid in money, hay, or anything else the man wants. The cows are fed by a field being assigned for all the cottiers of the farm. No instance of a cottier without a cow. The calves they rear till half a year old, and then sell them at 12s. to 20s., which will pay for the cow's hay. They keep no sheep, but every cabin has a pig, a dog, and some poultry. No difference in their circumstances for the last fifteen years. It is here thought that it would be very difficult to nurse up a race of little farmers from the cottiers, by adding land gradually to them at a fair rent; it would be also very difficult, if not impossible, to cut off the cottiers from a farm; nobody would be troubled with such tenants, and no farmer would hire a farm with the poor on it independent of him; their cattle and all their property would be in constant danger; as the kingdom increases in prosperity, such ideas it is to be hoped will vanish. Their food is potatoes and milk for ten months, and potatoes and salt the remaining two; they have however a little butter. They sell their pig, their calf, and their poultry, nor do they buy meat for more than ten Sundays in a year. Their fuel costs them about 14s. a year, or eighty kish of turf[165], an ample allowance. There is in every cabin a spinning-wheel, which is used by the women at leisure hours, or by a grown girl; but for twelve years nineteen in twenty of them breed every second year. *Vive la pomme de terre!*

Expenses of a Poor Family[1]

						£	s.	d.
Cabin and garden ...	...	...	...	...	...	1	10	0
Labour in the garden	...	...	...	...	...	1	10	0
2 cows ...	...	...	...	...	...	2	10	0
Hay for ditto	...	...	...	...	...	1	10	0
Turf ...	...	...	...	...	...		14	0
Clothing, 15s. a head	...	...	...	...	...	3	15	0
Tools ...	...	...	...	...	...		5	0
Hearth tax ...	...	...	...	...	...		2	0
						£11	16	0

The Receipt

The year ...	...	...	...	365 days			
Deduct Sundays ...	...	...	52				
Bad weather ...	...	...	30				
Holydays ...	...	...	10				
			—	92 ,,			
				273 ,, at 6d.	6	16	6

					£	s.	d.			
2 calves	...	...	...	...	1	10	0			
Pig	...	...	...	...	1	0	0			
Poultry	...	...	...	...		5	0			
								2	15	0

	£	s.	d.
Carried over	9	11	6
303 days' spinning between the wife and daughter at 3d.	3	15	3
	£13	6	9
EXPENSES ...	11	16	0
REMAINS for whisky, etc., etc. ...	£1	10	9

Potatoes are much more the food than formerly; there are full twice as many planted. The cottiers are all very much addicted to pilfering. Their general character, idleness and dirtiness, and want of attention. They are remarkable for a most inviolable honour in never betraying

[1] [In a similar budget given elsewhere in the *Minutes*, Arthur Young includes tithe money, and fees paid to the priest for confessions and christenings. *Ed.*]

each other, or even anybody else, which results from a general contempt of order and law, and a want of fear of everything but a cudgel; the reader will remember that maiming cattle, pulling down and scattering stacks, and burning the houses of those who take lands over their heads, are very well known. I am registering information, and that not from one or two persons, but several.

The bounty on the inland carriage of flour to Dublin has occasioned the building several mills, five considerable ones, four were immediately built in consequence. The quantity of tillage has increased double in twenty years. Probably from this cause, among others, has arisen the increase of whisky, the quantity of which is three times greater than fifteen years ago. Not less than 30,000 barrels of barley and bere are distilled yearly within eight miles of Gloster. The country in general is much improved in most national circumstances; buildings are much increased, on a larger scale, and of a far better sort than twenty years ago; there is also a rise in the price of almost all commodities.

SEPT. 30TH. Took my leave of Mr Lloyd, a gentleman from whose conversation I reaped equal instruction and amusement. Passed by Shinrone, Modreeny and Graigue, to Johnstown [House on Lough Derg], the seat of Peter Holmes, Esq. Much of this line a very beautiful country. For the following particulars I am indebted to Mr Holmes.

Through the whole barony of Lower Ormond, the soil is in general a dry limestone land. Farms are large, few less than 500 or 600 acres. The small farms are taken much in partnership; a parcel of labourers will take 100 or 200 acres. Flax is sown only by the cottiers in their gardens; very few that do not sow some. They proportion it very exactly to their own consumption; it is wove by weavers, who make it their business to weave for others;

and there are very few gentlemen that do not do the same for the coarse linen of their families. Very little lime used. No farm-yards; the hay is stacked in the fields where it is designed to be fed, and scattered about; and, shame on them! they do the same with their straw; but no wonder the farm-yard system is unknown, for they sell much of their corn in the stack in the field, which gentlemen buy for straw. In tillage, bullocks and heifers are generally used, four in a plough, and they do not quite half an acre a day. Labour is done by cottiers who have a cabin and a garden of one acre if only one man in family, but if the son is grown, 2 acres. The cabin and one acre is reckoned at 20s., also two *collops*, at 20s. each, which are generally cows. All this he works out at 5d. a day, all extra labour 6½d. a day, and 8d. in harvest. They all have from one to three pigs, and much poultry. Their food is potatoes for at least eleven months of the year, and one month of oat, barley, or bere bread. It is a general remark, that industrious and attentive men will earn £5 in the year. The circumstances of the poor are much better than they were twenty years ago, for their land and cabins are not charged to them by *gentlemen* higher than they were thirty years ago, while all they sell bears double the price.

Potatoes are rather more cultivated and eaten than twenty years ago, and are managed better. The poor in this neighbourhood are by no means to be accused of a general spirit of thieving. It arises from holding them in too much contempt, or from the improper treatment of their superiors. No Whiteboys have ever arisen in these baronies, nor any riots that last longer than a drunken bout at a fair; nothing that has obstructed the execution of justice. There is no objection to cutting off the cottiers from a farm, and making them tenants to the landlord, upon the score of difficulty in letting a farm without cottiers upon it, provided they were kept perfectly distinct

by a good fence. Nor is there any doubt but out of them a
race of little farmers might be gradually formed. Land at
improved rents sells at twenty years' purchase. Rents are
doubled in twenty years; they are not fallen since 1772.
Leases are usually for three lives, or thirty-one years. The
bounty on the inland carriage of corn has occasioned the
building some mills, which, united with the turnip husbandry, and the vast increase of whisky, have altogether
much increased tillage.

The Shannon adds not a little to the convenience and
agreeableness of a residence so near it. Besides affording
wild fowl, the quantity and size of its fish are amazing.
Pikes swarm in it, and rise in weight to 50 lb. In the little
flat spaces on its banks are small but deep lochs, which are
covered in winter and in floods; when the river withdraws,
it leaves plenty of fish in them, which are caught to put
into stews. Mr Holmes has a small one before his door at
Johnstown, with a little stream which feeds it; a trowling
rod here gets you a bite in a moment, of a pike from 20
to 40 lb. I had also the pleasure of seeing a fisherman
bring three trout, weighing 14 lb., and sell them for 6½d.
a piece. Perch swarm; they appeared in the Shannon for
the first time about ten years ago, in such plenty that the
poor lived on them. Bream of 6 lb. Eels very plentiful.
Upon the whole, these circumstances, with the pleasure of
shooting and boating on the river, added to the glorious
view it yields, render this neighbourhood one of the most
enviable situations to live in that I have seen in Ireland.
The face of the country gives every circumstance of
beauty. From Killodiernan Hill, behind the new house
building by Mr Holmes, the whole is seen to great advantage. The spreading part of the Shannon, called Lough
Derg, is commanded distinctly for many miles; it is in two
grand divisions of great variety. That to the north is a
reach of five miles leading to Portumna [Co. Galway].

The whole hither shore a scenery of hills, checkered by inclosures and little woods, and retiring from the eye into a rich distant prospect.

OCT. 3RD. Taking my leave of Johnstown and its agreeable and hospitable family, I took the road towards Derry [Co. Tipperary], the seat of Michael Head, Esq., through a country much of it bordering on the Shannon, and commanding many fine views of that river; but its nakedness, except at particular places, takes off much from the beauty of the scenery. It is to Mr Head's attention that I am indebted for the following particulars concerning the barony of Owney and Arra.

The soil is a light gravelly loam, on a slaty rock, which is almost general through the whole. The rent on an average 15s. for profitable land, and 1s. for mountain, and as there is about half and half, the whole will be 8s. The rise of rent, in twenty years, is about double. Estates are generally large, scarce any so low as £500 or £600 a year. Farms are all small, none above 300 or 400 acres; many are taken in partnership, three, four, or five families to 100 acres. They divide the land among themselves, each man taking according to his capital. The terms *rundale* and *changedale* unknown, as is the latter practice. There are no farms without buildings upon them. Laying out money in building better houses would pay no interest at all, as they are perfectly satisfied with their mud cabins. The tillage of the common people is done with horses, four in a plough, which do half an acre a day: gentlemen use four oxen. The price 8s. an acre. No paring and burning. They shut up their meadows for hay in March or April, and rarely begin to mow till September. I should remark that I saw the hay making or marring all the way from Johnstown hither, with many fields covered with water, and the cocks forming little islands in them. They are generally two months making it; the crop 1 to $1\frac{1}{2}$ ton per acre.

There is no regular system of cattle in this barony, there not being above four or five graziers, but gentlemen, in their domains, have all the different systems. The common farmers keep a few of most sorts of cattle. All keep pigs, which are much increased of late. The common mode of labour is that of cottiers, they have a cabin and an acre for 30s., and 30s. the grass of a cow, reckoning with them at 5d. a day the year round; other labour vibrates from 4d. to 6d. A cottier with a middling family will have two cows; there is not one without a cow. All of them keep as many pigs as they can rear, and some poultry. Their circumstances are rather better than twenty years ago.

Dancing is very general among the poor people, almost universal in every cabin. Dancing masters of their own rank travel through the country from cabin to cabin, with a piper or blind fiddler, and the pay is 6d. a quarter. It is an absolute system of education. Weddings are always celebrated with much dancing; and a Sunday rarely passes without a dance; there are very few among them who will not, after a hard day's work, gladly walk seven miles to have a dance. *John* is not so lively; but then a hard day's work with him is certainly a different affair from what it is with *Paddy*. Other branches of education are likewise much attended to, every child of the poorest family learning to read, write, and cast accounts.

There is a very ancient custom here, for a number of country neighbours among the poor people to fix upon some young woman that ought, as they think, to be married; they also agree upon a young fellow as a proper husband for her; this determined, they send to the fair one's cabin to inform her, that on the Sunday following she is *to be horsed*, that is, carried on men's backs. She must then provide whisky and cider for a treat, as all will pay her a visit after mass for a hurling match[166]. As soon as she is *horsed*, the hurling begins, in which the young fellow appointed for her husband has the eyes of all the company fixed on him; if he comes off conqueror, he is certainly married to the girl, but if another is victorious, he as certainly loses her; for she is the prize of the victor. These trials are not always finished in one Sunday, they take sometimes two or three; and the common expression when they are over is, such a girl was *goaled*. Sometimes one barony hurls against another, but a marriageable girl is always the prize. Hurling is a sort of cricket, but instead of throwing the ball in order to knock down a wicket, the aim is to pass it through a bent stick, the ends stuck in the ground. In these matches they perform such feats of activity, as ought to evidence the food they live on to be far from deficient in nourishment.

There is only one flour mill in the barony, and the increase of tillage is very trifling; but the whisky stills at Killaloe [Co. Clare] trebled in five or six years. In the hills above Derry are some very fine slate quarries, that employ sixty men. The slates are very fine, and sent by the Shannon to distant parts of the kingdom.

Mr Head has a practice in his fences which deserves universal imitation: it is planting trees for gate posts. Stone piers are expensive, and always tumbling down; trees are beautiful, and never want repairing. Within fifteen years this gentleman has improved Derry so much, that those who had only seen it before, would find it almost a new creation. He has built a handsome stone house, on the slope of a hill rising from the Shannon, and backed by some fine woods, which unite with many old hedges well planted to form a woodland scene, beautiful in the contrast to the bright expanse of the noble river below: the declivity, on which these woods are, finishes in a mountain, which rises above the whole. The Shannon gives a bend around the adjoining lands, so as to be seen from the house both to the west and north, the lawn falling gradually to a margin of wood on the shore, which varies the outline. The river is two miles broad, and on the opposite shore cultivated inclosures rise in some places almost to the mountain top, which is very bold.

OCT. 7TH. Took my leave of Mr Head, after passing four days very agreeably. Through Killaloe, over the Shannon, a very long bridge of many arches. Went out of the road to see a fall of that river at Castleconnell [Co. Limerick], where there is such an accompaniment of wood as to form a very pleasing scenery. The river takes a very rapid rocky course, around a projecting rock, on which a gentleman has built a summer-house, and formed a terrace; it is a striking spot. To Limerick. Laid at Bennis's, the first inn we had slept in from Dublin   God preserve us this journey from another!

OCT. 8TH. Leaving that place, I took the road through Pallas to Cullen [Co. Tipperary]. The first six or seven miles from Limerick has a great deal of corn, which shews that tillage is gaining even upon bullocks themselves. I observed with much pleasure, that all the cottiers had their little gardens surrounded with banks well planted with osiers. To the Rev. Mr Lloyd's, at Castle Lloyd [Co. Limerick], near Cullen. The following particulars, which I owe to him, concern more immediately the barony of Clanwilliam in Tipperary, the same [*i.e.* Clanwilliam] in Limerick, Small County, and the part of Coonagh next Clanwilliam [in Limerick].

Estates are generally very large, but some so low as £300 a year. Farms rise from small ones in partnership to 5000 or 6000 acres. The Tillage Acts have had the effect of lessening them evidently. The great system of this district

is that of grazing. Bullocks are bought in at the fairs of
Ballinasloe, Newport, Bannagher, Toomyvara, etc., in the
months of September, October, and November, the prices
from £5 to £8. As soon as bought, they are turned into
the coarsest ground of the farm; the fattening stock being
put into the after-grass, the lean ones are turned after
them; if the farmer has a tract of mountain, they will be
turned into that at first. They are put to hay after Christmas, and kept at it till May. About the 10th of May they
are put to grass for the summer; and in this, the method is
to turn into every field the stock which they imagine will
be maintained by it, and leave the whole there till fat. The
Cork butchers come in July and August to make their
bargains, and begin to draw in September, and continue to
take them till December. Some graziers keep them with
hay till the market rises, but it is not a common practice.
It is thought that they begin to lose flesh about the 20th
of November, and that after the first nothing is gained.
Average selling price £9. 10s. The number of sheep kept
in this neighbourhood has decreased, owing to the division
into smaller farms. The winter food for them in the rich
tracts is grass, except in snows, when they turn them to
their hay stacks. The rise in the price of wool, 5s. a stone
in thirty years. There are but few dairies; the little farmers
have the chief.

Respecting tillage, the chief is done by little farmers, for
the graziers apply themselves solely to cattle. It is entirely
connected with breaking up grass for potatoes—the
quantity small. There are many weavers about the
country, who make *bandle* cloth, and some a yard wide,
for the poor people; they live both in towns and villages.
All the women spin flax. Leases are for thirty-one years
or three lives. Land sells at twenty years' purchase. There
has been a fall of rents from 1772, to the American war,
but since that time they have been rising. The religion all
Roman Catholic.

Much of the labour is done by servants, hired into the house of little farmers, that keep dairies, etc. Much also by cottiers, who have a cabin and an acre and a half of potato garden, which are valued at three guineas; they have also two cows, at 50s. a cow. They all keep a pig, a dog, two cats, and some poultry Their circumstances are better than they were twenty years ago. Their pig they sell, but they eat some poultry, particularly geese. Some of them buy turf for fuel, but many depend on breaking and stealing hedge-wood; they are much given to pilfering. Many of the poor here have no cows. There are cabins on the road side that have no land; the inhabitants of them are called *spalpeens*, who are paid for their labour in cash, by the month, etc. Some of them pay no rent at all, others 10s. a year, and these are the people who hire grass land for their potatoes. It is certain that the cottiers are much better off than these *spalpeens*, who can get but little milk, buying it part of the summer half year only of the dairy farmers.

OCT. 10TH. Left Castle Lloyd, and took the road by Galbally to Mitchelstown [Co. Cork], through a country part of it a rich grazing tract; but from near Galbally, to the Galtee mountains, there are large spaces of flat lands, covered with heath and furze, that are exceedingy improvable, yet seem as neglected as if nothing could be made of them. The road leads immediately at the northern foot of the Galtees, which form the most formidable and romantic boundary imaginable; the sides are almost perpendicular, and reach a height, which, piercing the clouds, seem formed rather for the boundaries of two conflicting empires, than the property of private persons. The variety of the scenery exhibited by these mountains is great; the road, after passing some miles parallel with them, turns over a hill, a continuation of their chain, and commands an oblique view of their southern side, which has much more variety than the northern; it looks down at the same time upon a long plain, bounded by these and other mountains, several rivers winding through it, which join in the centre near Mitchelstown. I had been informed that this was a miserable place; it has at least a situation worthy of the proudest capital.

Upon my arrival, Lord Kingsborough, who possesses almost the whole country, procured me the information I requested in the most liberal manner, and a residence since has enabled me to perfect it. His Lordship's vast property extends from Kildorrery to Clogheen, beyond Ballyporeen [Co. Tipperary], a line of more than sixteen Irish miles, and it spreads in breadth from five to ten miles. It contains every variety of land, from the fertility of grazing large bullocks to the mountain heath the cover of grouse. The profitable land lets from 8s. to 25s. an acre, but the whole does not on an average yield more than 2s. 6d. Such a field for future improvements is therefore rarely to be found. On the cold and bleak hills of Scotland estates of greater extent may be found, but lying within twenty miles of Cork, the most southerly part of Ireland, admits a rational prophesy that it will become one of the first properties in Europe.

The size of farms held by occupying tenants is in general very small, Lord Kingsborough having released them from the bondage of the middlemen. Great tracts are held in partnership; and the amounts held by single farmers rise from £5 to £50 a year, with a very few large farms. The soils are as various as in such a great extent they may be supposed: the worst is the wet morassy land, on a whitish gravel, the spontaneous growth, rushes and heath; this yields a scanty nourishment to cows and half-starved young cattle. Large tracts of wet land has a black peat or a turf surface; this is very reclaimable, and there are immense tracts of it. The profitable soil is in general a sandy or a gravelly loam, of a reddish brown colour; and the principal distinction is its being on lime or grit stone, the former generally the best. It declines in value from having a yellow sand or a yellow clay near the surface under it. There are tracts of such incomparable land that I have seen very little equal to it, except in Tipperary, Limerick, and Roscommon. A deep friable loam, moist enough for the spontaneous growth to fat a bullock, and dry enough to be perfectly under command in tillage. If I was to name the characteristics of an excellent soil, I should say *that* upon which you may fat an ox, and feed off a crop of turnips. By the way I recollect little or no such land in England, yet is it not uncommon in Ireland. Quarries of the finest limestone are found in almost every part of the estate.

The tracts of mountain are of a prodigious extent; the Galtees only are six or seven miles long, from one to four miles across, and more improvable upon the whole than any land I have seen, turf and limestone being on the spot, and a gentle exposure hanging to the south. In every inaccessible cliff there are mountain ash, oak, holly, birch, willow, hazel, and white thorn, and even to a considerable height up the mountain, which, with the many old stumps scattered about them, prove that the whole was once a forest, an observation applicable to every part of the estate.

The tillage here extends no farther than what depends on potatoes, on which root they subsist as elsewhere. They sometimes manure the grass for them, and take a second crop; after which they follow them with oats, till the soil is so exhausted as to bear no longer, when they leave it to weeds and trumpery, which vile system has spread itself so generally over all the old meadow and pasture of the estate, that it has given it a face of desolation—furze, broom, fern, and rushes, owing to this and to neglect, occupy seven-eighths of it. The melancholy appearance of the lands arising from this, which, with miserable and unplanted mounds for fences, with no gate but a furze bush stuck in a gap, or some stones piled on each other, altogether form a scene the more dreary, as an oak, an ash or an elm, are almost as great a rarity (save in the plantations of the present Lord) as an olive, an orange, or a mulberry. There is no wheat, and very little barley. Clover and turnips, rape, beans, and peas, quite unknown.

The rents are paid by cattle, and of these dairy cows are the chief stock. The little farmers manage their own; the larger ones let them to dairymen for one cwt. of butter each cow, and 12s. to 15s. horn money; but the man has a privilege of four *collops*, and an acre of land and cabin to every twenty cows. Sheep are kept in very small numbers; a man will have two, or even one, and he thinks it worth his while to walk ten or twelve miles to a fair, with a straw band tied to the leg of the lamb, in order to sell it for 3s. 6d., an undoubted proof of the poverty of the country. Markets are crowded for this reason, for there is nothing too trifling to carry; a yard of linen, a fleece of wool, a couple of chickens, will carry an unemployed pair of hands ten miles. Hogs are kept in such numbers that the little towns and villages swarm with them; pigs and children bask and roll about, and often resemble one another so much, that it is necessary to look twice before the *human face divine* is confessed. I believe there are more pigs in Mitchelstown than human beings; and yet propagation is the only trade that flourished here for ages.

Labour is chiefly done in the cottier system, which has been so often explained. There are here every gradation of the lower classes, from the *spalpeens*, many among them strangers, who build themselves a wretched cabin in the road, and have neither land, cattle, nor turf, rising to the regular cottier, and from him to the little joint-tenant, who, united with many others, take some large farm in partnership; still rising to the greater farmer. The population is very great. It is but few districts in the North that would equal the proportion that holds on this estate; the cabins are innumerable, and, like most Irish cabins, swarm with children. Wherever there are many people, and little employment, idleness and its attendants must abound.

It is not to be expected that so young a man as Lord Kingsborough, just come from the various gaiety of Italy, Paris, and London, should, in so short a space as two years, do much in a region so wild as Mitchelstown; a very short narrative, however, will convince the reader that the time he has spent here has not been thrown away. He found his immense property in the hands of that species of tenant which we know so little of in England, but which in Ireland have flourished almost to the destruction of the kingdom, the *middleman*, whose business and whose industry consists in hiring great tracts of land as cheap as he can, and re-letting them to others as dear as he can, by which means that beautiful gradation of the pyramid, which connects the broad base of the poor people with the great nobleman they support, is broken; he deals only with his own tenant, the multitude is abandoned to the humanity and feelings of others, which to be sure may prompt a just and tender conduct; whether it does or not, let the misery and poverty of the lower classes speak, who are thus assigned over. This was the situation of nine-tenths of his property. Many leases being out, he rejected the trading tenant, and let every man's land to him, who occupied it at the rent he had himself received before. During a year that I was employed in letting his farms, I never omitted any opportunity of confirming him in this system, as far as was in my power, from a conviction that he was equally serving himself and the public in it; he will never quit it without having reason afterwards for regret.

In a country changing from licentious barbarity into civilized order, building is an object of perhaps greater consequence than may at first be apparent. In a wild, or but half cultivated tract, with no better edifice than a mud cabin, what are the objects that can impress a love of order on the mind of man? He must be wild as the roaming herds; savage as his rocky mountains; confusion, disorder, riot, have nothing better than himself to damage or destroy: but when edifices of a different solidity and character arise; when great sums are expended, and numbers employed to rear more expressive monuments of industry and order, it is impossible but new ideas must arise, even in the uncultivated mind; it must feel something, first to respect, and afterwards to love; gradually seeing that in proportion as the country becomes more decorated and valuable, licentiousness will be less profitable, and more odious. Mitchelstown, till his Lordship made it the place of his residence, was a den of vagabonds, thieves, rioters, and Whiteboys; but I can witness to its being now as orderly and peaceable as any other Irish town, much owing to this circumstance of building, and thereby employing such numbers of the people. Lord Kingsborough, in a short space of time, has raised considerable edifices; a large mansion for himself, beautifully situated on a bold rock; a quadrangle of offices; a garden of 5 English acres, surrounded with a wall, hothouses, etc. Besides this, three good stone and slate houses upon three farms, and engaged for three others, more considerable, which are begun; others repaired, and several cabins built substantially.

So naked a country as he found his estate, called for other exertions. He brought a skilful nurseryman from England, and formed 12 acres of nursery. It begins to shew itself; above 10,000 perch of hedges are made, planted with quick and trees; and several acres, filled with young and thriving plantations. Trees were given, gratis, to the tenantry, and premiums begun for those who plant most, and preserve them best, besides fourscore pounds a

year offered for a variety of improvements in agriculture
the most wanted upon the estate.

Those who are fond of scenes in which nature reigns
in all her wild magnificence should visit the stupendous
chain (of the Galtees). It consists of many vast mountains,
thrown together in an assemblage of the most interesting
features, from boldness and height of the declivities, freedom
of outline, and variety of parts; filling a space of about six
miles by three or four. Galtymore [3015 ft.] is the highest
point, and rises like the lord and father of the surrounding
progeny. From the top you look down upon a great extent
of mountain, which shelves away to the south, east, and
west; but to the north, the ridge is almost a perpendicular
declivity. On that side the famous Golden Vale of
Limerick and Tipperary spreads a rich level to the eye,
bounded by the mountains of Clare, King's and Queen's
counties, with the course of the Shannon, for many miles
below Limerick. To the south you look over alternate
ridges of mountains, which rise one beyond another, till in
a clear day the eye meets the ocean near Dungarvan. The
mountains of Waterford and Knockmealdown fill up the
space to the south-east. The western is the most extensive
view; for nothing stops the eye till Mangerton and Macgillicuddy's Reeks point out the spot where Killarney's
Lake calls for a farther excursion. The prospect extends
into eight counties, Cork, Kerry, Waterford, Limerick,
Clare, Queen's, Tipperary, King's. Nor are these immense outlines the whole of what is to be seen in this great
range of mountains. Every glen has its beauties; there is
a considerable mountain river, or rather torrent, in every
one of them. Nothing can exceed the beauty of the water.
Its lucid transparency shews, at considerable depths, every
pebble no bigger than a pin, every rocky basin alive with
trout and eels, that play and dash among the rocks, as if
endowed with that native vigour which animates, in a

superior degree, every inhabitant of the mountains, from the bounding red deer, and the soaring eagle, down even to the fishes of the brook. Every five minutes you have a waterfall in these glens, which in any other region would stop every traveller to admire it. Sometimes the vale takes a gentler declivity, and presents to the eye, at one stroke, twenty or thirty falls, which render the scenery all alive with the motion; the rocks are tossed about in the wildest confusion, and the torrent bursts by turns from above, beneath, and under them; while the background is always filled up with the mountains which stretch around.

*   *   *   *   *   *   *

Having heard much of the beauties of a part of the Queen's County I had not before seen, I took that line of country in my way on a journey to Dublin.

From Mitchelstown to Cashel [Co. Tipperary] the road leads as far as Galbally in the route already travelled from Cullen. Towards Cashel the country is various. The only objects deserving attention are the plantations of Thomastown, the seat of Francis Mathews, Esq. Found the widow Holland's inn at Cashel, clean and very civil. Take the road to Urlingford [Co. Kilkenny]. The rich sheep pastures, part of the famous Golden Vale, reach between three and four miles, from Cashel to the great bog by "Botany Hill," noted for producing a greater variety of plants than common. That bog is separated by only small tracts of land from the string of bogs which extend through the Queen's County, from the great Bog of Allen; it is here of considerable extent, and exceedingly improvable. Then enter a low marshy bad country which grows worse after passing the sixty-sixth milestone, and successive bogs in it.

Breakfast at Johnstown [Co. Kilkenny], a regular

village on a slight eminence built by Mr "Hayley" [Hely].
Enter a fine planted country, with much corn and good
thriving quick hedges for many miles. The road leads through
a large wood, which joins Lord Ashbrook's [167] plantations,
whose house [Castle Durrow] is situated in the midst of
more wood than almost any one I have seen in Ireland.
Pass Durrow [Queen's Co.]. The country for two or three
miles continues all inclosed with fine quick hedges, is
beautiful, and has some resemblance to the best parts of
Essex. Cross a great bog, within sight of Lord De Vesci's [168]
plantations. Slept at Ballyroan, at an inn kept by three
animals, who call themselves women; met with more
impertinence than at any other in Ireland. It is an
execrable hole.

In three or four miles pass Sir John Parnell's [169] [at Rath-
league], prettily situated in a neatly dressed lawn, with
much wood about it, and a lake quite alive with live fowl.
Pass Monasterevin [Co. Kildare], and cross directly a large
bog, drained and partly improved. Here I got again into
the road I had travelled before.

I must in general remark, that from near Urlingford to
Dawson's Court near Monasterevin, which is completely
across the Queen's County, is a line of above thirty English
miles, and is by much the most improved of any I have seen
in Ireland. It is generally well planted so as to give it the
richness of an English woodland scene. What a country
would Ireland be had the inhabitants of the rest of it
improved the whole like this!

END OF PART I

A TOUR IN IRELAND

PART II

PART II

GENERAL OBSERVATIONS

SOIL, FACE OF THE COUNTRY
AND CLIMATE

To judge of Ireland by the conversation one sometimes hears in England, it would be supposed that
one half of it was covered with bogs, and the other
with mountains filled with Irish ready to fly at the sight
of a civilized being. There are people who will smile when
they hear that, in proportion to the size of the two countries,
Ireland is more cultivated than England, having much less
waste land of all sorts. Of uncultivated mountains there are
no such tracts as are found in our four northern counties,
and the North Riding of Yorkshire, with the eastern line
of Lancaster, nearly down to the Peak of Derby, which
form an extent of above an hundred miles of waste. The
most considerable of this sort in Ireland are in Kerry,
Galway and Mayo, and some in Sligo and Donegal. But
all these together will not make the quantity we have in
the four northern counties; the valleys in the Irish mountains are also more inhabited, I think, than those of
England, except where there are mines, and consequently
some sort of cultivation creeping up the sides. Natural
fertility, acre for acre, over the two kingdoms, is certainly
in favour of Ireland; of this I believe there can scarcely
be a doubt entertained, when it is considered that some of
the more beautiful, and even best cultivated counties in
England, owe almost everything to the capital art and
industry of the inhabitants.

The circumstance which strikes me as the greatest
singularity of Ireland is the rockiness of the soil, which

should seem at first sight against that degree of fertility; but the contrary is the fact. Stone is so general, that I have great reason to believe the whole island is one vast rock of different strata and kinds rising out of the sea. I have rarely heard of any great depths being sunk without meeting with it. In general it appears on the surface in every part of the kingdom; the flattest and most fertile parts, as Limerick, Tipperary, and Meath, have it at no great depth, almost as much as the more barren ones. May we not recognise in this the hand of bounteous Providence, which has given perhaps the most stony soil in Europe to the moistest climate in it? If as much rain fell upon the clays of England (a soil very rarely met with in Ireland, and never without much stone) as falls upon the rocks of her sister island, those lands could not be cultivated. But the rocks here are clothed with verdure; those of limestone, with only a thin covering of mould, have the softest and most beautiful turf imaginable.

The rockiness of the soil in Ireland is so universal that it predominates in every sort. One cannot use with propriety the terms clay, loam, sand, etc., it must be a *stony* clay, a *stony* loam, a *gravelly* sand. Clay, especially the yellow, is much talked of in Ireland, but it is for want of proper discrimination. I have once or twice seen almost a pure clay upon the surface, but it is extremely rare. The true yellow clay is usually found in a thin stratum under the surface mould and over a rock; harsh, tenacious, stony, strong loams, difficult to work, are not uncommon, but they are quite different from English clays.

Friable sandy loams, dry but fertile, are very common, and they form the best soils in the kingdom for tillage and sheep. Tipperary and Roscommon abound particularly in them. The most fertile of all are the bullock pastures of Limerick, and the banks of the Shannon in Clare, called the *Corcasses*. These are a mellow, putrid, friable loam.

Sand which is so common in England is nowhere met with in Ireland, except for narrow slips of hillocks, upon the sea coast. Nor did I ever meet with or hear of a chalky soil.

The bogs, of which foreigners have heard so much, are very extensive in Ireland; that of Allen extends eighty miles, and is computed to contain 300,000 acres. There are others also, very extensive, and smaller ones scattered over the whole kingdom; but these are not in general more than are wanted for fuel.

Few countries can be better watered by large and beautiful rivers; and it is remarkable that by much the finest parts of the kingdom are on the banks of these rivers. Witness the Suir, Blackwater, the Liffey, the Boyne, the Nore, the Barrow, and part of the Shannon; they wash a scenery that can hardly be exceeded. From the rockiness of the country, however, there are few of them that have not obstructions, which are great impediments to inland navigation.

The mountains of Ireland give to travelling that interesting variety which a flat country can never abound with. And at the same time, they are not in such number as to confer the usual character of poverty which attends them. I was either upon or very near the most considerable in the kingdom. Mangerton and the Reeks in Kerry; the Galtees in Cork; those of Mourne in Down; Croagh Patrick and Nephin in Mayo; these are the principal in Ireland, and they are of a character, in height and sublimity, which should render them the objects of every traveller's attention.

Relative to the climate of Ireland, a short residence cannot enable a man to speak much from his own experience; the observations I have made myself, however, confirm the idea of its being vastly wetter than England; but the worst circumstance of the climate of Ireland is the constant moisture without rain. Wet a piece of leather and lay it in a room, where there is neither sun nor fire, and it will not in summer even be dry in a month. I have known gentlemen in Ireland deny their climate being moister than England—but if they have eyes let them open them, and see the verdure that clothes their rocks, and compare it with ours in England, where rocky soils are of a russet brown however sweet the food for sheep. Does not their island lie more exposed to the great Atlantic, and does not the West wind blow three-fourths of a year? If there was another island yet more to the westward, would not the climate of Ireland be improved? Such persons speak equally against fact and reason.

RENTAL

The proportion between the rent of land in England and Ireland is nearly as two to five. In other words, that space of land which in Ireland lets for 2s. would in England produce 5s. This is the resolution of that surprising inferiority in the rent of Ireland: the English farmer pays a rent for his land in the state he finds it, which includes, not only the natural fertility of the soil, but the immense expenditure which national wealth has in the progress of time poured into it, but the Irishman finds nothing he can afford to pay a rent for, but what the bounty of God has given, unaided by either wealth or industry. The second point is of equal consequence; when the land is to be let, the rent it will bring must depend on the capability of the cultivators to make it productive; if they have but half the capital they ought to be possessed of, how is it possible they should be able to offer a rent proportioned to the rates of another country, in which a variety of causes have long directed a stream of abundant wealth into the purses of her farmers?

TILLAGE

The products [of Ireland] upon the whole are much inferior to those of England, not from inferiority of soil, but the extreme inferiority of management. Tillage in Ireland is very little understood. In the greatest corn counties, such as Louth, Kildare, Carlow and Kilkenny, where are to be seen very fine crops of wheat, all is under the old system, exploded by good farmers in England, of sowing wheat upon a fallow, and succeeding it with as many crops of spring corn as the soil will bear. Where they do best by their land, it is only two of barley or oats before the fallow returns again, which is something worse than the open field management in England of one: fallow; two: wheat; three: oats; to which, while the fields are open and common, the farmers are by cruel necessity tied down.

The bounty on the inland carriage of corn to Dublin has increased tillage very considerably, but it has nowhere introduced any other system, and to this extreme bad management of adopting the exploded practice of a century ago, instead of turnips and clover, it is owing that Ireland with a soil acre for acre much better than England has its products inferior.

But keeping cattle of every sort is a business so much more adapted to the laziness of the farmer, that it is no wonder the tillage is so bad. It is everywhere left to the cottiers, or to the very poorest of the farmers, who are all utterly unable to make those exertions, upon which alone a vigorous culture of the earth can be founded; and were it not for potatoes, which necessarily prepare for corn, there would not be half of what we see at present. While it is in such hands, no wonder tillage is reckoned so unprofitable; profit in all undertakings depends on capital, and is it any wonder that the profit should be small when the capital is nothing at all? Every man that has one gets into cattle, which will give him an idle lazy superintendence, instead of an active attentive one.

OF THE TENANTRY OF IRELAND

It has been probably owing to the small value of land in Ireland before, and even through, a considerable part of the present century, that landlords became so careless of the interests of posterity, as readily to grant their tenants leases for ever. It might also be partly owing to the unfortunate civil wars, which for so long a space of time kept that unhappy country in a state rather of devastation than improvement. When a castle, or a fortified house, and a family strong enough for a garrison, were essentially necessary to the security of life and property among Protestants, no man could occupy land unless he had substance for defence as well as cultivation; short, or even determinable tenures were not encouragement enough for settling in such a situation of warfare. To increase the force of an estate, leases for ever were given of lands, which from their waste state were deemed of little value. The practice once become common, continued long after the motives which originally gave rise to it, and has not yet ceased entirely in any part of the kingdom. Hence therefore, tenants holding large tracts of land under a lease for ever, and which have been re-let to a variety of under tenants, must in this enquiry be considered as landlords.

The obvious distinction to be applied is, that of the occupying and unoccupying tenantry: in other words, the real farmer and the middleman. The very idea, as well as the practice, of permitting a tenant to re-let at a profit rent seems confined to the distant and unimproved parts of every empire. In the highly cultivated counties of England the practice has no existence, but there are traces

of it in the extremities. In Scotland it has been very common,
and I am informed that the same observation is partly
applicable to France. In proportion as any country becomes
improved the practice necessarily wears out.

It is in Ireland, a question greatly agitated, whether the
system has or has not advantages, which may yet induce
a landlord to continue in it. The friends to this mode of
letting lands contend, that the extreme poverty of the lower
classes renders them such an insecure tenantry, that no
gentleman of fortune can depend on the least punctuality
in the payment of rent from such people, and therefore to
let a large farm to some intermediate person of substance,
at a lower rent, in order that the profit may be his induce-
ment and reward for becoming a collector from the
immediate occupiers, and answerable for their punctuality,
becomes necessary to any person who will not submit to
the drudgery of such a minute attention. Also that such
a man will at least improve a spot around his own residence,
whereas the mere cottier can do nothing. If the intermediate tenant is, or from the accumulation of several
farms becomes, a man of property, the same argument is
applicable to his re-letting to another intermediate man,
giving up a part of his profit to escape that trouble which
induced the landlord to begin this system, and at the same
time accounts for the number of tenants one under another,
who have all a profit out of the rent of the occupying
farmer. In the variety of conversations on this point, of
which I have partook in Ireland, I never heard any other
arguments that had the least foundation in the actual state
of the country, for as to ingenious theories, which relate
more to what might be, than to what is, little regard should
be paid to them. That a man of substance, whose rent is
not only secure, but regularly paid, is in many respects a
more eligible tenant than a poor cottier, or little farmer,
cannot be disputed. If the landlord looks no farther than

those circumstances the question is at an end, for the argument must be allowed to have its full weight even to victory. But there are many other considerations.

I was particularly attentive to every class of tenants throughout the kingdom, and shall therefore describe these middlemen, from whence their merit may be the more easily decided. Sometimes they are resident on a part of the land, but very often they are not. Dublin, Bath, London, and the country towns of Ireland, contain great numbers of them. The merit of this class is surely ascertained in a moment. There cannot be a shadow of a pretence for the intervention of a man whose single concern with an estate is to deduct a portion from the rent of it. They are however sometimes resident on a part of the land they hire, where it is natural to suppose they would work some improvements; it is however very rarely the case. I have in different parts of the kingdom seen farms just fallen in after leases of three lives, of the duration of fifty, sixty and even seventy years, in which the residence of the principal tenant was not to be distinguished from the cottiered fields surrounding it. I was at first much surprised at this, but after repeated observation, I found these men very generally were the masters of packs of wretched hounds, with which they wasted their time and money, and it is a notorious fact, that they are the hardest drinkers in Ireland. Living upon the spot, surrounded by their little under-tenants, they prove the most oppressive species of tyrant that ever lent assistance to the destruction of a country. They re-let the land, at short tenures, to the occupiers of small farms; and often give no leases at all. Not satisfied with screwing up the rent to the uttermost farthing, they are rapacious and relentless in the collection of it.

Many of them have defended themselves in conversation with me, upon the plea of taking their rents partly in kind when their under-tenants are much distressed. "What," say they, "would the head landlord, suppose him a great nobleman, do with a miserable cottier who, disappointed in the sale of a heifer, a few barrels of corn, or firkins of butter, brings his five instead of his ten guineas? But we can favour him by taking his commodities at a fair price, and wait for reimbursement until the market rises. Can my lord do that?" A very common plea, but the most unfortunate that could be used to anyone who ever remarked that portion of human nature which takes the garb of an Irish land-jobber! For upon what issue does this remark place the question? Does it not acknowledge, that calling for their rents, when they cannot be paid in cash, they take the substance of the debtor at the very moment when he cannot sell it to another? Can it be necessary to ask what the price is? It is at the option of the creditor, and the miserable culprit meets his oppression, perhaps his ruin, in the very action that is trumpeted as a favour to him.

But farther, the dependence of the occupier on the resident middlemen goes to other circumstances. Personal service of themselves, their corn and horses is exacted for leading turf, hay, corn, gravel, etc., insomuch that the poor under-tenants often lose their own crops and turf, from being obliged to obey these calls of their superiors. Nay, I have even heard these jobbers gravely assert, that without under-tenants to furnish cars and teams at half or two-thirds the common price of the country, they could carry on no improvements at all; yet taking a merit to themselves for works wrought out of the sweat and ruin of a pack of wretches, assigned to their plunder by the inhumanity of the landholders. In a word, the case is reducible to a short compass; intermediate tenants work no improvements, if non-resident they *cannot*, and if resident they *do not*, but they oppress the occupiers, and render them as incapable as they are themselves unwilling. The kingdom is an aggregate proof of these facts; for if long leases, at low rents and profit incomes given, would have improved it, Ireland had long ago been a garden.

Here it is proper to observe that though the intermediate man is generally better security than the little occupier, yet it is not from thence to be concluded that the latter is beyond all comparison beneath him in this respect. The contrary is often the case, and I have known the fact, that the landlord disappointed of his rent, has *drove* (distrained) the under-tenants for it at a time when they had actually paid it to the middleman. If the profit rent is spent, as it very generally is in claret and hounds, the notion of good security will prove visionary, as many a landlord in Ireland has found it. Several very considerable ones have assured me, that the little occupiers were the *best* pay they had on their estates, and the intermediate *gentlemen* tenants by much the *worst*.

A very considerable part of the kingdom and the most enlightened landlords in it have discarded this injurious system, and let their farms to none but the occupying tenantry. Their experience has proved, that the apprehension of a want of security was merely ideal, finding their rents much better paid than ever. At the last extremity, it is the occupier's stock which is the real security of the landlord. It is that he distrains, and finds abundantly more valuable than the laced hat, hounds and pistols of the gentleman jobber, from whom he is more likely in such a case to receive a *message* than a remittance.

Having thus described the tenants that ought to be rejected, let me next mention the circumstances of the occupiers. The variety of these is very great in Ireland. In the North, where the linen manufacture has spread, the farms are so small, that 10 acres in the occupation of one person is a large one, 5 or 6 will be found a good farm, and all the agriculture of the country so entirely subservient to the manufacture, that they no more deserve the name of farmers than the occupier of a cabbage garden.

In Limerick, Tipperary, Clare, Meath and Waterford, there are to be found the greatest graziers and cow keepers perhaps in the world; some who rent and occupy from £3000 to £10,000 a year. These of course are men of property, and are the only occupiers in the kingdom who have any considerable substance. The effects are not so beneficial as might be expected. Rich graziers in England, who have a little tillage, usually manage it well, and are in other respects attentive to various improvements; though it must be confessed not in the same proportion with great arable farmers; but in Ireland these men are as errant slovens as the most beggarly cottiers. The rich lands of Limerick are in respect of fences, drains, buildings, weeds, etc. in as waste a state as the mountains of Kerry; the fertility of nature is so little seconded, that few tracts yield less pleasure to the spectator. From what I observed, I attributed this to the idleness and dissipation so general in Ireland. These graziers are too apt to attend to their claret as much as their bullocks, live expensively, and being enabled, from the nature of their business, to pass nine-tenths of the year without any exertion of industry, contract such a habit of ease, that works of improvement would be mortifying to their sloth.

In the arable counties of Louth, part of Meath, Kildare, Kilkenny, Carlow, Queen's, and part of King's, and Tipperary, they are much more industrious, but the farms are too small, and the tenants too poor, to exhibit any appearances that can strike an English traveller. Their manuring is trivial, their tackle and implements wretched, their teams weak, their profit small, and their living little better than that of the cottiers they employ. These circumstances are the necessary result of the smallness of their capitals, which even in these tillage counties do not usually amount to a third of what an English farmer would have to manage the same extent of land. The leases of these men are usually three lives to Protestants, and thirty-one years to Catholics.

The tenantry in the more unimproved parts, such as Cork, Wicklow, Longford, and all the mountainous counties, where it is part tillage, and part pasturage, are generally in a very backward state. Their capitals are smaller than the class I just mentioned, and among them is chiefly found the practice of many poor cottiers hiring large farms in partnership. They make their rents by a little butter, a little wool, a little corn, and a few young cattle and lambs. Their lands at extreme low rents are the most unimproved (mountain and bog excepted) in the kingdom. They have, however, more industry than capital, and with a very little management, might be brought greatly to improve their husbandry. I think they hold more generally from intermediate tenants than any other set; one reason why the land they occupy is in so waste a state. In the mountainous tracts, I saw instances of greater industry than in any other part of Ireland. Little occupiers who can get leases of a mountain side, make exertions in improvement, which, though far enough from being complete, or accurate, yet prove clearly what great effects encouragement would have among them.

In the King's County, and also in some other parts, I saw many tracts of land, not large enough to be re-let, which were occupied under leases for ever, very well planted and improved by men of substance and industry.

The poverty, common among the small occupying tenantry, may be pretty well ascertained from their general conduct in hiring a farm. They will manage to take one with a sum surprisingly small. They provide labour, which in England is so considerable an article, by assigning portions of land to cottiers for their potato gardens, and keeping one or two cows for each of them. To lessen the live stock necessary, they will, whenever the neighbourhood enables them, take in the cattle at so much per month, or season, of any person that is deficient in pasturage at home, or of any labourers that have no land. Next, they will let out some old lay for grass potatoes [*sic*] to such labourers; and if they are in a county where corn acres are known, they will do the same with some corn land. If there is any meadow on their farm, they will sell a part of it as the hay grows. By all these means the necessity of a full stock is very much lessened, and by means of living themselves in the very poorest manner, and converting every pig, fowl, and even egg into cash, they will make up their rent, and get by very slow degrees into somewhat better circumstances. Where it is the custom to take in partnership, the difficulties are easier got over, for one man brings a few sheep, another a cow, a third a horse, a fourth a car and some seed potatoes, a fifth a few barrels of corn, and so on, until the farm among them is tolerably stocked, and hands upon it in plenty for the labour.

It is from the whole evident that they are uncommon masters of the art of overcoming difficulties by practice and contrivance. Travellers, who take a superficial view of them, are apt to think their poverty and wretchedness, viewed in the light of farmers, greater than they are. Perhaps there is an impropriety in considering a man merely as the occupier of such a quantity of land, and that instead of the land, his capital should be the object of contemplation. Give the farmer of 20 acres in England no more capital than his brother in Ireland, and I will venture to say he will be much poorer, for he would be utterly unable to go on at all.

A few considerable landlords many years ago made the experiment of fixing, at great expense, colonies of Palatines on their estates. Some of them I viewed, and made many enquiries. The scheme did not appear to me to answer. They had houses built for them, plots of land assigned to each at a rent of favour, were assisted in stock, and all of them with leases for lives from the head landlord. I am convinced no country, whatever state it may be in, can be improved by colonies of foreigners, and whatever foreigner, as a superintendent of any great improvement, asks for colonies of his own countrymen to execute his ideas, manifests a mean genius and but little knowledge of the human heart. If he has talents he will find tools wherever he finds men, and make the natives of the country the means of increasing their own happiness. Whatever he does then, will live and take root, but if effected by foreign hands, it will prove a sickly and shortlived exotic, brilliant perhaps for a time in the eyes of the ignorant, but of no solid advantage to the country that employs him.

OF THE LABOURING POOR

Such is the weight of the lower classes in the great scale of national importance, that a traveller can never give too much attention to every circumstance that concerns them. Their welfare forms the broad basis of public prosperity, in proportion to their ease is the strength and wealth of nations, as public debility will be the certain attendant on their misery. Convinced that to be ignorant of their state and situation, in different countries, is to be deficient in the first rudiments of political knowledge, I have upon every occasion made the necessary enquiries, to get the best information circumstances would allow me. Many a question have I put to gentlemen upon these points, which were not answered without having recourse to the next cabin; a source of information the more necessary, as I found upon various occasions that some gentlemen in Ireland are infected with the rage of adopting *systems* as

well as those of England. With one party the poor are all
starving, with the other they are deemed in a very tolerable
situation, and a third, who look with an evil eye on the
administration of the British Government, are fond of
exclaiming at poverty and rags, as proofs of the cruel
treatment of Ireland. When truth is likely to be thus
warped, a traveller must be very circumspect to *believe* and
very assiduous to *see*.

The Cottier System [170]

It is necessary here to explain the common cottier
system of labour in Ireland, which much resembles that
of Scotland until very lately. If there are cabins on a farm
they are the residence of the cottiers. If there are none
the farmer marks out the potato gardens, and the labourers,
who apply to him on his hiring the land, raise their own
cabins on such spots; in some places the farmer builds, in
others he only assists them with the roof, etc. A verbal
compact is then made, that the new cottier shall have his
potato garden at such a rent, and one or two cows kept
him at the price of the neighbourhood, he finding the cows.
He then works with the farmer at the rate of the place,
usually $6\frac{1}{2}d$. a day, a tally being kept (half by each party),
and a notch cut for every day's labour; at the end of six
months, or a year, they reckon, and the balance is paid.
The cottier works for himself as his potatoes require.

There are a great many cabins, usually by the roadside
or in the ditch, which have no potato gardens at all.
Ireland being free from the curse of the English Poor
Laws, the people move about the country and settle where
they will [171]. A wandering family will fix themselves under
a dry bank, and with a few sticks, furze, fern, etc. make
up a hovel much worse than an English pigstye, support
themselves how they can, by work, begging and stealing;
if the neighbourhood wants hands, or takes no notice of

them, the hovel grows into a cabin. In my rides about Mitchelstown, I have passed places in the road one day, without any appearance of a habitation, and next morning found a hovel, filled with a man and woman, six or eight children and a pig. These people are not kept by anybody as cottiers, but are taken at busy seasons by the day or week, and paid in money.

Relative to the cottier system wherever it is found, it may be observed that the recompense for labour is the *means of living*. In England, these are dispensed in money, but in Ireland in land or commodities. The great question is, which system is most advantageous to the poor family. Generally speaking the Irish poor have a fair bellyful of potatoes, and they have milk the greatest part of the year. What I would particularly insist on here is the value of his labour being food not money; food not for himself only, but for his wife and children. An Irishman loves whisky as well as an Englishman does strong beer, but he cannot go on Saturday night to the whisky house and drink out the week's support of himself, his wife and his children, not uncommon in the ale house of the Englishman. That the Irishman's cow may be ill fed is admitted, but ill fed as it is, it is better than the no cow of the Englishman; the children of the Irish cabin are nourished with milk, which, small as the quantity may be, is far preferable to the beer or vile tea which is the beverage of the English infant, for nowhere but in a town is milk to be bought. Farther, in a country where bread, cheese or meat are the common food, it is consumed with great economy, and kept under lock and key where the children can have no resort, but the case with potatoes is different, they are in greater plenty, the children help themselves; they are scarce ever seen about a cabin without being in the act of eating them, it is their employment all day long. Another circumstance not to be forgotten is the regularity of the supply. The crop of potatoes, and the milk of the cow [*sic*] is more regular in Ireland than the *price* at which the Englishman buys his food. In England complaints rise even to riots, when the rates of provisions are high; but in Ireland the poor have nothing to do with prices, they depend not on prices, but crops of a vegetable very regular in its produce. Whether [the Irish system] is good or bad, or better or worse than that of England, it is what will necessarily continue until a great increase of national wealth has introduced a more general circulation of money. They will then have the English mode with its defects as well as its disadvantages.

Food

The food of the common Irish, potatoes and milk, have been produced more than once as an instance of the extreme poverty of the country, but this I believe is an opinion embraced with more alacrity than reflection. I have heard it stigmatised as being unhealthy, and not sufficiently nourishing for the support of hard labour, but this opinion is very amazing in a country, many of whose poor people are as athletic in their form, as robust, and as capable of enduring labour as any upon earth. The idleness seen among many when working for those who oppress them is a very contrast to the vigour and activity with which the same people work when themselves alone reap the benefit of their labour. To what country must we have recourse for a stronger instance than lime carried by little miserable mountaineers thirty miles on horses' backs to the foot of their hills, and up the steeps on their own. When I see the people of a country in spite of political oppression with well formed vigorous bodies, and their cottages swarming with children, when I see their men athletic and their women beautiful, I know not how to believe them subsisting on an unwholesome food. Of this food there is one circumstance which must ever recommend it, they have a bellyful, and that let me add is more than the superfluities of an Englishman leaves to his family. Let any person examine minutely into the receipt and expenditure of an English cottage, and he will find that tea, sugar and strong liquors can come only from pinched bellies. I will not assert that potatoes are a better food than bread and cheese, but I have no doubt of a bellyful of the one being much better than half a bellyful of the other, still less have I that the milk of the Irishman is incomparably better than the small beer, gin or tea of the Englishman, and this even for the father, how much better must it be for the poor infants; milk to them is nourishment, is health, is life.

If anyone doubts the comparative plenty, which attends the board of a poor native of England and Ireland, let him attend to their meals. The sparingness with which our labourer eats his bread and cheese is well known. Mark the Irishman's potato bowl placed on the floor, the whole family upon their hams around it, devouring a quantity almost incredible, the beggar seating himself to it with a hearty welcome, the pig taking his share as readily as the wife, the cocks, hens, turkeys, geese, the cur, the cat, and perhaps the cow—and all partaking of the same dish. No man can often have been a witness of it without being convinced of the plenty, and I will add, the cheerfulness that attends it.

Clothing

The common Irish are in general clothed so very indifferently, that it impresses every stranger with a strong idea of universal poverty. Shoes and stockings are scarcely ever found on the feet of children; and great numbers of men and women are without them: a change however in this respect, as in most others, is coming in, for there are many more of them with those articles of clothing now than ten years ago. An Irishman and his wife are much more solicitous to feed than to clothe their children; whereas in England, it is surprising to see the expense they put themselves to, to deck out children whose principal subsistence is tea. Very many of them in Ireland are so ragged that their nakedness is scarcely covered, yet are they in health and active. As to the want of shoes and stockings, I consider it as no evil, but a much more cleanly custom than the bestiality of stockings and feet that are washed no oftener than those of our own poor. I remarked generally, that they were not ill-dressed of Sundays and holidays.

Habitations

The cottages of the Irish, which are called cabins, are the most miserable looking hovels that can well be conceived; they generally consist of only one room. Mud kneaded with straw is the common material of the walls; these have only a door, which lets in light instead of a window, and should let the smoke out instead of a chimney, but they had rather keep it in. These two conveniences they hold so cheap, that I have seen them both stopped up in stone cottages built by improving landlords. The roofs of the cabins are rafters, raised from the tops of the mud walls, and the covering varies; some are thatched with straw, potato stalks, or with heath, others only covered with sods of turf. The bad repair of these roofs are kept in, a hole in the thatch being often mended with turf, and weeds sprouting from every part, gives them the appearance of a weedy dunghill, especially when the cabin is not built with regular walls, but supported on one, or perhaps on both sides by the banks of a broad dry ditch; the roof then seems a hillock, upon which perhaps the pig grazes. Some of these cabins are much less and more miserable habitations than I had ever seen in England. I was told they were the worst in Connacht, but I found it an error; I saw many in Leinster to the full as bad, and in Wicklow some worse than any in Connacht. When they are well roofed, and built not of stones ill put together, but of mud, they are much warmer, independently of smoke, than the clay or lath and mortar cottages of England, the walls of which are so thin, that a rat hole lets in the wind to the annoyance of the whole family.

The furniture of the cabins is as bad as the architecture, in very many consisting only of a pot for boiling their potatoes, a bit of a table, and one or two broken stools; beds are not found universally, the family lying on straw, equally partook of by cows, calves and pigs, though the luxury of styes is coming in in Ireland, which excludes the poor pigs from the warmth of the bodies of their master and mistress.

This is a general description, but the exceptions are very numerous. I have been in a multitude of cabins that had much useful furniture, and some even superfluous; chairs, tables, boxes, chests of drawers, earthernware, and in short most of the articles found in a middling English cottage; but upon enquiry, I very generally found that these acquisitions were all made within the last ten years, a sure sign of a rising national prosperity. I think the bad cabins and furniture the greatest instances of Irish poverty, and this must flow from the mode of payment for labour, which makes cattle so valuable to the peasant, that every farthing they can spare is saved for their purchase; from hence also results another observation, which is, that the apparent poverty of it is greater than the real; for the house of a man that is master of four or five cows will have scarce anything but deficiencies, nay I was in the cabins of dairymen and farmers, not small ones, whose cabins were not at all better furnished than those of the poorest labourer; before therefore we can attribute it to absolute poverty,

we must take into the account the customs and inclinations
of the people. In England a man's cottage will be filled
with superfluities before he possesses a cow. I think the
comparison much in favour of the Irishman; a hog is a
much more valuable piece of goods than a set of tea things,
and though his snout in a crock of potatoes is an idea not
so poetical as—

> Broken teacups, wisely kept for show,
> Ranged o'er the chimney, glistened in a row. [172]

yet will the cottier and his family at Christmas find the
solidity of it an ample recompense for the ornament of
the other.

Live Stock

In every part of the kingdom the common Irish have
all sorts of live stock. Pigs are more general (even than
cows), and poultry in many parts of the kingdom, especially
Leinster, are in such quantities as amazed me. This is
owing probably to three circumstances; first, to the plenty
of potatoes with which they are fed; secondly, to the
warmth of the cabins; and thirdly to the great quantity of
spontaneous white clover in almost all the fields, which
much exceeds anything we know in England. Upon the
seeds of this plant the young poultry rear themselves; much
is sold, but a considerable portion eaten by the family,
probably because they cannot find a market for the whole.

Oppression

It must be very apparent to every traveller, through that
country, that the labouring poor are treated with harshness,
and are in all respects so little considered, that their want
of importance seems a perfect contrast to their situation in
England, of which country, comparatively speaking, they
reign the sovereigns. The age has improved so much in
humanity, that even the poor Irish have experienced its

influence, and are every day treated better and better; but still the remnant of the old manners, the abominable distinction of religion, united with the oppressive conduct of the little country gentlemen, or rather vermin of the kingdom, who never were out of it, altogether still bear very heavy on the poor people and subject them to situations more mortifying than we ever behold in England[173]. The landlord of an Irish estate, inhabited by Roman Catholics, is a sort of despot who yields obedience, in whatever concerns the poor, to no law but that of his will. To discover what the liberty of a people is, we must live among them, and not look for it in the statutes of the realm. The language of written law may be that of liberty, but the situation of the poor may speak no language but that of slavery; there is too much of this contradiction in Ireland. A long series of oppressions, aided by very many ill-judged laws, have brought landlords into a habit of exerting a very lofty superiority, and their vassals into that of an almost unlimited submission; speaking a language that is despised, professing a religion that is abhorred, and being disarmed, the poor find themselves in many cases slaves even in the bosom of *written* liberty. Landlords that have resided much abroad are usually humane in their ideas, but the habit of tyranny naturally contracts the mind, so that even in this polished age, there are instances of a severe carriage towards the poor, which is quite unknown in England.

A landlord in Ireland can scarcely invent an order which a servant, labourer or cottier dares to refuse to execute. Nothing satisfies him but an unlimited submission. Disrespect or anything tending towards sauciness he may punish with his cane or his horsewhip with the most perfect security; a poor man would have his bones broken if he offered to lift his hand in his own defence. Knocking down is spoken of in the country in a manner that makes an Englishman stare. It must strike the most careless traveller to see whole strings of cars whipt into a ditch by a gentleman's footman to make way for his carriage; if they are overturned or broken in pieces, no matter, it is taken in patience; were they to complain they would perhaps be horsewhipped.

Consequences have flowed from these oppressions which ought long ago to have put a stop to them. In England we have heard much of Whiteboys, Steelboys, Oakboys, Peep-o-Day Boys, etc., but these various insurgents are not to be confounded, for they are very different[174]. The proper distinction in the discontents of the people is into Protestant and Catholic. All but the Whiteboys were among the manufacturing Protestants in the North. The Whiteboys, Catholic labourers in the South. From the best intelligence I could gain, the riots of the manufac-turers had no other foundation, but such variations in the manufacture as all fabrics experience, and which they had themselves known and submitted to before. The case, however, was different with the Whiteboys; who being labouring Catholics met with all those oppressions I have described, and would probably have continued in full sub-mission had not very severe treatment in respect of tithes, united with a great speculative rise of rents about the same time, blown up the flame of resistance; the atrocious acts they were guilty of made them the object of general indignation, Acts were passed for their punishment which seemed calculated for the meridian of Barbary. This arose to such height, that by one they were to be hanged under certain circumstances without the common formalities of a trial, which though repealed the following sessions marks the spirit of punishment; while others remain yet the law of the land, that would if executed tend more to raise than quell an insurrection. From all which it is manifest that the gentlemen of Ireland never thought of a radical cure from overlooking the real cause of the disease, which in fact lay in themselves, and not in the wretches they doomed to the gallows. A better treatment of the poor in Ireland is a very material point to the welfare of the whole British Empire. Events may happen which may convince us fatally of this truth. If not, oppression must have broken all the spirit and resentment of men.

Emigrations

Before the American war broke out, the Irish and Scotch emigrations were a constant subject of conversation in England, and occasioned much discourse even in Parliament. The common observation was, that if they were not stopped, these countries would be ruined, and they were generally attributed to a great rise of rents. Upon going over to Ireland I determined to omit no opportunities of discovering the cause and extent of this emigration. The spirit of emigrating in Ireland appeared to be confined to two circumstances, the Presbyterian religion, and the linen manufacture. I heard of very few emigrants except among manufacturers of that persuasion. The Catholics never went, they seem not only tied to the country but almost to the parish in which their ancestors lived. As to the emigration in the North, it was an error in England to suppose it a novelty which arose with the increase of rents. The contrary was the fact, it had subsisted perhaps, forty years, in-so-much that at the ports of Belfast, Derry, etc., the *passenger trade*, as they called it, had long been a regular branch of commerce, which employed several ships, and consisted in carrying people to America. The increasing population of the country made it an increasing trade, but when the linen trade was low the *passenger trade* was always high. At the time of Lord Donegall's letting his estate in the North, the linen business suffered a temporary decline, which sent great numbers to America, and gave rise to the error that it was occasioned by the increase of his rents[175]. The fact, however, was otherwise, for great numbers of those who went from his lands actually sold those leases for considerable sums, the hardship of which was supposed to have driven them to America.

RELIGION

The history of the two religions in Ireland is too generally known to require any detail introductory to the subject. The conflict for two centuries occasioned a scene of devastation and bloodshed, till at last, by the arms of King William, the decision left the uncontrolled power in the hands of the Protestants. The landed property of the kingdom had been greatly changed[176] in the period of the reigns of Elizabeth and James I. Still more under Cromwell, who parcelled out an immense proportion of the kingdom to the officers of his army, the ancestors of great numbers of the present possessors. The last forfeitures were incurred in that war which stripped and banished James II. Upon the whole, nineteen-twentieths of the kingdom changed hands from Catholic to Protestant. The lineal descendants of great families, once possessed of vast property, are now to be found all over the kingdom, in the lowest situation, working as cottiers for the great-grandsons of men, many of whom were of no greater account in England than these poor labourers are at present on that property which was once their own. So entire an overthrow, and change of landed possession, is within the period to be found in scarce any country in the world. In such great revolutions of property the ruined proprietors have usually been extirpated or banished, but in Ireland the case was otherwise. Families were so numerous and so united in clans, that the heir of an estate was always known; and it is a fact that in most parts of the kingdom the descendants of the old landowners regularly transmit by testamentary deed the memorial of their right to those estates which once belonged to their families. From hence it results that the question of religion has always in Ireland been intimately connected with the right to and possession of the landed property of the kingdom, and has probably received from this source a degree of acrimony, not at all wanting to influence the superstitious prejudices of the human mind.

The Penal Laws

If the exertions of a succession of ignorant legislatures have failed continually in propagating the religion of government, or in adding to the internal security of the kingdom, much more have they failed in the great object of national prosperity. The only considerable manufacture in Ireland which carries in all its parts the appearance of industry, is the linen, and it ought never to be forgotten that this is solely confined to the Protestant parts of the kingdom; yet we may see from the example of France and other countries that there is nothing in the Roman Catholic religion itself that is incompatible with manufacturing industry. The poor Catholics in the south of Ireland spin wool very generally, but the purchasers of their labour and the whole worsted trade is in the hands of the Quakers of Clonmel, Carrick, Bandon, etc. The fact is, the professors of that religion are under such discouragements that they cannot engage in any trade which requires both industry and capital. If they succeed and make a fortune, what are they to do with it? They can neither buy land, nor take a mortgage, nor even sign down the rent of a lease. Where is there a people in the world to be found industrious under such a circumstance? The system pursued in Ireland has had no other tendency but that of driving out of the kingdom all the personal wealth of the Catholics, and prohibiting their industry within it. The face of the country, every object in short which presents itself to the eye of the traveller, tells him how effectually this has been done.

Oppression has (moreover) reduced the major part of the Irish Catholics to a poor ignorant rabble; you (Irish gentlemen) have made them ignorant, and then it is cried "your ignorance is a reason for keeping you so. You shall live and die, and remain in ignorance, for you are too wretched to be enlightened." In all other parts of Europe the Catholic religion has grown mild and even tolerant; a softer humanity is seen diffused in those countries, once the most bigoted. Had property taken its natural course in Ireland, the religion of the Catholics there would have improved with that of their neighbours. Ignorance is the child of poverty, and you cannot expect the modern improvements, which have resulted from disseminated industry and wealth, should spread among a sect whose property you have detached, and whose industry you have crushed. To stigmatise them with ignorance and bigotry, therefore, is to reproach them with the evils which your own conduct has entailed; it is to bury them in darkness, and villify them because they are not enlightened.

Has the rod of oppression obliterated the memory or tradition of better days? Would protection, favour and encouragement add fresh stings to their resentment? None can assert it. The laws have weakened instead of strengthening the Protestant interest; had a milder system encouraged their industry and property, they would have had something to lose, and would, with an enemy in the land, have thought twice before they joined him. Give them an interest in the kingdom, and they will use their arms, not to overturn but to defend it. Let it in general be remembered, that no country in the world has felt any inconveniences from the most liberal spirit of toleration: that on the contrary, those are universally acknowledged to be the most prosperous, and the most flourishing, which have governed their subjects on the most tolerating principles, other countries, which have been actuated by the spirit of bigotry, have continued poor, weak, and helpless. Ireland will never prosper to any great degree until she profits by the example of her neighbours. Let her dismiss her illiberal fears; let her keep pace with the mild spirit of European manners, let her transfer her anxiety from the faith to the industry of her subjects; let her embrace, cherish and protect the Catholics as good subjects, and they will become such; let her, despising every species of religious persecution, consider all religious as brethren, employed in one great aim, the wealth, power and happiness of the general community; let these be the maxims of her policy, and she will no longer complain of poverty and debility, she will be at home prosperous, and abroad formidable.

TIMBER AND PLANTING[177]

The greatest part of the kingdom exhibits a naked, bleak, dreary view for want of wood, which has been destroyed for a century past with the most thoughtless prodigality, and still continues to be cut and wasted as if it was not worth the preservation.

In conversation with gentlemen, I found they very generally laid the destruction of timber to the common people, who they say have an aversion to a tree; at the earliest age they steal it for a walking stick; afterwards, for a spade handle; later for a car shaft, and later still for a cabin rafter. That the poor do steal, it is certain, but I am clear the gentlemen of the country may thank themselves. Is it the consumption of sticks and handles that has destroyed millions of acres? absurdity! The profligate, prodigal, worthless landowner cuts down his acres, and leaves them unfenced against cattle, and then he has the impudence to charge the scarcity of trees to the walking sticks of the poor.

I have made many very minute calculations of the expense, growth and value of plantations in Ireland, and am convinced from them that there is no application of the best land in that kingdom will equal the profit of planting the worst in it. A regard for the interest of posterity call for the oak and other trees which require more than an age to come to maturity, but with other views the quick growing ones are of profit much superior; these come to perfection so speedily that three-fourths of the landlords of the kingdom might expect to cut where they planted, and reap those great profits, which most certainly attend it.

TITHES

That there are abuses in the modes of levying (tithes) is undoubted. The greatest that I heard of were the notes and bonds taken in some parts of that kingdom (Ireland) by the proctors for the payment of tithes, which bear interest, and which are sometimes continued for several years, principal and interest being consolidated until the sum becomes too great for the poor man to pay, when great extortions are complained of, and formed the grievance which seemed most to raise the resentment of the rioters, called Whiteboys. The great power of the Protestant gentlemen render their compositions very light, while the poor Catholic is made in too many cases to pay severely for the deficiencies of his betters. This is a great abuse, but not to be remedied till the whole kingdom is animated with a different spirit.

ABSENTEES

There are very few countries in the world that do not experience the disadvantage of remitting a part of their rents to landlords who reside elsewhere, and it must ever be so while there is any liberty left to mankind of living where they please. In Ireland the amount proportioned to the territory is greater probably than in most other instances, and not having a free trade with the kingdom in which such absentees spend their fortunes, it is cut off from that return which Scotland experiences for the loss of her rents. It is not the simple amount of the rental being remitted into another country, but the damp on all sorts of improvements, and the total want of countenance and encouragement which the lower tenantry labour under. The landlord at such a great distance is out of the way of all complaints, or which is the same thing, of examining into, or remedying evils; miseries of which he can see nothing, and probably hear as little of, can make no impression. All that is required of the agent is to be punctual in his remittances, and as to the people who pay him, they are too often welcome to go to the devil, provided their rents could be paid from his territories.

This is the general picture. God forbid it should be universally true! There are absentees who expend large sums upon their estates in Ireland. The Earl of Shelburne has made great exertions for the introduction of English agriculture. Mr Fitzmaurice has taken every means to establish a manufacture [at Ballymote]. The church and other buildings at Belfast do honour to Lord Donegall, nor are many other instances wanting, equally to the advantage of the kingdom, and the honour of the individuals.

POPULATION[178]

There are several circumstances in Ireland extremely favourable to population, to which must be attributed that country being so much more populous than the state of manufacturing industry would seem to imply. There are five causes, which may be particularised among others of less consequence. First, there being no Poor Laws. Second, the habitations. Third, the generality of marriage. Fourth, children not being burdensome. Fifth, potatoes the food.

The Laws of Settlement in England, which confine the poor people to what is called their legal settlements, one would think framed with no other view than to be a check on the national industry; it was however a branch of, and arose from, those monuments of barbarity and mischief, our poor rates, for when once the poor were made what they ought never to be considered, a burden, it was incumbent on every parish to lessen as much as possible their numbers. These laws were therefore framed in the very spirit of depopulation, and most certainly have for near two centuries proved a bar to the kingdom's becoming as populous as it would otherwise have done. Fortunately for Ireland, it has hitherto kept free from these evils, and from thence results a great degree of her present population. Whole families in that country will move from one place to another with freedom, fixing according to the demand for their labour, and the encouragement they receive to settle. The liberty of doing this, is certainly a premium on their industry, and consequently to their increase.

The cabins of the poor Irish being such apparently miserable habitations, is another very evident encouragement to population. In England, where the poor are in many respects in such a superior state, a couple will not marry unless they can get a house, to build which, take the kingdom through, will cost from £25 to £60; half the life, and all the vigour and youth of a man and woman are passed before they can save such a sum; and when they have got it, so burdensome are poor to a parish, that it is twenty to one if they get permission to erect their cottage. But in Ireland, the cabin is not an object of a moment's consideration; to possess a cow and a pig is an earlier aim;

the cabin begins with a hovel, that is erected with two day's labour, and the young couple pass not their youth in celibacy for want of a nest to produce their young in.

Marriage is certainly more general in Ireland than in England. I scarce ever found an unmarried farmer or cottier; but it is seen more in other classes, which with us do not marry at all; such as servants. The generality of footmen and maids, in gentlemen's families, are married, a circumstance we very rarely see in England.

Another point of importance, is their children not being burdensome. In all the enquiries I made into the state of the poor, I found their happiness and ease generally relative to the number of their children, and nothing considered as great a misfortune as having none. Whenever this is the fact, or the general idea, it must necessarily have a considerable effect in promoting early marriages, and consequently population.

The food of the people being potatoes is a point not of less importance; for when the common food of the poor is so dear as to be an object of attentive economy, the children will want that plenty which is essential to rearing them; the article of milk, so general in the Irish cabins, is a matter of the first consequence in rearing infants. The Irish poor in the Catholic parts of that country are subsisted entirely upon land, whereas the poor in England have so little to do with it, that they subsist almost entirely from shops, by a purchase of their necessaries. In the former case it must be a matter of prodigious consequence, that the product should be yielded by as small a space of land as possible; this is the case with potatoes more than with any other crop whatever.

MANNERS AND CUSTOMS

There are three races of people in Ireland, so distinct as to strike the least attentive traveller; these are the

Spanish which are found in Kerry, and a part of Limerick and Cork, tall and thin, but well made, a long visage, dark eyes and long black lank hair. The Scotch race is in the North, where are to be found the features which are supposed to mark that people, their accent, and many of their customs. In a district near Dublin [Fingal], but more particularly in the baronies of Bargy and Forth, in the county of Wexford, the Saxon tongue is spoken without any mixture of the Irish, and the people have a variety of customs which distinguish them from their neighbours. The rest of the kingdom is made up of mongrels. The Milesian race of Irish, which may be called *native*, are scattered over the kingdom, but chiefly found in Connacht and Munster; a few considerable families, whose genealogy is undoubted remain, but none of them with considerable possessions, except the O'Briens and Mr O'Neill; the former have near twenty thousand pounds a year in the family, the latter half as much, the remnant of a property once his ancestors, which now forms six or seven of the greatest estates in the kingdom. O'Hara and MacDermot are great names in Connacht, and O'Donoghue a con-siderable one in Kerry, but I heard of a family of O'Driscolls in Cork who claim an origin prior in Ireland to any of the Milesian race.

The only divisions which a traveller, who passed through the kingdom without making any residence, could make, would be into people of considerable fortune and mob. The intermediate division of the scale, so numerous and respectable in England, would hardly attract the least notice in Ireland. A residence in the kingdom convinces one, however, that there is another class in general, of small fortune—country gentlemen and renters of land.

The manners, habits, and customs of people of con-siderable fortune are much the same everywhere, at least there is very little difference between England and Ireland, it is among the common people one must look for those traits by which we discriminate a national character. The circumstances which struck me most in the common Irish were, vivacity and a great and eloquent volubility of speech; one would think they could take snuff and talk without tiring till Doomsday. They are infinitely more cheerful and lively than anything we commonly see in England, having nothing of that incivility of sullen silence with which so many Englishmen seem to wrap themselves up, as if retiring within their own importance. Lazy to an excess at *work*, but so spiritedly active at *play*, that at *hurling*, which is the cricket of savages, they shew the greatest feats of agility. Their love of society is as remarkable as their curiosity is insatiable; and their hospitality to all comers, be their own poverty ever so pinching, has too much merit to be forgotten. Pleased to enjoyment with a joke, or witty repartee, they will repeat it with such expression, that the laugh will be universal. Warm friends and revengeful enemies; they are inviolable in their secrecy, and inevitable in their resentment; with such a notion of honour, that neither threat nor reward would induce them to betray the secret or person of a man, though an oppressor, whose property they would plunder without ceremony. Hard drinkers and quarrelsome; great liars, but civil, submissive, and obedient. Dancing is so universal among them, that there are everywhere itinerant dancing-masters, to whom the cottiers pay 6*d.* a quarter for teaching their families. Besides the Irish jig, which they can dance with a most *luxuriant* expression, minuets and country dances are taught; and I even heard some talk of cotillions coming in.

Some degree of education is also general, hedge schools as they are called (they might as well be termed *ditch* ones, for I have seen many a ditch full of scholars) are everywhere to be met with, where reading and writing are taught[179].

Schools are also common for men, I have seen a dozen great fellows at school, and was told they were educating with an intention of being priests. Many strokes in their character are evidently to be ascribed to the extreme oppression under which they live. If they are as great thieves and liars as they are reported, it is certainly owing to this cause.

If from the lowest class we rise to the highest, all there is gaiety, pleasure, luxury and extravagance. The town life at Dublin is formed on the model of that of London. Every night in the winter there is a ball or a party, where the polite circle meet, not to enjoy but to sweat each other; a great crowd crammed into 20 feet square gives a zest to the *agréments* of small talk and whist. There are four or five houses large enough to receive a company commodiously, but the rest are so small as to make parties detestable. There is however an agreeable society in Dublin, in which a man of large fortune will not find his time heavy. The style of living may be guessed from the fortunes of the resident nobility and great commoners; there are about thirty that possess incomes from seven to twenty thousand pounds a year. The Court has nothing remarkable or splendid in it, but varies very much, according to the private fortune or liberality of disposition in the Lord Lieutenant.

In the country their life has some circumstances which are not commonly seen in England. Large tracts of land are kept in hand by everybody to supply the deficiencies of markets; this gives such a plenty, that, united with the lowness of taxes and prices, one would suppose it difficult for them to spend their incomes, if Dublin in the winter did not lend assistance. Let it be considered that the prices of meat are much lower than in England; poultry only a fourth of the price; wild fowl and fish in vastly greater plenty; rum and brandy not half the price; coffee, tea, and wines far cheaper; labour not above a third; servants' wages upon an average thirty per cent. cheaper. That taxes are inconsiderable, for there is no land tax, no poor rates, no window tax, no candle or soap tax, only half a wheel-tax, no servants' tax, and a variety of other articles heavily burdened in England, but not in Ireland. Considering all this, one would think they could not spend their incomes; they do contrive it, however. In this business they are assisted by two customs that have an admirable tendency to it, great numbers of horses and servants. The excess in the latter are in the lower sort, owing not only to the general laziness, but also to the number of attendants everyone of a higher class will have. This is common in great families in England, but in Ireland a man of £500 a year feels it. The number of horses may almost be esteemed a satire upon common sense, were they well fed enough to be useful they would not be so numerous, but I have found a good hack for a common ride scarce in a house where there were a hundred. Another circumstance to be remarked in the country life is the miserableness of many of their houses. There are men of £5000 a year in Ireland, who live in habitations that a man of £700 a year in England would disdain. An air of neatness, order, dress and *propreté* is wanting to a surprising degree around the mansion; even new and excellent houses have often nothing of this about them. But the badness of the houses is remedying every hour throughout the whole kingdom, for the number of new ones just built, or building, is prodigiously great.

The tables of people of fortune are very plentifully spread; many elegantly, differing in nothing from those of England. Claret is the common wine of all tables, and so much inferior to what is drunk in England, that it does not appear to be the same wine; but their port is incomparable, so much better than the English, as to prove, if

DUBLIN

The Parliament House in College Green

proof was wanting, the abominable adulterations it must undergo with us. Drinking and duelling are two charges which have long been alleged against the gentlemen of Ireland, but the change of manners which has taken place in that kingdom is not generally known in England[180]. Drunkenness ought no longer to be a reproach, for at every table I was at in Ireland I saw a perfect freedom reign, every person drank just as little as they pleased, nor have I ever been asked to drink a single glass more than I had an inclination for; I may go farther and assert that hard drinking is very rare among people of fortune. Duelling was once carried to an excess, which was a real reproach and scandal to the kingdom; it of course proceeded from excessive drinking; as the cause has disappeared, the effect has nearly followed; not however entirely, for it is yet far more common among people of fashion than in England. Let me however conclude what I have to observe on the conduct of the principal people residing in Ireland, that there are great numbers among them who are as liberal in all their ideas as any people in Europe.

But I must now come to another class of people, to whose conduct it is almost entirely owing that the character of the nation has not that lustre abroad which I dare assert it will soon very generally merit: this is the class of little country gentlemen*; tenants, who drink their claret by means of profit rents; jobbers in farms; bucks; your fellows with round hats, edged with gold, who hunt in the day, get drunk in the evening, and fight the next morning. I shall not dwell on a subject so perfectly disagreeable, but remark that these are the men among whom drinking, wrangling, quarrelling, fighting (and) ravishing are found as in their native soil; once to a degree that made them

* God forbid I should give this character of all country gentlemen of small fortunes in Ireland: I have myself been acquainted with exceptions.—*Author's Note*.

the pest of society; they are growing better, but even now, one or two of them got by accident (where they have no business) into better company are sufficient very much to *derange* the pleasures that result from a liberal conversation. A new spirit; new fashions; new modes of politeness exhibited by the higher ranks are imitated by the lower, which will, it is to be hoped, put an end to this race of beings; and either drive their sons and cousins into the army or navy, or sink them into plain farmers like those we have in England, where it is common to see men with much greater property without pretending to be gentlemen. I repeat it from the intelligence I received, that even this class are very different from what they were twenty years ago, and improve so fast that the time will soon come when the national character will not be degraded by any set.

That character is upon the whole respectable: it would be unfair to attribute to the nation at large the vices and follies of only one class of individuals. Those persons from whom it is candid [*i.e.* fair] to take a general estimate do credit to their country. That they are a people learned, lively, and ingenious, the admirable authors they have produced will be an eternal monument; witness their Swift, Sterne, Congreve, Boyle, Berkeley, Steele, Farquhar, Southerne, and Goldsmith. Their talent for eloquence is felt, and acknowledged in the parliaments of both the kingdoms. Our own service both by sea and land, as well as that (unfortunately for us) of the principal monarchies of Europe, speak their steady and determined courage[181]. Every unprejudiced traveller who visits them will be as much pleased with their cheerfulness, as obliged by their hospitality, and will find them a brave, polite, and liberal people.

TRADE AND COMMERCE

Ireland being a dependent country, the British legislature has upon all occasions controlled its commerce, sometimes

with a very high hand, but universally upon the principles
of monopoly, as if the poverty of that country was to form
the wealth of Britain. I have upon every occasion endeavoured to show the futility of such an idea, and to
prove that the wealth of Ireland has always been, and is,
the wealth of England; that whatever she gets is expended
in a very large proportion in the consumption of British
fabrics and commodities. Whenever old prejudices wear
out, it will certainly be found for the interest of England
to give every freedom possible to the trade of Ireland.

Trade of Great Britain with Ireland[182]

			£		£
In the year	1700	Imports	233,853	Exports	261,115
„	1710	„	310,846	„	285,424
„	1720	„	282,812	„	328,583
„	1730	„	294,156	„	532,698
„	1740	„	390,565	„	628,288
„	1750	„	612,808	„	1,316,600
„	1760	„	904,180	„	1,050,401
„	1770	„	1,214,398	„	2,125,466

* * * * * * *

Before I conclude this section, I must observe one circumstance, which though not important enough to stop
the progress of commercial improvement in Ireland, yet
must very much retard it, and that is the contempt in
which trade is held by those who call themselves gentlemen.
I heard a language common in Ireland which, if it was to
become universal, would effectually prevent her ever
attaining greatness. I have remarked the houses of country
gentlemen being full of brothers, cousins, etc., idlers whose
best employment is to follow a hare or fox; *why are they
not brought up to trade or manufacture? Trade!* (the answer
has been), *they are gentlemen:*—to be poor till Doomsday;
a tradesman has not a right to the point of honour—you
may refuse his challenge. Trinity College at Dublin

swarms with lads who ought to be educated to the loom and the counting house. Many ill effects flow from these wretched prejudices. One consequence, manifest over the whole kingdom, is commercial people quitting trade or manufactures when they have made from five to ten thousand pounds to *become gentlemen*. Where trade is dishonourable it will not flourish, this is taking people from industry at the very moment they are the best able to command success. Many Quakers, who are (take them for all in all) the most sensible class of people in that kingdom, are exceptions to this folly; and mark the consequence, they are the only wealthy traders in the island. The Irish are ready enough to imitate the vices and follies of England; let them imitate her virtues; her respect for commercial industry which has carried her splendour and her power to the remotest corners of the earth.

GENERAL STATE OF IRELAND

It may not be disadvantageous, to a clear idea of the subject at large, to draw into one view the material facts which throw a light on the general state of the kingdom, that we may be able to have a distinct notion of that degree of prosperity which appears to have been of late years the inheritance of her rising industry.

Buildings

These improving or falling into decay are unerring signs of a nation's increasing grandeur or declension. Ireland has been absolutely new built within these twenty years, and in a manner far superior to anything that was seen in it before. It is a fact universal over the whole kingdom; cities, towns, and country seats; but the present is the era for this improvement, there being now far more elegant seats rising than ever were known before.

Roads

The roads of Ireland may be said all to have originated
from Mr French's Presentment Bill [empowering the
Grand Juries to make roads], and are now in a state that
do honour to the kingdom. There has probably been expended in consequence of that Bill considerably above a
million sterling.

Towns

The towns of Ireland have very much increased in the
last twenty years; a strong mark of rising prosperity.
Towns are markets which enrich and cultivate the
country, and can therefore never depopulate it, as some
visionary theorists have pretended. The country is always
the most populous within the sphere of great cities, and
the increased cultivation of the remotest corners shows that
this sphere extends like the circulating undulations of water
until they reach the most distant shores. Besides towns can
only increase from an increase of manufactures, commerce
and luxury. All three are other words for riches and employment, and these again for a general increase of people.

Rise of Rents

The rents of land have at least doubled in twenty-five
years, which is a most unerring proof of a great prosperity.
The rise of rents proves a variety of circumstances all
favourable; that there is more capital to cultivate land;
that there is a greater demand for the products of the
earth, and consequently a higher price; that towns thrive,
and are therefore able to pay higher prices; that manufactures and foreign commerce increase. The present
rental of Ireland appears to be £5,293,312.

Commerce

Trade in Ireland, in all its branches, has increased
greatly in twenty-five years. This has been a natural

effect from the other articles of prosperity already enumerated.

	£
The Irish exports to Great Britain, on an average of 25 years before 1748, were	438,665
Ditto on 25 years since	965,050
Increase	£526,385

This greatest article of her trade has therefore more than doubled.

	£
Exports to Great Britain per annum for the last 7 years	1,240,677
The preceding 7 years	917,088
Increase	£323,589

The greatest exports of Ireland, on an average of the last 7 years, are:

	£
Linen	1,615,654
The product of oxen and cows	1,218,902
Ditto of sheep	200,413
Ditto of hogs	150,631
Ditto of corn	64,871
	£3,250,471

Her total exports are probably three millions and a half.

Consumption

A people always consume in proportion to their wealth, hence an increase in the one marks clearly that of the other. The articles of beer, rum, and sugar are greatly increased; tea quadrupled; wine having lessened is certainly owing to the increased sobriety of the kingdom, which must have made a difference in the import. The imports of silks and woollen goods speak the same language of increased consumption.

Population

It is perfectly needless to speak of population, after showing that agriculture is improved, manufactures and commerce increased, and the general appearance of the kingdom carrying the face of a rising prosperity. It follows inevitably from all this, that the people must have increased, and accordingly, the information from one end of the island to the other confirmed it. The hearth tax in 1778 produced £61,646 which cannot indicate a less population, exceptions included, than three millions.

Upon the whole, we may safely determine, that judging by those appearances and circumstances which have been generally agreed to mark the prosperity or declension of a country, that Ireland has since the year 1748 made as great advances as could possibly be expected, perhaps greater than any other country in Europe. Since that period her linen exports have just *trebled*. Her general exports to Great Britain more than *doubled*. The rental of the kingdom *doubled*. And, I may add, that her linen and general exports have increased proportionately to this in the last seven years, consequently her wealth is at present on a like increase.

END OF PART II

EDITOR'S
NOTES

EDITOR'S NOTES

1. DUNLEARY. Named Kingstown in honour of George IV in 1821, and now known as Dun Laoghaire.

2. "A CITY WHICH MUCH EXCEEDED MY EXPECTATION." The eighteenth century was the period of Dublin's greatest development. Although the magnificent Custom House and the Four Courts were not built until the end of the century, the city in 1776 possessed several important public buildings and many imposing private houses. The Parliament House (now the Bank of Ireland) was erected 1729–39, the east and west wings being added between 1785 and 1794. The West Front of Trinity College (founded in 1591) was erected 1752–60. The first stone of the Exchange was laid in 1769. The Royal Barracks was built in 1704. Leinster House was built by the first Duke of Leinster about 1745. Charlemont House, in Rutland Square, was erected by James Caulfield, Earl of Charlemont, in 1773. The Rotunda Rooms in the Rotunda Gardens (Rutland Square) were built in 1764, and the Phoenix Park, which was formed in the reign of Charles II to provide the Viceroy with a field for sport, had been laid out and planted for public use in 1745. The population of Dublin was estimated by Whitelaw in 1798 at 172,091.

3. LORD HARCOURT. Simon Harcourt (1714–77), first Earl of Harcourt, succeeded Lord Townshend as Viceroy in 1772. He resigned in 1777.

4. COLONEL BURTON. William Burton became Teller of the Exchequer. In 1776 he was acting as aide-de-camp to Lord Harcourt. On the death of his uncle, Henry, Earl Conyngham (see note 23), without heirs in 1781, he inherited Slane Castle and assumed the name of Conyngham.

5. ROBERT FITZGERALD (The Knight of Kerry). A judge of the Admiralty Court and M.P. for Dingle (see p. 123).

6. MR LA TOUCHE. The Huguenot family of La Touche settled in Ireland after the Revocation of the Edict of Nantes. The gentleman referred to was David La Touche (1703–85), head of the bank established by his father in Dublin (see p. 30).

7. LA BUONA FIGLIUOLA, ETC. There were two theatres in Dublin at this time, one in Crow Street, the other in Smock Alley. The operas referred to, all very popular in their day, were by Piccinni, Guglielmi, and Anfossi respectively.

8. MR FLOOD. Henry Flood (1732–91) was the leader of the popular party until he accepted the Vice-Treasurership in 1775. He resigned this post in 1781.

9. MR DALY. Denis Daly of Dunsandle, Co. Galway, was M.P. for Co. Galway, 1768–90.

10. MR GRATTAN. Henry Grattan (1746–1820) carried the amendment to the address in favour of Free Trade in 1779 and moved the address to the Crown demanding legislative independence in 1782.

11. SIR WILLIAM OSBORNE. The Rt. Hon. William Osborne, 8th Bart. of Newtownanner, Co. Tipperary, was M.P. for Dungarvan, 1768–83. He was a supporter of Irish legislative independence (see p. 131).

12. PRIME SERJEANT BURGH. Walter Hussey Burgh (1742–83) became Prime Serjeant in 1777 and Chief Baron of the Irish Exchequer in 1782. He was an advocate of Free Trade and opposed the Union.

13. "THE ATTORNEY-GENERAL OF ENGLAND, WITH A DASH OF HIS PEN...." The subordination of the Irish Parliament was ensured by Poynings' Act (1494) by which Irish Bills had to be submitted to the English Privy Council, and by an Act of George I by which the English Parliament asserted the right to legislate for Ireland. Legislative independence was strongly advocated throughout the eighteenth century by Molyneux, Swift, Flood, Grattan, etc. and was finally granted in 1782.

14. LORD IRNHAM. Simon Luttrell was created Baron Irnham of Luttrellstown, Co. Dublin, in 1768 and Earl of Carhampton in 1785. His son, Henry Lawes Luttrell, the COLONEL LUTTRELL referred to in the text, was the well-known opponent of Wilkes.

15. MR WYNN BAKER. John Wynn Baker was a Yorkshireman who bought a farm at Loughlinstown, near Celbridge, Co. Kildare, in 1763, for the purpose of making agricultural experiments under the patronage of the Dublin Society (see below). He educated a number of boys for husbandry, manufactured

EDITOR'S NOTES 217

agricultural implements, and wrote several treatises on agriculture.

16. THE DUBLIN SOCIETY. This society, which is one of the oldest of its kind in Europe, was founded in 1731 to promote husbandry and other "useful arts." After 1820 it was known as the *Royal Dublin Society*.

17. AGMONDISHAM VESEY, ESQ. He was appointed Accountant-General of Ireland in 1761 and was M.P. for Kinsale in 1776. His wife had a literary salon in London, and was a friend of Dr Johnson's.

18. LEIXLIP. This was originally a Danish settlement. Old Norse, *Laxhlaup*, a salmon leap.

19. THE DEAN OF DERRY. Thomas Barnard became Dean of Derry in 1769 and Bishop of Killaloe in 1780. He was an intimate friend of Johnson, Goldsmith and Sir Joshua Reynolds. ST WOLSTAN'S was the property of his wife, and was at this time used as a summer residence by the Viceroy.

20. MR CONOLLY. Thomas Conolly was M.P. for Malmesbury and Chichester as well as for Co. Londonderry. He possessed great political influence in Ireland through his wealth and various family connections. He was an advocate of the Union.

21. THE DUKE OF LEINSTER. William Robert Fitzgerald became 2nd Duke of Leinster in 1773. He was a prominent leader of the Irish Volunteers.

22. LORD MORNINGTON. Garret Wesley (*or* Wellesley) was created Viscount Wellesley and Earl of Mornington in 1760. He was the father of the great Duke of Wellington.

23. LORD CONYNGHAM. Henry Conyngham (1705–81) of Slane, Co. Meath, and Mountcharles, Co. Donegal, was created Viscount Conyngham in 1756, and Earl Conyngham in 1781. Colonel Burton (see note 4) was his nephew.

24. ABSENTEE LANDLORDS. Owing to repeated and extensive confiscations of Irish land (see note 176) many of the landlords were English and spent most of their time in England. According to two estimates quoted by Dr O'Brien (*Economic History of Ireland in the 18th Century*) the absentee rents amounted to £632,200 in 1769; and to £1,500,000 in 1797. Young himself put the figure at £732,200. An absentee tax was frequently

suggested, but nothing was done owing to the opposition of the landed interest.

25. LORD CHIEF BARON FOSTER. Anthony Foster was appointed Lord Chief Baron of the Exchequer in Ireland in 1766. His son was John Foster, Lord Oriel, last Speaker of the Irish House of Commons.

26. LORD BOYNE. Gustavus Hamilton, a distinguished officer in the service of William III, was created Baron of Stackallan in 1715, and Viscount Boyne in 1717. The gentleman referred to was Richard (Hamilton), 4th Viscount Boyne (1724–87).

27. MELLIFONT ABBEY. This monastery (the first Cistercian house established in Ireland) was founded by a Prince of the O'Carrolls, about the year 1142. After its dissolution at the Reformation, the lands passed to Sir Edward Moore, ancestor of the Earls of Drogheda.

28. JOHN BAKER HOLROYD. He was a prolific writer on economic subjects and his estate in Sussex (purchased in 1769) was regarded as a model of farming. He became President of the Board of Agriculture in 1803, and was created Earl of Sheffield in 1816.

29. THE MIDDLEMAN. Agents were often employed by the absentees to collect rents and manage their estates. The landlords let their lands at low rents and long leases to save themselves trouble and gave the middlemen a free hand to make their own profits. As rents rose as a result of growing prosperity at the end of the century, the owners were generally anxious to resume direct control and the middlemen tended to disappear.

30. CUSTOM OF PLOUGHING UP LANDS AT THE END OF A LEASE. When a lease fell in, it was the custom to put up the farm for auction. Those who hoped to get their leases renewed, often "broke up" the land at the end of the term to reduce its value.

31. IRISH ROADS. At the beginning of the eighteenth century the roads were maintained by the joint effort of the landowners and labourers in each parish, but after 1765 road-making was entrusted to the county Grand Juries with excellent results. Young praises Irish roads and compares them favourably with the English highways.

32. LORD BECTIVE. Sir Thomas Taylour of Headfort, Co. Meath, was created Viscount Headfort in 1762 and Earl Bective in 1766.

33. SPALPEENS. Young's explanation of the Irish *spailpín* is generally held to be incorrect, although the origin and exact meaning of the word is unknown.

34. LORD LONGFORD. Edward Michael Pakenham became 2nd Baron Longford in 1766.

35. LORD BELVIDERE. George (Rochfort), Earl of Belvidere and Viscount Belfield, succeeded his father in 1774.

36. LORD SHELBURNE. Sir William (Petty), 2nd Earl of Shelburne, was the elder son of the Hon. John Fitzmaurice, who assumed the name of Petty, and was subsequently created Earl of Shelburne. He was President of the Board of Trade and became Prime Minister in 1782. In 1784 he was created Marquis of Landsdowne (see p. 112).

37. DEAN COOTE. Charles Coote, brother of Sir Eyre Coote the distinguished soldier, was Dean of Kilfenora, 1764–96 (see p. 145).

38. ARTHUR YOUNG'S VIEWS ON THE UNION. Young approached the subject of a Union with some doubt, for though he appears to advocate it here, he elsewhere observes that if England granted Ireland Free Trade and relaxed the restrictions on her Parliament (while maintaining control over military resources), no legislative union would be necessary.

39. PREMIUMS ON THE INLAND CARRIAGE OF CORN. An Act was passed by the Irish Parliament in 1759 which gave a bounty on the inland carriage of corn from all parts of Ireland to Dublin. The idea was to encourage tillage by bringing the Dublin market to the farmer's door by paying the carriage at the public expense. This bounty, although it stimulated agriculture, was a heavy charge on the revenue and was discontinued after 1796.

40. GERVAS PARKER BUSHE. He was High Sheriff for Co. Kilkenny in 1768. He married the sister of Henry Grattan.

41. LORD CARRICK. Henry Thomas (Butler), 2nd Earl of Carrick, took his seat in the House of Lords in 1774.

42. FARMS TAKEN IN PARTNERSHIP. The practice of taking lands in joint-ownership was a relic of *gavelkind*, the old Irish system of landholding abolished in James I's reign. See note on *rundale* and *changedale*, p. 224.

43. NEW ROSS. This was a place of considerable commercial importance in the Middle Ages. At this time it possessed a trade in butter and beef. It was one of the staple ports for exporting wool.

44. THE WHITEBOYS. These first arose in the West of Ireland in 1711 and again made their appearance in the South in October 1761. They were so-called because they wore white shirts over their clothes to prevent description. They objected to the enclosing of common lands, to the tithe system (see note 46), and to the extortions of the middlemen. In 1765 and 1775 severe Acts were passed against them, and Whiteboyism, the ancestor of all Irish agrarian crime, was temporarily controlled.

45. "THE LANDING OF THUROT," ETC. In 1756, war broke out between Great Britain and France and there were rumours of an invasion of Ireland. The chances of this were lessened by the defeat of Conflans at Quiberon, Nov. 20th, 1759, but Thurot early the next year managed to reach the town of Carrickfergus which he occupied for several days. On the approach of troops he withdrew, and his squadron was defeated.

46. TITHES AND TITHE PROCTORS. Tithes were felt to be a heavy burden by the Roman Catholic peasantry, for they had to be paid to the clergy of the Protestant Church, who rented them to tithe farmers, who collected their own commission. Sometimes they accepted payment by bonds bearing interest (see pp. 53, 197); sometimes they exacted payment in labour and kind.

47. BARONIES OF BARGY AND FORTH. These are situated at the southern end of Co. Wexford, and are bounded on two sides by the sea and on the third by Bannow Bay and the Forth Mountains. The inhabitants are said to be descended from Norman colonists, and until recent times preserved a distinct dialect and separate customs and folklore.

48. THE QUAKERS. The missions of the Quakers to Ireland commenced at the end of the Commonwealth period. Once established, they applied themselves to trade, and became as noted for their wealth as for their philanthropy. In Clonmel, they monopolised the corn supply, and founded the provision trade (see note 152). They showed similar enterprise at Carrick and elsewhere.

49. IRISH FISHERIES. Although these were stimulated by bounties, the trade as a whole did not flourish, as is shown by

the statistics of imported fish. Lecky attributed this to the disappearance of the fish from their old haunts and to a lack of enterprise and skill among the fishermen.

50. LORD COURTOWN. James (Stopford), 2nd Earl of Courtown, took his seat in the House of Lords in 1771.

51. POWERSCOURT. The district takes its name from the De La Poer family who built a castle on the site of the present Powerscourt House. Sir Richard Wingfield, first Viscount Powerscourt, was granted the lands of Powerscourt by James I.

52. "AN IMMENSE CONICAL MOUNTAIN." The Great Sugar Loaf, 1659 feet.

53. BARON HAMILTON. The Hon. George Hamilton, Baron of the Exchequer, was M.P. for Belfast for many years.

54. FINGAL. This northern portion of Co. Dublin was originally a Danish settlement. It was always an important part of the English Pale, the inhabitants being noted for their excellent husbandry.

55. DROGHEDA. One of the oldest towns in Ireland and one which had always enjoyed important municipal privileges. At this time it manufactured coarse linen and exported provisions.

56. BATTLE OF THE BOYNE. Fought on the 1st July (old style) 1690, between William III and James II. The issues at stake were: the principles of the English Revolution; the triumph of Protestantism; and the overthrow of the ambition of Louis XIV, who was supporting James. An obelisk to commemorate the victory of King William and to mark the site of the battlefield was erected in 1736.

57. THE LINEN MANUFACTURE. Linen cloth was made all over Ireland in the Middle Ages and exported abroad. The trade was stimulated by an influx of Protestant weavers into Ireland after the Revocation of the Edict of Nantes. It was free from English commercial restrictions and was encouraged by the Irish parliament. In 1708 spinning schools were established in every county, and an Irish Linen Board was appointed to watch over the interests of manufacturers (1711). The industry grew rapidly. In 1710, 1,688,574 yards of linen cloth were exported, while in 1779 the figure had risen to 18,836,042 yards. About the time of Young's visit the trade was becoming localised in Ulster.

58. "THE POPERY LAWS." Under the Penal Code, which came into force after the Williamite Wars, the Irish Catholics were excluded from parliament and all civil offices. They might not keep school, or enter the university. They were not allowed to buy land, or to hold leases for more than 31 years, or upon such terms that the profits exceeded one-third of the rents. The Code had the most pernicious effect upon the national development, in that it preserved the monopoly of power obtained by the new landlords under the confiscations, and formed them into a dominant caste cut off from healthy contact with the mass of the people, who were rendered poor, ignorant and discontented. Although it was often said that the laws were not strictly enforced, there is much evidence to the contrary. With the growth of toleration, the Code was condemned by public opinion, and Catholic Relief Acts were passed in 1778, 1782 and 1793.

59. EMIGRATION. This was mainly among the Presbyterians in the North, and was due to the restrictions placed on the woollen industry, the Test Act, the distress caused by high rents and tithes, and later to the depression in the linen trade at the time of the American war. In the first three-quarters of the eighteenth century about 200,000 persons left Ulster for the New World.

60. DUNDALK. This town had suffered in the Rebellion of 1641. In 1737 the Irish Linen Board established a cambric manufactury here, and brought over a number of French weavers to start the industry. In 1767 the Irish Parliament voted considerable sums for the improvement of the harbour.

61. NEWRY. Originally peopled by Protestant settlers in the reign of James I, the town was burnt by the Duke of Berwick in 1689. It received special protection from William III and developed a trade with the Continent in linen goods and raw materials. The canal from Newry, which connects Lough Neagh with the sea, was begun in 1730 as the result of the encouragement given by the Irish Parliament to inland navigation.

62. LORD GOSFORT. Sir Archibald Acheson, was created Baron Gosfort of Markethill in 1776.

63. ARMAGH. This town, the see of the Primate of all Ireland, had often suffered from the effects of war. Richard Robinson, the son of a Yorkshire gentleman, who was educated at Westminster and Oxford, was its most princely benefactor. He came to Ireland

in 1751 as Chaplain to the Lord Lieutenant, and became Primate in 1765. He was created Lord Rokeby in 1777.

64. OAKBOYS AND STEELBOYS. See note 174.

65. MR BROWNLOW. The Rt. Hon. William Brownlow was M.P. for Co. Armagh, 1753–94. Lurgan was founded by his ancestor, Sir William Brownlow, who received a grant of lands in the Plantation of Ulster (1610).

66. LORD HILLSBOROUGH. Wills Hill was created Earl of Hillsborough in 1751 and Marquess of Downshire in 1789. He was Registrar of the High Court of Chancery in Ireland and was Secretary of State for the Colonies.

67. "LEAVING LISBURN TOOK THE ROAD TO BELFAST." Young did not remain in Belfast on this occasion, as the persons to whom he had letters of introduction were absent.

68. BARONY OF THE ARDS. The Lower and Upper Ards form a peninsula between Strangford Lough and the sea. The Anglo-Norman family of Savage were once hereditary Seneschals of the County of Ulster, but were expelled from the Lower Ards by the Irish in the Middle Ages and became associated with the districts round Portaferry. The MR SAVAGE referred to above was High Sheriff in 1763.

69. "THE PRINCIPAL RELIGION IS PRESBYTERIAN." Presbyterianism was introduced into Ulster by Scottish settlers early in the seventeenth century.

70. BELFAST. For a long time Belfast, which was planted with English settlers in James I's reign, ranked low among Irish towns. It came into prominence in the reign of William III, who patronised the linen industry with which the fortunes of the place were henceforth linked. By the end of the eighteenth century, it ranked as the third town in Ireland. The growth of prosperity is shown by the linen exports, and the growth of population. In a return quoted by Benn (*History of Belfast*) the population was 8549 in 1757, 13,105 in 1782, and 18,320 in 1791. See notes on Lord Donegall, pp. 224, 234.

71. LORD ANTRIM. Randal William (MacDonnell), 6th Earl of Antrim and Viscount Dunluce.

72. LOUGH NEAGH. The largest lake in the British Isles, being 18 miles in length, 11 in breadth and 65 in circumference.

73. MR O'NEILL. John O'Neill of Shanes Castle, Co. Antrim, was created Baron O'Neill in 1793 and Viscount O'Neill in 1795.

74. RUNDALE. *Rundale* or *runrig* were the scattered strips of arable land owned by small holders who held land in common. When the fields went out of cultivation the various holdings were changed to give all the joint owners an equal share of good and bad soil. This practice was known as *changedale*.

75. THE HEARTS OF STEEL. See note 174.

76. THE GIANT'S CAUSEWAY. This natural formation consists of more than 40,000 basaltic columns supposed to have been built up as the result of the contraction and cooling of lava. The idea that the columns were formed by regular crystallisation is now generally abandoned.

77. LONDON COMPANIES. At the Plantation of Ulster (1608–10) the City of London undertook to plant the district covered by the modern county of Londonderry. The initial capital outlay was met by means of a rate levied upon the London Livery Companies, to each of which grants of land were apportioned.

78. LORD DONEGALL. Arthur (Chichester), 5th Earl of Donegall, was created Earl of Belfast and Marquis of Donegall in 1791. See note 175.

79. THE BISHOP OF DERRY. Frederick (Hervey), 4th Earl of Bristol and Bishop of Derry (1730–1803), was a benefactor to his diocese and played an important part in the Volunteer movement.

80. LONDONDERRY. Derry dates its rise as a town from the time when it was planted by the City of London, from whence it derives its name. The shipping of the port in 1760 consisted of 67 sail from 30 to 350 tons. In 1776 it was only two-thirds of this; the decline being due to the slackening of emigration and diminished import of flax seed.

81. THE BISHOP OF RAPHOE. John Oswald, Bishop of Dromore, was translated to Raphoe in 1763.

82. IRISH CARS. There is a picture of a typical "Irish car" in the 2nd edition of the *Tour* showing a pair of long shafts, block wheels and a wooden platform, which could be fitted with side boards to carry grain. The sledge type of car noticed here was also to be found in the Highlands.

83. "LEAD MINES MIXED WITH SILVER." Minerals in Ireland were not extensively worked in the eighteenth century owing to lack of capital.

84. SIR JAMES CALDWELL. He was Sheriff of Co. Fermanagh in 1756 and raised a regiment of horse for the defence of Ireland in 1760. In early life he distinguished himself in the Austrian service and was created a *Count of Milan in the Holy Roman Empire* by the Empress Maria Theresa.

85. THE EARL OF ROSS. Sir Ralf Gore was created Earl of Ross in 1771. The Peerage became extinct on his death in 1802.

86. LORD ENNISKILLEN. William Willoughby Cole was created Viscount Enniskillen in 1776 and Earl of Enniskillen in 1789. He was an eloquent speaker and was opposed to the Union.

87. THE SPA AT SWANLINBAR. This was a resort of the Irish fashionable world especially towards the end of the eighteenth century, when many Continental resorts were closed to foreigners. The *Post-Chaise Companion* (1786) describes the waters as excellent for "scurvy, nerves, low spirits and bad appetite." Marcus Beresford, Archbishop of Armagh, related how his father and a party of friends, who had arranged to spend the summer of 1806 here with their families, were kept waiting in their coaches before the hotel for many hours before rooms were ready for their reception.

88. THE BISHOP OF KILMORE. George Jones, fellow of King's College, Cambridge, was consecrated Bishop of Kilmore in 1775.

89. THE EARL OF FARNHAM. Robert Maxwell, 2nd Baron Farnham, was created Earl of Farnham in 1763.

90. PLOUGHING BY THE TAIL. The custom of attaching horses by their tails to the plough was prohibited by an Act of Charles I's reign. The practice of pulling wool off live sheep and burning corn from the chaff was condemned at the same time. Pennant found the first of these barbarous customs prevailing in Skye as late as 1772 and Dr Johnson describes how the Highlanders pulled their barley and burnt the oats from the husk.

91. THE WOOLLEN INDUSTRY. This reached its zenith in 1687 when the value of exports amounted to £70,521. In 1699 the English Parliament passed an Act by which the exportation of manufactured woollens from Ireland was totally prohibited. This

led to a great decline in the industry and to a smuggling trade, chiefly with France.

92. RODERICK O'CONNOR. He became King of Connacht in 1156 and King of all Ireland in 1166. The Priory at Roscommon was founded by Felin O'Connor, King of Connacht in 1257, and the tomb in the church is generally held to be his.

93. THE MILESIANS. This race was one of several that immigrated to Ireland in very early times. According to legend, the Milesians came from Spain.

94. MACDERMOT, PRINCE OF COOLAVIN. The MacDermot's country once included a considerable portion of the counties of Sligo and Roscommon and some districts in Mayo, but after the Williamite wars the family was confined to the district on the shores of Lough Gara. This is one of the few Irish titles that still survives.

95. MR PONSONBY. John Ponsonby, son of the Earl of Bessborough, was Speaker of the Irish House of Commons, 1756–71.

96. LORD KINGSTON. Sir Edward King was created Baron Kingston of Rockingham in 1764, Viscount Kingsborough in 1766, and Earl of Kingston in 1768.

97. SLIGO. The chief exports at this time were linen and butter. Seward described it in 1795 as "a town of considerable trade," *Topographia Hibernica* (1795).

98. THE BISHOP OF KILLALA. Samuel Hutchinson, Dean of Dromore, was consecrated Bishop of Killala in 1759.

99. "TO HOWL THE CORPSE TO THE GRAVE." Funeral wails dating from Pagan times have always drawn comment from travellers in Ireland. Professional keening at funerals went out of fashion in the first decade of the nineteenth century.

100. LORD LUCAN. Sir Charles Bingham was created Baron Lucan of Castlebar in 1776, and Earl of Lucan in 1795.

101. LORD ALTAMONT. Peter (Browne), 2nd Earl of Altamont, succeeded his father in 1776. His son was a strong supporter of the Union, and was created Marquis of Sligo.

102. JOYCE'S COUNTRY. This is the description given to that part of the barony of Ross, Co. Galway, which lies between the Killaries and Lough Mask, from the prevailing name of its

inhabitants who are descended from a Welsh family settled there in the reign of Edward I.

103. LACK-CLAY. Young describes this hard substance elsewhere as being "like baked clay, the thickness of a tile."

104. CHANGE FROM IRISH TO ENGLISH NAMES. "Stranaghan" is evidently a misprint for *ÓHéanachdin* which was anglicised into *Bird* (Ir. *éan*, a bird); *ÓMarcachdin* became *Ryder* (Ir. *marcach*, a rider); *ÓCoiledin* became *Collins* and perhaps *Whelp* (Ir. *coiledn*, a whelp); though *Whelp* as a surname is hardly known in Ireland to-day. *Mac Conraoi* became *King* (Ir. *rí* a king); *Mac an Rudaire* means "the knight's son" and so became *Knight* or *MacKnight*. I am indebted to Professor O'Rahilly of Trinity College, Dublin, for the information contained in this note.

105. THE ARCHBISHOP OF TUAM. Jemmet Browne, Bishop of Elphin, became Archbishop of Tuam in 1775.

106. BANDLE LINEN. A narrow cloth named after an Irish measure.

107. CHARTER SCHOOLS. These were founded under the auspices of Primate Boulter in 1733, for the education and conversion of the children of the Catholic poor, who were excluded under the Penal Code from other educational establishments. They were characterised by many abuses.

108. GALWAY. At one time this town had a flourishing foreign trade, but it suffered in the Cromwellian wars and at this period was in a state of decay.

109. OSNABURGS. Coarse linen originally made in Osnabrück, North Germany.

110. SIR LUCIUS O'BRIEN. He was a member of a younger branch of the O'Briens, Earls of Thomond and Inchiquin, and was a prominent member of the Popular Party.

111. THE CORCASSES. These pastures on the banks of the Shannon and Fergus were long noted for their luxuriance. (Irish, *corçach* a marsh, or *curcas* a reed or bulrush.)

112. LAWS FOR THE INCREASE OF TILLAGE. The first of several Acts in Ireland for the encouragement of tillage was passed in 1708 when a bounty was given on the export of wheat. In 1759

a premium was granted on the inland carriage of corn (see note 39). A final impetus to tillage was given by Foster's Corn Law in 1784.

113. ENGLISH RESTRICTIONS UPON IRISH TRADE. These were put into force in accordance with the economic theory of the period which held that a colony might lawfully be exploited in the interests of the mother-country. An agitation for Free Trade began in 1776 owing to the outbreak of war with America, which involved an embargo on the Irish provision trade, and practically all restrictions were removed between 1779 and 1782.

114. CASTLES OF BUNRATTY AND ROSMANAGHER. Bunratty was erected by the Anglo-Norman, Robert de Muscegros, about 1251. It was held by the O'Briens, later Earls of Thomond, between 1318 and 1642, when it was burnt by the Irish Confederates. Rosmanagher was also a seat of the Earls of Thomond.

115. LIMERICK. Through Mr Pery's influence £27,500 was voted by the Irish Parliament for the improvement of Limerick between 1755–61. A commodious Custom House was erected and new roads were made in the neighbourhood. A theatre was built in 1770 where Garrick and other leading actors played. The population according to an estimate quoted by Lecky was 25,480 in 1760.

116. MR PERY. Edmond Sexton Pery was M.P. for Limerick and Speaker of the Irish House of Commons. He was created Viscount Pery in 1785. His great-nephew became Earl of Limerick.

117. "THE POOR PEOPLE RECKON THEIR CATTLE BY COLLOPS." The *collop* was the animal unit which an Irish acre of pasture could support. Irish *colpa*, a full grown beast (horse or cow).

118. "IT WAS WITH REGRET I LEFT SO AGREEABLE AND LIBERAL A FAMILY." Young supplies further information about his visit to the Aldworth's in his *Autobiography*.

119. LORD DONERAILE. Richard Aldworth of Newmarket, Co. Cork, who was the grandfather of the MR ALDWORTH mentioned above, married a daughter of Arthur St Leger, first Lord Doneraile. When the Doneraile title became extinct in 1767 their second son St Leger Aldworth was elevated to the peerage, and created Viscount Doneraile in 1785.

120. THE SPA AT MALLOW. In his *History of Cork* (1750) Smith says of Mallow: "the town being well-situated, and the company agreeable, it hath obtained among some the name of the *Irish Bath*."

121. MR GORDON OF "NEW GROVE." "New Grove" lay between Cork and Mallow, three miles from Whitechurch. Mr Gordon was Surveyor-General of Munster.

122. BLARNEY CASTLE. This was built by Cormac MacCarthy about 1446. The MacCarthys were created Lords of Muskerry and Earls of Clancarty, but their lands were forfeited in consequence of their adherence to the cause of James II. The Blarney estate was purchased in 1703 by Lord Chief Justice Pyne who sold it to General Sir James Jefferys.

123. DOMINICK TRANT, ESQ. He was M.P. for St Canice, Kilkenny from 1776–83, and the author of a pamphlet advocating Catholic claims. He married the sister of the notorious Lord Clare.

124. COVE HARBOUR. Named Queenstown after a landing made here by Queen Victoria in 1849, and now known as *Cobh.*

125. LORD INCHIQUIN. William (O'Brien), 4th Earl of Inchiquin. His son was created Earl of Thomond.

126. THE EARL OF SHANNON. Richard (Boyle), 2nd Earl of Shannon, succeeded his father in 1765. He became Vice-Treasurer of Ireland.

127. CORK. This ranked as the second city in Ireland and was the centre of the provision trade. In 1750 the population was estimated by Smith (*History of Cork*) at 70,000.

128. THE DEAN OF CORK. George Chinnery, became Dean of Cork in 1763 and Bishop of Killaloe in 1779.

129. SHALLOONS. Light cloths originally made at Chalôns in France. For CARRICK see note 155.

130. SMUGGLING. See note on the WOOLLEN INDUSTRY, pp. 225–26.

131. SHAG. A long napped rough cloth.

132. THE REV. ARCHDEACON OLIVER. John Oliver, became Archdeacon of Ardagh in 1762.

133. SIR JOHN COLTHURST. He succeeded to the Baronetcy in 1774. He was killed in a duel by Dominick Trant. See note 123.

134. LORD SHELBURNE. See note 36.

135. THE IRISH LOY. The *laighe* was a species of spade.

136. LORD KENMARE. Thomas (Browne), 4th Viscount Kenmare, was descended from Sir Valentine Browne who purchased lands in Cork and Kerry in Queen Elizabeth's reign. His son was created Earl of Kenmare in 1800.

137. MUCKROSS ABBEY. This so-called "Abbey" was in reality a Franciscan Friary founded about 1440 by a MacCarthy on the site of an older establishment. Young did not appreciate the architectural merits of the ruins.

138. GLENA. This forms part of the Purple Mountain (2739 ft.) which lies west of Muckross.

139. "MANGERTON CASCADE AND DRUMAROURK HILL." Young evidently is referring here to Torc Cascade and Drumrourk Hill which lies about a mile and a half to the east of Torc Mountain. Mangerton is farther to the south.

140. ROSS CASTLE. Built by the O'Donoghues in the fourteenth century, and occupied by them for several hundreds of years. It was the last fortress in Ireland to hold out against the Cromwellians.

141. LORD CROSBIE. William (Crosbie), 2nd Baron Branden, was created Viscount Crosbie of Ardfert in 1771, and Earl of Glandore in 1776.

142. "A BEAUTIFUL CISTERCIAN ABBEY." Ardfert Abbey, a Franciscan Friary founded in 1253 by Thomas Fitzmaurice, first Lord of Kerry.

143. WOODFORD. Later known as Bedford House.

144. MRS QUIN. Windham Quin was M.P. for Kilmallock 1769–76. He married Frances, daughter of Richard Dawson of Dawson Grove, Co. Monaghan. His eldest son was created Earl of Dunraven.

145. THE PALATINES. In 1709 a number of Germans from the Rhine, tired of being continually harried by war, emigrated to England. Several hundred families of these were settled in different parts of Ireland with the object of improving agriculture and of strengthening the Protestant interest. They do not seem to have exercised any permanent influence upon their surroundings,

and when their leases fell in, they merged into the condition of the ordinary Irish tenant.

146. "THREE RUINS OF FRANCISCAN FRIARIES." These must have been: the Trinitarian Friary founded in 1272; an Augustinian Friary attributed to John, first Earl of Kildare (1315); and a Franciscan Friary founded in 1464 by Thomas, Earl of Kildare. The manor of Adare came into the possession of the Quin family in 1683.

147. "IN THE BREED OF CATTLE HE HAS BEEN VERY ATTENTIVE." Stockbreeding in England was making rapid progress at this time, under the influence of the Leicestershire farmer Robert Bakewell.

148. THE GOLDEN VALE. The part of the great plain of Tipperary watered by the Suir, in the centre of which the town of Tipperary is situated; so called on account of the richness of its soil. The name is also applied to the district in Co. Limerick which extends from Kilfinnane to Pallaskenry.

149. EARL OF CLANWILLIAM. John Meade, son of Sir Richard Meade of Ballintober, Co. Cork, was created Earl of Clanwilliam in 1776.

150. LORD DE MONTALT. Sir Thomas Maude was M.P. for Tipperary, 1761–76. He was created Baron de Montalt in 1776.

151. THE ROCK OF CASHEL. This rises steeply to the height of about 300 feet and has upon it a number of interesting ecclesiastical buildings. These include the Cathedral, part of which dates from the thirteenth century; Cormac's Chapel (twelfth century); a Round Tower (tenth century); and an ancient cross which marks the place where the Kings of Munster were crowned.

152. CLONMEL. The channel of the Suir was deepened in the middle of the eighteenth century by means of a grant from the Irish Parliament, and this enabled the town to become the collecting centre for an extensive export trade in corn and provisions. MR MOORE was descended from a Cromwellian settler, the senior branch of whose family became Lords of Mountcashel. His enterprises collapsed some years later when the milling trade of Clonmel was monopolised by the Quakers.

153. SIR WILLIAM OSBORNE. See note 11.

154. THE EARL OF TYRONE. George De la Poer (Beresford), 2nd Earl of Tyrone, was created Marquis of Waterford in 1789.

155. CARRICK-ON-SUIR. In 1670 the woollen manufacture was established here by the great Duke of Ormonde. By the end of the eighteenth century 3000 persons were employed in making ratteens of which about 6000 pieces were produced annually. A good trade also passed up the Suir to Clonmel and down the river to Waterford. The prosperity of the place disappeared early in the nineteenth century.

156. WATERFORD. Described in the sixteenth century as the "second city in Ireland," Waterford declined during the Cromwellian and Williamite wars. At this time the trade in beef, butter, tallow and hides had revived.

157. FAITHLEGG HILL. Now known as Cheekpoint Hill (437 ft.).

158. MONAVULLAGH. Seefin (2387 ft.) is the highest point of the Monavullagh range which lies to the south-west of the Comeragh Mountains.

159. INDUSTRY OF THE IRISH PEASANT. This has often been called in question, a fact which adds interest to the observations of Young in this and other passages. Under the Penal Laws the people reaped no reward for industry and had therefore no reason for exerting themselves. A pamphleteer (R. S. Tighe) writing on popular education (1787) remarked, "It is a mistake to conceive that the people of Ireland are by nature more lazy [than those] of other countries. Transport them and the reverse of the assertion is more near to truth. The hardest labour (that of coal heaving and the carrying of sedan chairs) is performed in London chiefly by Irishmen."

160. THE JOURNEY FROM PASSAGE TO MILFORD HAVEN. Wesley used to suffer similar irritation at these undue delays and in his *Journal* gives three rules for those who sailed between England and Ireland: "(1) Never pay till you set sail; (2) go not on board till the captain goes on board; (3) send not your baggage on board till you go yourself." The post-office packets sailed, weather permitting, on fixed dates; but the advantage to the public from the circumstance as compared with the service performed by private ships was not great, for the duration of the voyage was uncertain.

161. MITCHELSTOWN, CO. CORK. This estate came into the possession of Sir John King of Boyle, Co. Roscommon, ancestor

of the Earls of Kingston, in the seventeenth century. Robert (King) Viscount Kingsborough, son of the Earl of Kingston (see note 96), invited Young to be his agent at Mitchelstown in 1777. The latter remained here until 1779 when he left owing to dissensions with the Kingsborough family.

162. HEARTH-MONEY. A yearly tax on each hearth first imposed on Ireland in the reign of Charles II. Those who occupied a house of less than the annual value of 8s. were exempt.

163. THE CURRAGH. This great plain was the site in very early mes of games and chariot races (Irish, *currach*, a race-course).

164. LORD CARLOW. William Dawson was created Viscount Carlow in 1776. His son was the first Earl of Portarlington.

165. A KISH. A large wickerwork basket used in Ireland for carrying turf.

166. HURLING. The game of hurley in Ireland dates from very early times. It is played with wooden clubs and a hard ball. It resembles the English hockey, but has nothing in common with cricket as Young suggests.

167. LORD ASHBROOK. William (Flower), 2nd Viscount Ashbrook and 3rd Baron Castle Durrow, Co. Kilkenny.

168. LORD DE VESCI. Sir Thomas Vesey was created Viscount de Vesci of Abbey-Leix, Queen's Co. in 1776.

169. SIR JOHN PARNELL. He was M.P. for Maryborough. His son became Chancellor of the Irish Exchequer.

170. THE COTTIER SYSTEM. The cottier had no security and no permanent interest in the soil. When he had paid his rack-rent to the middleman, his tithe to the Protestant clergyman, and his dues to his own priests, he had no surplus for himself and was forced to live on the margin of subsistence. The labourer's budget detailed on p. 148 speaks for itself.

171. THE ENGLISH AND IRISH LABOURER COMPARED. The Irish labourer was not tied down to his parish by the Settlement Laws which caused distress in England, but on the other hand he missed the benefits of parochial relief. With the changes produced by the Industrial Revolution, the position of the English agricultural labourer deteriorated and in the last quarter of the eighteenth century he was in some respects no better off than his Irish neighbour.

172. "BROKEN TEA CUPS," ETC. These lines are taken from Goldsmith's *Deserted Village* (1770).

173. OPPRESSIONS OF THE LESSER GENTRY. Wesley remarked in his *Journal*: "the poor in Ireland in general are well-behaved; all the ill-breeding is among well dressed people." He was much shocked at the "knocking down" process noted by Young, and the free use which certain gentlemen made of their sticks.

174. OAKBOYS, STEELBOYS AND PEEP-O-DAY BOYS. The *Oakboys*, who appeared in Ulster in 1763, were so called from the oaken branches that they wore in their hats. They objected to the compulsory labour which the peasantry were forced to give on the roads and committed various outrages. The *Hearts of Steel* (so called to express a firmness of resolution) arose in Antrim and Down about 1771. They objected to the raising of rents by Lord Donegall and others (see below), which led to eviction, and resorted to violence. The *Peep-o-Day Boys* formed an anti-Catholic organisation in Co. Armagh where the Roman Catholics with a lower standard of living were out-bidding the Protestants for farms. They became the *Orange Boys* of a later period. See note on the WHITEBOYS, p. 220.

175. LORD DONEGALL AND HIS RENTS. When Lord Donegall's leases fell in 1771–72, he raised large fines from his tenants, and as they were unable to pay, let the lands to Belfast merchants. Lecky did not accept the verdict of those who declared that Lord Donegall was not at fault.

176. "THE LANDED PROPERTY OF THE KINGDOM HAD BEEN GREATLY CHANGED." The first regular plantation was carried out in King's and Queen's Counties in Philip and Mary's reign. Under Elizabeth, there was a plantation in Munster, following the Desmond rebellion. The plantation in Ulster took place after the war with Hugh O'Neill (1610). The Cromwellian Settlement resulted from the Rebellion of 1641. According to Sir William Petty, one-third of the best lands in Ireland was before 1641 in the hands of the Protestants, while after the Act of Settlement (1662), they held more than two-thirds of these lands. Further confiscations followed the Williamite wars, so that at the beginning of the eighteenth century it is estimated by Mr W. F. Butler in his *Confiscation in Irish History* that the Roman Catholics did not own more than one-twentieth of the soil.

177. TIMBER AND PLANTING. In early times Ireland was thickly wooded, but an immense quantity of timber was destroyed in the wars of Elizabeth and by settlers in the seventeenth century, for iron works and other purposes. Despite a number of Acts to encourage planting passed by the Irish Parliament, reafforestation made little progress.

178. POPULATION. Lecky estimated that in 1700 the population of Ireland was about two million, and that in 1800 it was roughly four and a half million. During the first half of the century, as a result of famine, disease, and emigration, it remained stationary, but increased rapidly from about 1750.

179. HEDGE SCHOOLS. Schools for the children of the peasantry which were maintained by the poorer classes themselves. John Howard, the prison reformer, contrasted them favourably with some of the Protestant Charter Schools.

180. DRINKING AND DUELLING. Young's testimony as to the diminution of these evils is borne out by Twiss, Luckombe, and others. The smaller gentry however were still drinking heavily and large quantities of whisky were consumed by the lower classes.

181. THE IRISH IN FOREIGN SERVICE. After the Treaty of Limerick (1691) large numbers of Irish Roman Catholics entered the service of Foreign Powers. In France they formed the nucleus of the famous Irish Brigade and fought against the English in the Wars of the Spanish and Austrian Successions.

182. TRADE OF GREAT BRITAIN WITH IRELAND. The figures given in the text bearing on this subject, as also those relating to the trade of Sligo on p. 76, are extracted from fuller lists given by Young.

END OF NOTES

INDEX

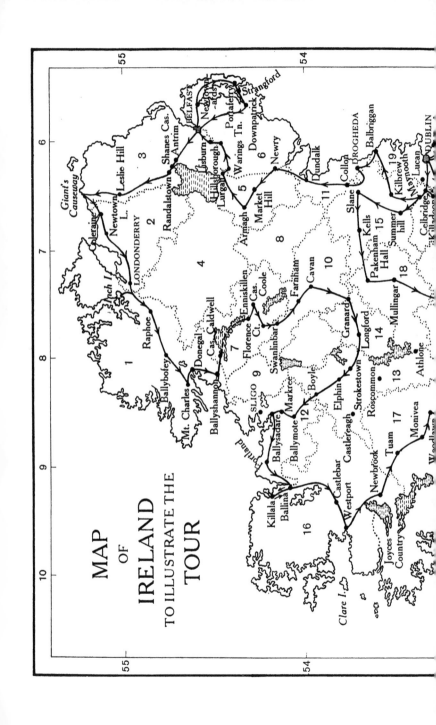

MAP
OF
IRELAND
TO ILLUSTRATE THE
TOUR

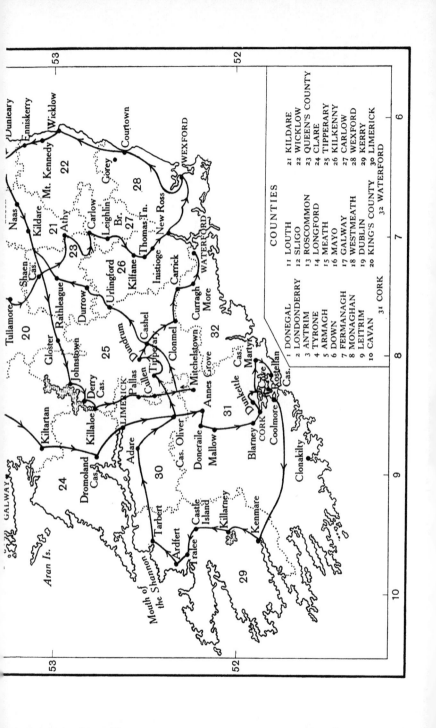

COUNTIES

1 DONEGAL
2 LONDONDERRY
3 TYRONE
4 ARMAGH
5 DOWN
6 FERMANAGH
7 MONAGHAN
8 CAVAN
9 LEITRIM
10 CAVAN

11 LOUTH
12 SLIGO
13 ROSCOMMON
14 LONGFORD
15 MEATH
16 MAYO
17 GALWAY
18 WESTMEATH
19 DUBLIN
20 KING'S COUNTY

21 KILDARE
22 WICKLOW
23 QUEEN'S COUNTY
24 CLARE
25 TIPPERARY
26 KILKENNY
27 CARLOW
28 WEXFORD
29 KERRY
30 LIMERICK

31 CORK

32 WATERFORD

For EU product safety concerns, contact us at Calle de José Abascal, 56–1°,
28003 Madrid, Spain or eugpsr@cambridge.org.

www.ingramcontent.com/pod-product-compliance
Ingram Content Group UK Ltd.
Pitfield, Milton Keynes, MK11 3LW, UK
UKHW020320140625
459647UK00018B/1941